Grade 3

The Complete Year
in Reading and Writing

Daily Lessons • Monthly Units • Yearlong Calendar

Abi Gotthelf and Pam Allyn

Includes CD–ROM in pocket

■SCHOLASTIC

NEW YORK • TORONTO • LONDON • AUCKLAND • SYDNEY
MEXICO CITY • NEW DELHI • HONG KONG • BUENOS AIRES

To all third-grade teachers, who care so much, and:

To my family for their constant and unconditional love,
support, and encouragement.
~ *Abi Gotthelf*

To Lois Bridges and Danny Miller
~ *Pam Allyn*

Scholastic Inc. grants teachers permission to photocopy the activity and stationery pages from this book for classroom use only. No other part of this publication may be reproduced in whole or in part, or stored in a retrieval system, or transmitted in any form or by any means, electronic, mechanical, photocopying, recording, or otherwise, without written permission of the publisher. For information regarding permission, write to Scholastic Inc., 557 Broadway, New York, NY 10012.

Cover design by Jay Namerow

Interior design by Maria Lilja

Photos by LitLife Archives (interior and cover), Maria Lilja (inside cover)

Acquiring Editor: Lois Bridges

Development and Production Editor: Danny Miller

Copy Editor: Chris Borris

ISBN 13: 978-0-545-04637-4

ISBN 10: 0-545-04637-8

Copyright © 2008 by LitLife Publishing LLC

Contents

As a bonus, use our Spotlight Units to journey through day-by-day lessons in all the Complete 4 components.

Acknowledgments

We would like to thank the teachers, the children, and our colleagues in the LitLife network of schools who believe in the power of words.

There was a team of people who gave of themselves in the deepest and most generous of ways to this project. We are full of gratitude for the wise and thoughtful Delia Coppola, Janet Knight, Debbie Lera, and Michelle Yang. Their insights, feedback, and creations glow brightly throughout this series.

We are grateful for the support of our extraordinary LitLife team: the remarkable and talented Jenny Koons, who understands life and people and kids and curriculum and enriched the books with her careful eye, and the marvelous Rebekah Coleman, whose spirit kept us going and whose wise attention completed us. With thanks to our dedicated interns Jen Estrada and Alyssa McClorey, and to Deb Jurkowitz, LitLife grammarian and in-house linguist. We deeply appreciate our agent, the magical Lisa DiMona, for shining the light that guides our way.

Danny Miller may very well be one of the funniest people on earth. He is also a brilliant editor. His dedicated efforts to this series are appreciated beyond compare by us all. Lois Bridges: inspiration, mentor, friend, champion of children and humanistic education, connector of all dots, editor extraordinaire, we thank you. All our appreciation to the team at Scholastic: the creative Maria Lilja, and Terry Cooper for her vision and dedication to the work of supporting teachers. In addition, we thank Eileen Hillebrand for her genius way of getting the word out there and Susan Kolwicz for her genius in getting the message heard.

And with thanks to Fiona and Muriel, two magical girls who helped us to know what third and fourth graders really like to read and write.

This experience of writing six books together has been by turns precious, wild, funny, exhausting, scary, joyous, and deeply satisfying. We collectively gave birth to three babies during this process, visited hundreds of schools, took our own kids to school, and tried to have dinner with our husbands once in a while. From the beginning, we committed to one another that when the work felt hard we would always remember that relationships come first. We are most proud of this and hope our readers can feel the power of our bonds in every page of every book in this series. We thank one another, always.

Pam Allyn sends boundless gratitude to Jim, Katie, and Charlotte Allyn for their love and for their countless inspirations. She would like to thank her coauthor Abi Gotthelf for her dedication to this project and, as a mother and teacher, to children.

Abi Gotthelf would like to thank all of the people who have helped make this book become a reality, particularly Delia Coppola and Michelle Yang, whose brilliant unit-writing skills and astute knowledge of third graders and how they learn helped shape many units in this book. Thanks to Kelly Brennan for sharing her wonderful work. She would also like to extend her thanks to teachers in Bronxville, New York, Bedford, New York, Westwood, New Jersey, and PS 183 and Girls Prep in Manhattan, whose keen knowledge of their grade levels guided their thoughtful feedback on content for this book. She would like to extend a special thank-you to Pam Allyn for including Abi in her quest to bring meaningful and engaging learning opportunities to children everywhere through work at LitLife and the development of this series. Finally, it is with all of her love that she acknowledges her biggest cheerleaders: husband Josh, sons Sam and Zachary, and her mother and father for their tireless support, encouragement, and confidence in her throughout this process.

Chapter 1

All About the Complete Year

Dear Third-Grade Teacher,

Third grade is a deeply significant year during which your students' growing abilities on multiple fronts—academic, social, and physical—come together in an intense evolution in their emotional growth and understanding of the world.

Your third graders are, right now, entering the age of real awareness of themselves in the world. One third grader tells us the story of being on the playground and having a revelation: "I was just standing there while everyone was running around me, and suddenly it was the first time I could picture myself outside myself."

In a similar vein, one day we watched a third grader draw a road around a castle in a picture and then he sat there just staring at it. When we asked, "What are you thinking about?" he said, "This is the first time I have drawn something that disappears from my view."

Perhaps, then, this is the beginning of conscious awareness of one's self—as a learner and as a person. It is a profound year, a year of discovery and growth.

Your third graders are facing the task of integrating their evolving understanding of the "reality" of the world with their still-evolving emotional, imaginative sides. Many still believe in magic, although they are beginning to question it more and more. Their attention shifts to the more concrete realties of friendships, playdates, and a variety of outside involvements—everything from soccer practice to piano lessons. Their worlds are expanding from core home events to the events of the outside world. They are attentive to all the nuances of the grown-ups around them.

They are still demonstrative in their affection and appreciation for you and greet you with hugs. They may drift to sleep at night thinking about their new learning while still holding their favorite stuffed animals.

There are many mental demands on a child of eight. Content area work, for example, is suddenly more complex. They are reading primary-source materials in the content areas, taking their first standardized tests, having to make connections across genres, and reading books with multiple themes and a more complex sense of time.

The process work this year is about thinking ahead. Third graders are able to set goals for reading and writing. They are thinking about friendship in dynamic, lively, and complex ways. This year, we create opportunities for collaboration that are fluid, so as to match rapidly changing developmental reading and writing levels.

Your third graders are capable of being deeply strategic in their reading and writing. Series books and reading across an author's work enable them to make connections across texts, studying the themes that run across them. This quest for strategies becomes paramount as their ever-increasing knowledge of the world develops, and they crave becoming more proficient at interacting with the world through the written word.

Your students' fascination with the sound and nature of words as they explore more complex texts makes poetry an important unit this year. Given the intensity of some of the issues that come into their consciousness, they gravitate genuinely to poetry. The repetition and rhythm in poetry are steady foundations upon which they can build bigger themes and ideas.

Let us take care to create test-preparation opportunities for third graders that are reasonable, rigorous, and actually even fun. You can help them prepare for future challenges they will encounter in life, rather than approach these challenges with dread.

Third graders see writing conventions as the tools of their new worlds as they write in new genres, from nonfiction to poetry to narrative. The comma, the quotation mark, and other forms of punctuation hold power, and your third graders want to know exactly what that power is and how they can use it to shape ideas.

They are more aware than ever of their immediate experiences as well as the world outside of themselves, of what is and is not real, and of their growing, evolving place in the world.

And yet, they still skip to lunch.

Warmly,

Abi Gotthelf   Pam Allyn

At-a-Glance Overview of the Complete Year

Organized around the Complete 4 components (Process, Genre, Strategy, and Conventions) and four unit stages (Immersion, Identification, Guided Practice, and Commitment), each book in the Complete Year series features a year's worth of integrated reading and writing curriculum. Because we honor your professional decision-making, you will find that the Complete Year provides a flexible framework, easily adapted to your state standards and to the needs and goals of your community, your students, and your teaching style.

Pam Allyn's *The Complete 4 for Literacy* and Debbie Lera's *Writing Above Standard* are foundational texts for the Complete Year. LitLife and RealeBooks provide innovative professional and technological support for the Complete Year.

What Will You Find Inside the Complete Year Series?

Yearlong Curricular Calendar

Units of Study
- More than 25 detailed unit outlines spanning every season of the school year.
- 8 Spotlight Units including more than 100 day-by-day lessons
- 2 ARCH units to start your year right
- 2 reflective units to end your year on a powerful note

Assessment
- Individualized assessments for every unit
- Complete 4 Assessment (C4A)

Lists of Anchor Texts for Each Unit

Parent Letters

Resource Sheets and Homework Assignments

Professional Reading Lists

Glossary of Terms

DVD that features Pam Allyn sharing the benefits of the Complete 4 for the Complete Year as well as ALL downloadable assessment forms and resources. You will also find helpful links to professional development support from LitLife and easy-to-use technological support from RealeBooks to help you publish your students' work.

The Complete Year Supports...

Individual teachers wanting a clear road map and detailed lessons for reading and writing and for reading/writing connections.

School or district teams wanting to plan a continuum together with specific lessons and units that address the needs of all students—ELL, gifted, and special needs.

Administrative leaders and literacy coaches wanting to guide their school to a consistent, standards-rich plan for reading and writing instruction.

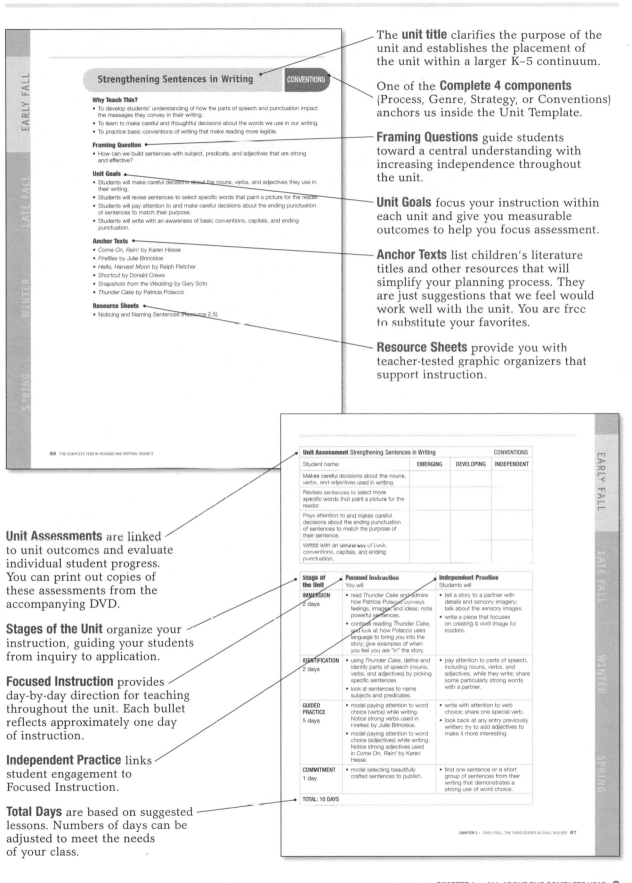

The **unit title** clarifies the purpose of the unit and establishes the placement of the unit within a larger K–5 continuum.

One of the **Complete 4 components** (Process, Genre, Strategy, or Conventions) anchors us inside the Unit Template.

Framing Questions guide students toward a central understanding with increasing independence throughout the unit.

Unit Goals focus your instruction within each unit and give you measurable outcomes to help you focus assessment.

Anchor Texts list children's literature titles and other resources that will simplify your planning process. They are just suggestions that we feel would work well with the unit. You are free to substitute your favorites.

Resource Sheets provide you with teacher-tested graphic organizers that support instruction.

Unit Assessments are linked to unit outcomes and evaluate individual student progress. You can print out copies of these assessments from the accompanying DVD.

Stages of the Unit organize your instruction, guiding your students from inquiry to application.

Focused Instruction provides day-by-day direction for teaching throughout the unit. Each bullet reflects approximately one day of instruction.

Independent Practice links student engagement to Focused Instruction.

Total Days are based on suggested lessons. Numbers of days can be adjusted to meet the needs of your class.

Strengthening Sentences in Writing — CONVENTIONS

Why Teach This?
- To develop students' understanding of how the parts of speech and punctuation impact the messages they convey in their writing.
- To learn to make careful and thoughtful decisions about the words we use in our writing.
- To practice basic conventions of writing that make reading more legible.

Framing Question
- How can we build sentences with subject, predicate, and adjectives that are strong and effective?

Unit Goals
- Students will make careful decisions about the nouns, verbs, and adjectives they use in their writing.
- Students will revise sentences to select specific words that paint a picture for the reader.
- Students will pay attention to and make careful decisions about the ending punctuation of sentences to match their purpose.
- Students will write with an awareness of basic conventions, capitals, and ending punctuation.

Anchor Texts
- *Come On, Rain!* by Karen Hesse
- *Fireflies* by Julie Brinckloe
- *Hello, Harvest Moon* by Ralph Fletcher
- *Shortcut* by Donald Crews
- *Snapshots from the Wedding* by Gary Soto
- *Thunder Cake* by Patricia Polacco

Resource Sheets
- Noticing and Naming Sentences (Resource 2.5)

56 THE COMPLETE YEAR IN READING AND WRITING: GRADE 3

Unit Assessment Strengthening Sentences in Writing — CONVENTIONS

Student name:	EMERGING	DEVELOPING	INDEPENDENT
Makes careful decisions about the nouns, verbs, and adjectives used in writing.			
Revises sentences to select more specific words that paint a picture for the reader.			
Pays attention to and makes careful decisions about the ending punctuation of sentences to match the purpose of their sentence.			
Writes with an awareness of basic conventions, capitals, and ending punctuation.			

Stage of the Unit	Focused Instruction You will	Independent Practice Students will
IMMERSION 2 days	• read *Thunder Cake* and admire how Patricia Polacco conveys feelings, images, and ideas; note powerful sentences. • continue reading *Thunder Cake*, and look at how Polacco uses language to bring you into the story; give examples of when you feel you are "in" the story.	• tell a story to a partner with details and sensory imagery; talk about the sensory images. • write a piece that focuses on creating a vivid image for readers.
IDENTIFICATION 2 days	• using *Thunder Cake*, define and identify parts of speech (nouns, verbs, and adjectives) by picking specific sentences. • look at sentences to name subjects and predicates.	• pay attention to parts of speech, including nouns, verbs, and adjectives, while they write; share some particularly strong words with a partner.
GUIDED PRACTICE 5 days	• model paying attention to word choice (verbs) while writing. Notice strong verbs used in *Fireflies* by Julie Brinckloe. • model paying attention to word choice (adjectives) while writing. Notice strong adjectives used in *Come On, Rain!* by Karen Hesse.	• write with attention to verb choice; share one special verb. • look back at any entry previously written; try to add adjectives to make it more interesting.
COMMITMENT 1 day	• model selecting beautifully crafted sentences to publish.	• find one sentence or a short group of sentences from their writing that demonstrates a strong use of word choice.
TOTAL: 10 DAYS		

CHAPTER 2 · EARLY FALL, THE THIRD GRADER AS SKILL BUILDER 57

EARLY FALL

LATE FALL

WINTER

SPRING

How This Book Will Support You

The Complete Year in Reading and Writing: Grade 3 is written by two authors: Abi Gotthelf, a team leader at LitLife and experienced classroom teacher, and Pam Allyn, the executive director of LitLife. Together, we have spent thousands of hours in third-grade classrooms, pondering the unique experience that comprises this year.

LitLife is a global organization dedicated to teacher training in the area of literacy education. Every lesson in this book has been field tested in a wide variety of classrooms. LitLife team leaders coach teachers and work alongside students to create a practical, meaningful curriculum that is well suited to each grade level because it exists inside a broader continuum. See this book as a compass you can use to chart a course in reading and writing instruction that feels true to your beliefs about the developmental needs and interests of third graders.

Many programs do not differentiate sufficiently by grade level. Third-grade teachers are often combined into a 3–5 grouping in professional literature and workshops. And yet the span between these grades is gigantic psychologically, socially, and intellectually. A curriculum for third grade needs to match the development of the learner and the uniqueness of this age student.

In creating this book for you, we also keep in mind the entirety of the child's learning experience throughout the elementary grades. While specifically written for third graders, the units presented here were created with the big picture in mind, children's entire K–5 experience.

The Complete 4

The Complete 4 was devised in response to the need expressed to us by teachers for balance in literacy instruction. We believe students should be well-rounded readers and writers. This means they should learn about reading and writing strategies. They should also develop a strong understanding of genre and a working knowledge of the conventions of the English language and begin to take on the passions, habits, and behaviors of lifelong readers and writers. The Complete 4 includes four key components of literacy instruction that will help us teach into these varied expectations: Process, Genre, Strategy, and Conventions.

The Complete 4 components help us to plan the school year by balancing the types of units across the year. Knowing whether a unit falls under the category of Process, Genre, Strategy, or Conventions, helps us to focus the unit so that all our lessons lead up to several key understandings.

Here is what we mean by the Complete 4:

Process	Your students will practice the processes shared by all successful readers and writers, at an appropriate developmental level. These include fluency, stamina, and independence.
Genre	Your students will learn to identify and use various literary containers, including narrative, nonfiction, poetry, and standardized tests.
Strategy	Your students will learn to be strategic readers and writers, practicing how writers make plans on a page, and how readers approach text differently depending on their needs.
Conventions	Your students will learn grammar and punctuation in contexts that are real, practical, and relevant to their reading and writing experiences.

In planning a Complete Year of literacy instruction for third grade, we have created reading and writing units that reflect a deep balance. All four Complete 4 components are represented. Take a look at the color-coded calendar on the inside front cover of this book to see how these units are organized across the year. We have arranged them so that they build on one another.

Will this book help me connect other aspects of the curriculum to the Complete 4?

Absolutely! One of the best features of the Complete 4 system is its flexibility. It has the capacity to help you integrate all these areas of your curriculum. For example, in third grade, your students are studying history and science topics of all kinds. They are expanding their research skills. Our units on nonfiction reading and writing support cross-content work. You can teach the skills and strategies for reading and writing in the content areas inside one or more of these units. This book will help you forge these connections, and our sample units will give you the resources to make those connections successfully and comfortably.

Alignment to standards is critical, and these units are constructed in such a way as to reflect the standards and to allow for your adjustments for your state standards.

Can this book help me if I have other demands in my day and cannot teach all the units?

Yes, it can. Here are three suggestions for how you could adapt this calendar to your particular situation:

- You can choose one reading and one writing unit from each Complete 4 component to teach during the year.
- You can focus on the units of study that pair well with your existing themes.
- You can teach only the reading or writing strand.

Will the Complete 4 help me forge reading and writing connections with my students?

This is another great aspect of the Complete 4 program: we link reading and writing units as "companions." Although the instruction may not always be identical, the units should be "talking" to one another. You will see how we take special care to make sure reading and writing units echo and parallel each other, or to stagger them so students see, feel, and understand those essential connections. Indeed, reading and writing are interrelated processes that are mutually supportive when taught together. You may have noticed that your strongest writers are typically your most passionate readers.

Can I use this book to support just my writing instruction since I already use another reading program?

Yes. You can use this book to guide you in either reading or writing. Take a look at the writing calendar only; with your grade-level team, you can look into your reading program and see where you can link the writing units into your instruction. For example, if your reading program has a set of stories on friendship, you could link that set to our Exploring Elements of Craft: Writing About Characters unit in the late fall. This calendar is designed so that you can use it flexibly—you can use either the reading calendar or the writing calendar on its own or if you want the "complete" package, you can use both of them together. And the Complete 4 is also a way to reintroduce quality children's literature into your classroom even if you use a core reading program.

Can I still benefit from this yearlong approach if my school has commitments that must be addressed at different times of the year?

One of the most exciting aspects of the Complete 4 is that the reading and writing units are interconnected and follow a logical sequence. However, we have also constructed the calendars to allow for flexibility. If, for example, your standardized testing comes earlier in the year, you can easily move units around to suit your test preparation schedule. Or if your entire school studies poetry together in the fall rather than the spring, you can move the units to accommodate that. The calendar is designed to be used either as a whole unit, as a step-by-step program, or as building blocks to construct your own unique program.

Will the Complete 4 help me meet the needs of all learners in my classroom?

The range of ability levels and learning modalities in each of our classrooms reminds us to balance our own teaching. The Complete 4 can help us accomplish this. For example, we tend to work with our English language learners mostly on conventions of print, while we work with writers whose first language is English more on strategies or genre. The Complete 4 reminds us that our English language learners flourish with exposure to the habits and passions of readers and writers, the study of different genres, and practice with complex strategies. Similarly, your students who have a comparatively strong sense of conventions are often not given intensive instruction in that area, but they too would enjoy and benefit greatly from inspiring lessons on the construction of a sentence or the artful use of a punctuation mark. The Complete 4 guides us to teach with an eye to creating a Complete Year for all students.

Will this book help me with the flow of my day?

Yes! We are very aware of your time constraints and the benefits of predictable routines. We have created a very simple, easy-to-follow outline for each day's work during reading and writing time that follows a whole/small/whole pattern. These are the three parts of every lesson:

- Focused Instruction: the whole-class lessons

- Independent Practice: individualized or small-group work

- Wrap-Up: more whole-class teaching with planning for the next day's lesson

Focused Instruction	Students gather for a period of Focused Instruction for 5 to 15 minutes.
	• Warm up your students with a reference to prior teaching and learning.
	• Teach one clear point.
	• Ask students to quickly try your point.
	• Clarify your teaching point.
	• Set the stage for Independent Practice.
Independent Practice	Students practice independently while you confer with students and/or conduct small instructional groups.
	• Encourage students to read or write independently (at their level).
	• Have students practice your teaching point as they read and write.
	• Meet with individual students, partnerships, and/or groups regularly for informal assessment and instruction.
	• Look for future teaching points or an example to use in the Wrap-Up.
Wrap-Up	Students return for a focused, brief discussion that reflects on the day's learning.
	• Restate your teaching point.
	• Share examples of students' work or learning.
	• Set plans for the next day and make connections to homework.

What are my students actually doing during Independent Practice?

As you will see from the scripted lessons in our Spotlight Units, during Independent Practice, students practice a skill you have demonstrated. In addition, they are doing something that seems fairly simple on the surface but in fact is the heart of our work and the driving energy for all the lessons in this book: **They are reading and writing independently**, every day. We suggest that 50 percent of all reading and writing time is Independent Practice. Of this time, approximately 20 percent should be spent practicing a specific skill associated with their reading, and 80 percent of the time should be spent actually reading and writing! Students should be given time every day to read and write in a comfortable manner, at their reading and writing levels, and in books and topics that are of great personal interest to them. Here are the approximate amounts of time your students can and should be reading and writing for each day (you may have to work toward these minutes as the year unfolds):

Grade Level	Actual Reading Time	Actual Writing Time
KINDERGARTEN	10–15 minutes	10–20 (writing/drawing)
FIRST GRADE	10–20	10–20
SECOND GRADE	20–30	20–25
THIRD GRADE	30–40	25–30
FOURTH GRADE	35–45	25–30
FIFTH GRADE	40–45	30–40

Are there essential materials I must use in order to make the Complete 4 program a success?

You can use any of your support materials, including a core reading program or a phonics program, alongside the Complete 4 approach. The heart of our approach is that every child has time to practice skills, strategies, and processes through reading and writing that is at his level and is as authentic as possible. A seminal National Endowment for the Arts study (2007) found, not surprisingly, that "students who read for fun nearly every day performed better on reading tests than those who reported reading never or hardly at all." The study points to the "failure of schools and colleges to develop a culture of daily reading habits." In addition, an analysis of federal Department of Education statistics found that those students who scored lower on all standardized tests lived in homes with fewer than ten books. (Rich, 2007). This study then points to two pivotal factors in ensuring lifelong literacy: children must have time to read a lot, and children must have easy, continual access to books.

Our work throughout this book and this series is designed to focus on daily Independent Practice: Students are reading authentic literature and reading a lot, every day, at their own level. Students are writing about topics of authentic interest and writing a lot, every day, at their own level. Students are navigating texts and have easy access to understandable texts throughout the day, especially during literacy time. These, then, are the two keys to our work: giving students time to practice reading and writing, and giving them access to texts that inspire them both as readers and as writers.

The access is critical and is best accomplished by establishing a well-stocked classroom library. Your library should have a variety of genres: nonfiction, fiction, and poetry. Approximately 20 to 30 percent of your library should be leveled in a clearly organized system in which children can find books that are truly comfortable for them to read at their independent reading levels.

Your students should have a way to bring their books between home and school and to store the stack of books they have been reading most recently, either in baggies or baskets. Organization is one of two keys to life (the other being passion!). Don't let disorder get in the way of helping your children do a lot of reading in your classroom. They can help you organize your library, too.

It is also crucial for students to have a way to record thinking about reading, either in a reading notebook, or a folder, or even a binder. The important thing to remember is that this should be a system that works for you and your students. It does not matter so much what you select or what you call it, as long as you know your children can easily access it, and they feel comfortable writing in it and, if they are our youngest readers and writers, drawing in it.

During writing time, your students need order as well. Keep a separate writing area neat and stocked, equipped with all the helpful tools a writer loves: sticky notes, staplers, tape, and date stamps. And as with reading time, your students should have a clearly identified, easy-to-use container to capture their writing. In this series, we use writing notebooks with our students from second grade to fifth grade, and writing folders with students in kindergarten and first grade. Using folders allows us to provide our students with a variety of paper choices if they need them. The key to keeping containers for students' writing work is that it is easy for them to revisit, reread, and reflect upon, and it is easy for you to look at before conferences and to assess on an ongoing basis. Again, it does not matter what you call these containers, or which ones you choose, as long as they are truly useful for both you and your students.

I don't have access to all the anchor texts you recommend in this book or there are other texts I prefer to use instead. Will my units be as effective if my anchor text selections are somewhat different from yours?

We want to give you as many specific suggestions as we can and so we have recommended many anchor texts for each unit. You can find them both in the unit templates and also in the back of the book in a seasonally organized bibliography so you can order all of them for your classroom library if you wish. However, if you can't find them all, or you have others you wish to use instead, you are more than welcome and the units will absolutely be as successful. Take a close look at why we chose the texts we did so you can replace them with selections that will still match the outcomes for the units and will feel comfortable for you.

I use the elements of balanced literacy: shared reading, guided reading, read-aloud, and more. Where do they fit in to the Complete 4 system?

See your elements of balanced literacy as the "how" of your teaching and the Complete 4 as the "what." Teachers who use balanced literacy elements are still asking: But WHAT do I teach tomorrow? The Complete 4 answers that age-old question. Your balanced literacy structures, then, can truly become the engines that drive your content home. For example, shared reading and the read aloud are structures you can use present your content, both in the Focused Instruction and in the Wrap-Up.

Guided reading is a structure you can use to practice content with smaller groups of children. This can be done during Independent Practice, so while some of your children are reading independently others are meeting with you in small groups.

What if I've never taught in units like this before?

In a Complete Year unit of study, students learn about one aspect of reading or writing (Process, Genre, Strategy, or Conventions) in a one- to six-week cycle of learning. Inside this book, you will find all the units for a Complete Year of reading and writing instruction. In each unit, we have set a specific focus for instruction and created framing questions to guide you and your students. We have set a time frame and established goals for each unit and put together a list of anchor texts that you can use to teach the lessons. Most important, we have provided helpful templates to take you through *all* the units.

To help you implement and pace your instruction, we have divided the instruction in each unit into four key lesson stages: Immersion, Identification, Guided Practice, and Commitment. The premise behind this concept was inspired by the work of Pearson and Gallagher (1983). They delineated a gradual release of responsibility from teacher to student as the ideal conditions for learning. These stages help us make the necessary turns in our teaching so that we move in an efficient and effective way through any unit of study and our students have the best chance for success.

Immersion	We immerse our students in a topic of study.
Identification	We name or define what students must know about the topic by the end of the unit.
Guided Practice	We model reading and writing for our students and give them time for practice, so that we can guide them toward the goals of the unit.
Commitment	We ask students to reflect on their learning and commit to the use of this knowledge in their future reading and writing.

You use specific language to identify the parts of a unit and the parts of a lesson. How can I be sure I can follow along easily?

The language in this book is extremely user-friendly. We try to steer clear of jargon as much as we can. To best help teachers plan units and teach lessons, we have identified terms that help us all move forward easily. We have included a helpful Glossary of Terms for you on page 234.

What is the role of the Spotlight Units in the Complete Year books?

Each Complete Year book features eight bonus Spotlight Units, designed to help you understand what each unit of study can look and feel like in your classroom—both in terms of the concrete day-to-day details as well as the "learning energy" that you create through your instructional language and strategies. During the Spotlight Units, we invite you into our classrooms to sit by our sides and listen as we interact with our students. While we know you'll use your own language that reflects your unique teaching personality, we provide examples of language we use in our classrooms as a model for you to adapt. Learning how to craft our teaching language in artful ways that encourage active student participation takes practice; for example, knowing how to design open-ended questions rather than questions that just elicit a yes–no response is an art, typically learned through classroom-tested trial and error. Sometimes it's helpful to listen in on another teacher and notice how she uses language to frame each teaching moment.

Inside the Spotlight Units, you'll find one reading unit and one writing unit in each of the Complete 4 components (Process, Genre, Strategy, and Conventions). Our Spotlight Units also include unit templates, so you can see how we translate the templates into day-by-day lesson plans. You'll notice that not all bullets are translated directly into lessons and that the flow of the unit is fluid and flexible so you can adapt it in ways that fit your students' unique needs and interests.

How do I use the unit templates?

We envision teachers taking the templates we provide for each unit and adapting them to their students. Perhaps you have favorite books you love to read in your nonfiction unit. Or perhaps your students need more than one day on a bulleted lesson. Although the templates offer guidelines for the overall structure of a unit and suggestions for how the unit might be paced, we see them as a road atlas, a guide that leads you toward your goal but also gives you the opportunity to add your own special touches along the way. Many teachers like to keep these unit templates on their desks as a reminder of where they are going, to help them plan each day's lesson.

How will I assess my students through the Complete Year?

The structure of the Complete 4 classroom gives you a rich opportunity to assess your students during their Independent Practice. Units of study give you regular, frequent opportunities to take stock of your students' progress. At the end of each unit is an assessment form for you to use.

Chapter 6 is dedicated to the C4 Assessment (C4A): a comprehensive tool designed for your grade level. You can use the C4A three times a year for both reading and writing. Quick and easy, the C4A will provide valuable information on your students' progress in all areas of reading and writing instruction.

The Complete Year in Grade 3

Our learning time with our students, bound by the parameters of the school year, is organized by seasons, so we thought it would be helpful to organize our books that way, too.

As the year begins, some of your third graders have great confidence about their place in school. They are excited to be upper graders! Others still hang back—they like the warmth and safety of the second-grade hallway. It will take them a bit longer to settle in. In the fall, they are establishing relationships and incorporating routines. The ARCH helps them to set goals for their reading and writing experiences. They are developing a much greater capacity to think ahead and make plans. Winter brings much new learning to stimulate their inquisitive minds: story and character explorations as well as nonfiction reading and writing. The spring brings with it more blooming possibilities. There is a new hum in the room—the potential of fast friendships lead to book clubs and writing clubs, poetry fills the air and inspires them to be creative and expressive. They are developing a new confidence in themselves and can look forward to the summer as readers and writers in the world. With their poems, their songs, their writing, their stacks of chapter books under their arms, they still skip holding hands at times. Growing, growing, but still so blessedly young.

Get ready now for the Complete Year experience. It's timely and timeless (and won't cost YOU time). Flexible and friendly (and fun). Easy to use and easy to navigate (and easy to explain to parents). Standards-based and field tested (in hundreds of classrooms). Made for you (to simplify your teaching life and to reconnect you with the joy of teaching). Made for your third graders (especially).

Have a great year!

Chapter 2

EARLY FALL

The Third Grader as Skill Builder

"I was eight. I knew the green damp, dark smells that bloomed on the hill. I could track the places where black ash grew. Eight must be old enough."
—from *The Basket Moon* by Mary Lyn Ray

For your third graders, every moment has its potential for learning. Every moment can be transformative. In this first season, choice brings its own mysteries and joys. A sentence is a beautiful thing and can help us construct new ideas. Journey with us into this first season, with units of study that will support skill-building and provide plenty of fun, too.

EARLY FALL UNITS

SPOTLIGHT UNITS

Beginning the Year With the ARCH

Our first units, known as the ARCH, are designed to bring our students together into a reading and writing community. This acronym stands for Assessment, Routines, Choice, and Healthy Community. The units balance the need to assess students as readers and writers with lessons on the routines of reading and writing time, the community-building aspects of reading and writing time, and how to make choices both in terms of topics and texts.

We must actively construct this community, by establishing the daily routines for reading and writing time, discovering personal and shared interests, and introducing our students to our libraries and writing tools. Fountas and Pinnell (2001) remind us that during the first month of school you have two important goals: to help your students think of themselves as readers and to establish roles and routines. They remind us to repeat key lessons, chart the routines and roles of the reader and writer, and refer our students back to these reference points regularly.

As teachers, we are always a bit uncertain about how to begin the year in terms of content. We want to get to know our students, and we know we need to establish these routines, but we wonder what the content and outcomes are for this work. The ARCH is designed to blend both process and products: the beautiful work we do in coming together for the first time, as well as the important work we do in generating products that represent our students and move them forward at the very beginning of this school year's journey.

Each Complete 4 year begins with an ARCH unit at every grade level, but each year should feel different because of your students' changing developmental needs. (See page 112 of *The Complete 4 for Literacy* to see all the ARCH articulations for each grade level.) In third grade, our ARCH focus is setting reading and writing goals. In the reading and writing units that follow, we continue to build upon that theme with units that help our students discover the value of thinking and working across text.

The ARCH units set the foundation for the entire year. The ARCH incorporates teaching of all of those routines and habits you long for and need when you are in the midst of your work with your students. If you set the stage now, you are guaranteed a happy, truly productive year in the teaching of reading and writing.

How to Make Smart Book Choices

1. Read the title and think about the picture on the cover.
2. Choose an author we are familiar with or choose a series we want to continue with.
3. Read the blurb on the back cover or the inside flap.
4. Do a *book walk* (pictures, table of contents, chapter titles, etc.) to see if the book interests you.
5. Turn to a random page or the first few pages and read.
6. Use the "5 Finger Rule."

You can give your students helpful tips for choosing books to post inside their notebooks.

The ARCH: Setting Personal Reading Goals

PROCESS

Why Teach This?

- To establish a collegial and supportive community of readers.
- To help students internalize the routines for independent reading practice.
- To determine students' strengths and needs as the year begins.
- To help students learn about themselves as readers and use this information to develop new goals for their learning in the coming months.

Framing Question

- How do readers reflect on their reading lives to set goals for learning?

Read-alouds help build community.

Unit Goals

- Students will co-construct a collegial, vibrant community of readers.
- Students will internalize the routines and structures of independent reading practice.
- Students will make book choices that represent interests, level, and purpose.
- Students will develop stamina, fluency, and confidence as readers.

Anchor Texts

- *The Boy Who Loved Words* by Roni Schotter
- *The Hundred Dresses* by Eleanor Estes
- *I Want to Be* by Thylias Moss
- *Whales* by Seymour Simon
- *What You Know First* by Patricia MacLachlan

Unit Assessment The ARCH: Setting Personal Reading Goals			PROCESS
Student name:	EMERGING	DEVELOPING	INDEPENDENT
Actively participates in a collegial, vibrant community of readers.			
Demonstrates an understanding of the routines and structures of reading time.			
Makes book selections that reflect interests, level, and purpose.			
Develops stamina, fluency, and confidence as a reader.			
Sets realistic reading goals.			

Stage of the Unit	Focused Instruction You will	Independent Practice Students will
IMMERSION 5 days	• read *The Boy Who Loved Words* and discuss how we will grow to love words this year together; share what words and books have meant to you. • read aloud from *The Hundred Dresses* and show how you practice reading for longer periods of time by setting goals; demonstrate using an egg timer to build capacity to read longer each day (start with smaller increments and increase the length of time each day). • read aloud from *The Hundred Dresses* and demonstrate routines of reading time, including the roles of student and teacher in a conference. • read aloud *The Hundred Dresses* and discuss how together you will build a community of trust, care, and mutual affection where everyone is included (you will finish reading this book aloud at other times of the day going forward). • invite school guests in to talk about their reading goals: what they plan to read this year, what they plan to read this month, what they plan to read this week, along with genres they would like to read and topics they would like to explore.	• write their reading histories/timelines—times when reading has mattered to them. • talk and write about readers they admire. • explore their book preferences by touring the library and talking with other readers. • respond to *The Hundred Dresses* by talking about what it means to create an inclusive community. • read independently for growing increments of time.

IDENTIFICATION
3 days
	• identify routines of the classroom library and how the class will use it to access independent reading materials.
	
	• read *Whales* and discuss the goal of reading both fiction and nonfiction; set goals for your own reading life and write them down in front of your students.
		• practice routines such as finding comfortable reading spots and making good use of reading supplies, including the classroom library and book baskets.
		
		• select a short stack of books for this month's reading based on interest and level.
		
		• discuss and record goals for reading that include:
		  • what they plan to read this year
		  • what they plan to read this month

IDENTIFICATION *(continued)*	• identify what makes a reading experience feel strong and successful; record ideas on a chart.	• what they plan to read this week • genres they would like to read • topics they would like to explore
GUIDED PRACTICE 5 days	• create anchor charts of what effective readers do to make wise book choices (consider genre, interests, comfortable length of book, level). • read aloud *What You Know First* and model what readers do during and after reading time (jot down ideas in reader's notebooks, talk with a partner). • continue reading *The Hundred Dresses* (or another picture book, poem, or excerpt from nonfiction text) and model what readers do to share ideas with others (talk with a partner, enter thinking into reader's notebook). • revisit *Whales* and discuss reading in multiple genres and show how to plan reading choices: have a short stack for active reading and another book "on deck." • read aloud *The Boy Who Loved Words* and discuss how you can save words you love in your reader's notebook as you read.	• think about the effective readers they know and discuss with one another what they do as readers. • practice daily routines and increase time on the egg timer. • read independently and practice what readers do during and after reading time. • think aloud with partners about texts they are reading. • plan reading goals by creating a set of "books on deck."
COMMITMENT 3 days	• name the five essential qualities of strong reading (fluency, stamina, independence, word attack, passion). • read *I Want to Be* and celebrate reading goals by talking about how we are all different in our goals but we belong to the same community. • celebrate commitment to creating a strong and supportive community of readers by admiring what you have seen readers do this month to support one another.	• share what they have read this month with a partner; share what they notice about their reading preferences and habits. • write a list of reading goals to share on walls of the classroom and in the hallway. • compliment one another as readers on notecards—"I admired when"—and share them with one another.
TOTAL: 16 DAYS		

EARLY FALL

LATE FALL

WINTER

SPRING

The ARCH: Setting Personal Writing Goals

PROCESS

Why Teach This?

- To establish a collegial and supportive community of writers.
- To help students learn and become independent in the routines and management of writing time.
- To help students develop the skills to sustain independent writing for an extended period of time.
- To help students learn about themselves as writers and use this information to develop new goals for their learning in the coming months.

Framing Question

- How do writers reflect on their writing lives to set goals for learning?

Unit Goals

- Students will co-construct a collegial, vibrant writing community.
- Students will internalize writing routines.
- Students will develop an awareness of writing in multiple genres.
- Students will develop stamina, fluency, and confidence as writers.
- Students will set writing goals.

Anchor Texts

- *The Basket Moon* by Mary Lyn Ray
- *Emma's Rug* by Allen Say
- *A Family of Poems: My Favorite Poetry for Children*, edited by Caroline Kennedy
- *In Daddy's Arms I Am Tall* by Javaka Steptoe
- *Miss Rumphius* by Barbara Cooney
- *Nothing Ever Happens on 90th Street* by Roni Schotter
- *The Tarantula in My Purse and 172 Other Wild Pets* by Jean Craighead George
- *Wolves* by Seymour Simon
- *Wordsworth the Poet* by Frances H. Kakugawa

Unit Assessment The ARCH: Setting Personal Writing Goals			PROCESS
Student name:	EMERGING	DEVELOPING	INDEPENDENT
Actively participates in a collegial, vibrant writing community.			
Demonstrates understanding of the routines and structures of independent writing time.			
Writes in multiple genres.			
Develops stamina, fluency, and independence.			
Sets realistic writing goals.			

Stage of the Unit	Focused Instruction You will	Independent Practice Students will
IMMERSION 5 days	• read aloud *Nothing Ever Happens on 90th Street* and discuss how writers find ideas from memories, wonderings, observations, and imagination. • read aloud *Miss Rumphius* and talk about how writers make the world more beautiful with their words. • read aloud *Emma's Rug* and discuss the power of imagination to fuel writing. • read aloud *The Basket Moon* and discuss conditions for creation (a community of support, a goal that you have, what you do when you face challenges). • demonstrate how you personalize your writer's notebook.	• respond to the question: "Where do you think writers get their ideas?" • respond in writing and in partner conversations from *Miss Rumphius*: "What could you do to make the world more beautiful through your writing?" • record ideas: create a "Welcome to my World" list of things they like and dislike, along with their passions and interests. • respond in writing to *The Basket Moon*: "What are my best conditions for creation?" • personalize their writer's notebook.
IDENTIFICATION 3 days	• read aloud from *In Daddy's Arms I Am Tall* and demonstrate and chart purposes for writing (create a beautiful gift with poetry, explain or share information with nonfiction, tell a story that matters to you with narrative). • read *Wordsworth the Poet* and name the qualities of an effective writer (strong process, knowledge of genres, practicing craft, and using conventions). • identify writing goals for this community of writers.	• identify their own purpose for writing this month. • talk with a partner about the qualities of an effective writer and choose one quality to focus on in their writing. • identify four personal writing goals in the Complete 4.

GUIDED PRACTICE 7 days	• read aloud from *The Tarantula in My Purse* and model how writers write about genuine interests and passions. • model how to use a writing partner to explore ideas. • by reading a poem from Caroline Kennedy's collection, demonstrate how to write ideas as a poem (could be 2 days). • by reading a piece from *The Tarantula in My Purse* demonstrate how to write an idea as nonfiction (could be 2 days). • by reading a snippet from *Basket Moon* demonstrate how to write an idea as a narrative story.	• begin to write about what they wonder about, what they remember, what they observe, and what they imagine. • share writing with a partner. • practice writing an idea as a poem. • practice writing an idea as a nonfiction text. • practice writing an idea as a narrative story. • reread with a partner. • edit one piece for spelling, punctuation, and grammar.
COMMITMENT 3 days	• demonstrate your community goals as a commitment. • celebrate the creation of class goals for establishing a strong writing community by asking the children to read them aloud. • celebrate by creating small groups to read one another's writing.	• make a commitment to one writing goal for each Complete 4 component. • share goals with a partner and with the class and hang them up inside the classroom or in the hallway.
TOTAL: 18 DAYS		

Becoming Resourceful as Readers and Writers

This set of units that come next is integral to the entire year. It is all about supporting our students as choice-makers, both as readers and as writers. Third graders are faced with a dizzying variety of possibilities for their reading experiences: series books, biographies, realistic fiction. They are also more and more influenced by their peers' decisions and the desire to "look good" as readers. This reading unit is designed to help your students make wise choices not only about what they read but how they read. In writing, topic choice is also a huge issue. It is difficult to face a blank page. Third graders are more susceptible than ever to the eagle eye of their neighbors. Watching a friend zip his pen down the page or his cursor down the computer screen, they are liable to feel a pang—why is finding ideas so hard? The Four Prompts unit gives our students very concrete ways to tap into all their own resources for writing. Our students need ongoing support on the concept of choices: how readers make them and how writers make them, scaffolding their independence as they enter new worlds.

Making Choices in Reading: Strategies for Comprehension

STRATEGY

Why Teach This?

- To help students make independent book choices.
- To help students become active readers.
- To name and refine how students use comprehension strategies.

Framing Question

- How do readers make wise book choices and read with strong understanding?

Unit Goals

- Students will make wise book choices.
- Students will make effective predictions.
- Students will make effective connections.
- Students will use prior knowledge to help with text understanding.

Anchor Texts

- *The Firekeeper's Son* by Linda Sue Park
- *Hey, Al* by Arthur Yorinks
- *Sixteen Years and Sixteen Seconds: The Sammy Lee Story* by Paula Yoo
- *Super-Completely and Totally the Messiest* by Judith Viorst

Unit Assessment Making Choices in Reading: Strategies for Comprehension			STRATEGY
Student name:	EMERGING	DEVELOPING	INDEPENDENT
Uses strategies for making wise book choices (level, interest, genre).			
Uses prediction as a way to prepare for one's reading.			
Makes connections to heighten comprehension of overall text.			
Forms opinions about texts.			

Stage of the Unit	Focused Instruction You will	Independent Practice Students will
IMMERSION 2 days	• discuss times when a book you are reading feels level, downhill, or uphill and why you make certain reading choices (level for books you want to read really smoothly, downhill for books you want to cruise through or revisit, and uphill for topics you want to investigate but you know may be a bit difficult for you); demonstrate how you select books (level, genre, interest). • begin reading *Sixteen Years and Sixteen Seconds: The Sammy Lee Story* and use reading strategies of prediction, making connections, and forming opinions through a think-aloud.	• create a short stack of books and talk with a partner about book choices. • revisit stack of books and revise book choices as needed.
IDENTIFICATION 4 days	• notice that effective readers make wise book choices, and have books both in a short stack and books on deck—the books you are planning to read later on or next. • read *Super-Completely and Totally the Messiest* and identify how effective readers use the cover and title to make predictions about a book and then read to test a prediction. • read *Hey, Al* and identify how effective readers make connections between texts and their lives. • read *The Firekeeper's Son* and identify how effective readers form opinions about what they read.	• read independently and share with a partner times when reading felt hard and which strategies they used to get through the hard parts. • use the cover and title to make a prediction about a text before they begin reading. • read with an eye toward making a meaningful connection between an event in the book and an event from their lives. • record an opinion that they have about an event or character in their books.

GUIDED PRACTICE 7 days	• model how effective readers use the cover, title, prior knowledge about an author, and friends' recommendations to enhance immediate understanding of text. • model how effective readers monitor for meaning and use self-correcting strategies to ensure that they understand a text. • model how effective readers make connections to big ideas in the text and their own lives to help them understand ideas in a text. • model how effective readers make connections to other texts or something in the book to help them better understand the ideas in the text. • model how effective readers form opinions about what they read. • model how effective readers use sticky notes to track their thinking; model a think-aloud or revisit any texts from previous days to review sticky notes.	• use cover and title to make predictions about a text. • read to test predictions. • notice when meaning breaks down and find a strategy to correct the problem. • work to make thoughtful predictions that move their reading forward. • form opinions about characters and events in stories. • collect ideas about texts and share with a partner. • note connections to other texts as they read and when they share with a partner.
COMMITMENT 1 day	• review how readers make wise book selections and how readers check for meaning initially and throughout text.	• reflect on how book choices are made that feel wise and effective. • celebrate one book they have read by sharing thoughts about it with the class.
TOTAL: 14 DAYS		

Organizing your library helps your students make thoughtful reading choices and builds independence.

Idea Makers

Great writers will say that they return to similar themes over and over in their writing. Langston Hughes observed his beloved Harlem many times in his poetry. Charlotte Zolotow wondered about parent-child relationships. Patricia Polacco remembers times from her childhood. Roald Dahl imagined worlds where magic came to life. Having choices as writers is both daunting and liberating all at the same time. But to cultivate choice with a group of 20 or more children can be downright intimidating! We know this all too well, and so we have developed a system both for helping children find freedom in finding writing ideas and also for helping them, within a set of prompts, to write about matters of interest and importance to them. The key to all great writing, and great teaching, is both structure and freedom. That's what the Four Prompts unit is all about.

Making Choices in Writing: The Four Prompts

STRATEGY

Why Teach This?

- To develop students' independence as writers.
- To reinforce the understanding that writers use core topics to write inside a variety of genres.

Framing Questions

- How do writers find ideas?
- How do writers use their ideas in a variety of ways?

Unit Goals

- Students will identify how ideas for writing come from four key areas: wondering, remembering, imagining, observing.
- Students will understand that writers experiment with their ideas in a variety of genres.
- Students will recognize key (anchor) texts as providing inspiration to locate writing ideas.

Anchor Texts

- *All the Small Poems and Fourteen More* by Valerie Worth (observing)
- *Aunt Flossie's Hats (and Crab Cakes Later)* by Elizabeth Fitzgerald Howard (remembering)
- *The Best Pet of All* by David LaRochelle (imagining)
- *Calling the Doves/ El Canto de las Palomas* by Juan Felipe Herrera (remembering)
- *A Drop of Water* by Walter Wick (wondering)
- *How I Spent My Summer Vacation* by Mark Teague (imagining)
- *Snowmen at Night* by Caralyn Buehner and Mark Buehner (imagining)

Unit Assessment Making Choices in Writing: The Four Prompts			STRATEGY
Student name:	EMERGING	DEVELOPING	INDEPENDENT
Recognizes that ideas for writing come from a variety of places, including wondering, remembering, observing, and imagining.			
Generates writing ideas within each of the Four Prompts.			
Experiments with writing ideas across genres.			
Uses anchor texts to inspire and impact own writing.			

Stage of the Unit	Focused Instruction You will	Independent Practice Students will
IMMERSION 2 days	• read aloud from the anchor text selections and ask the question: "Where do writing ideas come from?" • categorize writing ideas into the Four Prompt categories (observing, remembering, wondering, imagining).	• work with a partner to discover patterns in writing (ideas they return to, when writing feels comfortable, what ideas they are writing about). • categorize writing into the Four Prompts categories to notice patterns in writing.
IDENTIFICATION 4 days	• focus on remembering by reading aloud from *Aunt Flossie's Hats (and Crab Cakes Later)*; create a list of memories that students have that they would like to write about. • focus on wondering by reading *A Drop of Water* and talk about what we wonder about; chart students' wonderings. • focus on imagining by reading aloud *The Best Pet of All* and talk about where the author got his idea; create a list of things that students imagine. • focus on observing by reading some of Valerie Worth's poems; discuss the kinds of things that she observes and how she describes them.	• write about memories inspired by *Aunt Flossie's Hats (and Crab Cakes Later)* or about their own memories. • write about a wondering that they have. • write about something from their imagination. • observe and draw something in their classroom or outside that they have closely examined; list words that describe their observation.

GUIDED PRACTICE 5 days	• model creating a brainstorm list for each of the Four Prompts. • model writing in different genres even as you wonder, observe, remember, or imagine. • model writing a piece and then rewriting it in another genre (e.g., narrative to poetry) or produce a new piece to experiment in a new genre. • model how you reread your writing notebook to find a new topic in an old piece of writing. • demonstrate using your brainstorm list to find ideas when you are stuck on what to write.	• listen to texts written in response to each of the Four Prompts, make a connection with each text and use it as inspiration for their own writing ideas. • brainstorm a list of ideas inspired by each prompt. • take an idea they have written about already and try to rewrite it in another genre or produce a new piece to experiment in a new genre. • reread writing to find a new idea in an old piece of writing. • use brainstorm list to find writing ideas.
COMMITMENT 1 day	• discuss which category is most comfortable for you and which is least comfortable; select one piece to revise and edit.	• share writing with a partner and reflect in writing upon where writers get ideas; celebrate writing with a share.
TOTAL: 12 DAYS		

The Power of Story Elements

Your students have been reading fiction for all of their primary years. These units take them to the next step along the Complete 4 continuum: to begin to explore theme and time through their readings. Time may already be giving your readers a challenge. As they enter third grade, time presents a new kind of confusion in their reading texts. It is not just linear; it may move backward and forward, or even inside and out if they are reading science fiction. We wonder why our third graders, who appear so fluent and skilled in decoding, seem to have difficulty with the longer texts. Time is often the hidden roadblock. It is critical for us to teach into this essential ingredient of time so students feel empowered by it rather than controlled. We need to provide them with a sense of mastery over both the large abstractness of theme and the slippery and often elusive mystery of time. Time is embedded in the subject of theme. The theme of friendship in a picture book may unfold over a one-day period, whereas the theme of friendship in a longer chapter book may go across years of two friends' lives. Time and theme are connected, and this unit offers our students an opportunity to explore both.

Growing an Awareness of Theme and Time: Reading Fiction

 GENRE

Why Teach This?

- To review the elements of fiction and how they help readers' understanding.
- To teach students how to recognize the sense of time in a story.
- To teach students that some stories are written around a central theme.

Framing Question

- How can understanding the elements of fiction help us become stronger readers of fiction?

Unit Goals

- Students will understand that fictional stories include characters, setting, passage of time, problem, solution, and plot/theme.
- Students will identify words in a story that indicate a sense of time.
- Students will be introduced to the meaning of theme and how to understand it in a story.

Anchor Texts

- *The Art Lesson* by Tomie dePaola
- *Big Sister and Little Sister* by Charlotte Zolotow
- *The Chicken-Chasing Queen of Lamar County* by Janice N. Harrington
- *Crickwing* by Janell Cannon
- *Fly Away Home* by Eve Bunting
- *A Frog Thing* by Eric Drachman
- *Oliver Button Is a Sissy* by Tomie dePaola
- *The Other Side* by Jacqueline Woodson

Unit Assessment Growing an Awareness of Theme and Time: Reading Fiction			GENRE
Student name:	EMERGING	DEVELOPING	INDEPENDENT
Identifies elements of fiction.			
Makes connections across texts.			
Uses words that indicate a sense of time in retelling a story.			
Is aware of theme and describes theme efficiently.			

Stage of the Unit	Focused Instruction You will	Independent Practice Students will
IMMERSION 2 days	• read *A Frog Thing*; demonstrate how you look for theme in books—the big ideas in text. • demonstrate how you are aware of time; read *Big Sister and Little Sister* and discuss both theme and the passage of time.	• read and talk with a partner about what they notice about big ideas in their texts. • read and talk with a partner about the passage of time.
IDENTIFICATION 2 days	• read aloud *The Chicken-Chasing Queen of Lamar County* and define theme—a big idea or feeling that goes across the whole book. • read aloud *The Art Lesson* and define how books mark time (characters changing, seasons changing, picture clues).	• read independently and notice a big idea or feeling that is emerging in their book; place a sticky note in one place where they find a clue about a feeling or big idea. • read independently and notice clues about time and passage of time in their book; place a sticky note on one place where they find a clue.
GUIDED PRACTICE 5 days	• model how to identify the idea of time using clues from the text. • model how you uncover secrets of theme as you read; use *Fly Away Home* to demonstrate. • model how books are built around a theme; use *The Other Side* to demonstrate. • create a chart of the themes found in books. • create a chart of clues readers find in books to indicate passage of time.	• read with a partner to notice clues about the passage of time. • read with a partner to notice clues about theme. • read through known picture books with a partner, stopping to discuss what they think the theme is and what their evidence is. • read independently, noticing themes that emerge in the text. • read through known picture books and mark the passage of time with sticky notes.

COMMITMENT 2 days	• have each student select one of their favorite picture books and name a theme in it using one word (e.g., *loneliness*, *sisterhood*, *courage*, etc.). • have students select a favorite picture book to share with the class that calls attention to the passage of time.	• share a book that reflects their understanding of theme. • share a book that reflects their awareness of the passage of time.
TOTAL: 11 DAYS		

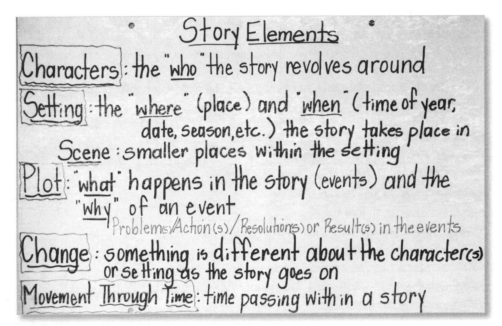

Class charts help students keep track of learning.

Growing an Awareness of Theme and Time: Writing Fiction

GENRE

Why Teach This?

- To show students how to write a narrative, paying attention to the role of story elements.
- To encourage students to incorporate a sense of time in their stories.
- To teach students how to center their story around one big idea or strong feeling.

Framing Question

- How can understanding two elements of story, theme and time, help us write strong narratives?

Unit Goals

- Students will write an original narrative using the following elements: character, setting, movement through time, and theme.
- Students will use descriptive words to give the reader a sense of time.
- Students will center their stories around one theme.

Anchor Texts

- *The Art Lesson* by Tomie dePaola
- *Big Sister and Little Sister* by Charlotte Zolotow
- *Crickwing* by Janell Cannon
- *Fly Away Home* by Eve Bunting
- *Morning on the Lake* by Jan Bourdeau Waboose
- *Oliver Button Is a Sissy* by Tomie dePaola
- *Once Upon a Cool Motorcycle Dude* by Kevin O'Malley
- *The Other Side* by Jacqueline Woodson
- *Previously* by Allan Ahlberg

Unit Assessment Growing an Awareness of Theme and Time: Writing Fiction			GENRE
Student name:	EMERGING	DEVELOPING	INDEPENDENT
Writes an original narrative text in sequential order.			
Includes theme and evidence of theme.			
Uses descriptive words to give the reader a sense of time.			
Uses time to demonstrate theme.			

Stage of the Unit	Focused Instruction You will	Independent Practice Students will
IMMERSION 2 days	• share a story about your childhood that moves quickly through time; share a story about your childhood that moves slowly through time. • model how you are wondering about the themes in your stories.	• revisit notebook entries to find examples of where they moved quickly through time or slowly through time. • revisit notebook entries to find themes in stories.
IDENTIFICATION 2 days	• review the idea that narratives have themes; highlight *Oliver Button Is a Sissy* and *The Art Lesson*, both by Tomie dePaola. • read aloud *Morning on the Lake* and model how to organize and develop ideas for a narrative. • demonstrate how you can play with time in one piece: show time moving quickly or slowly.	• select a theme and begin writing a narrative from their life or based on their imagination. • try writing one piece where time moves quickly or slowly.
GUIDED PRACTICE 5 days	• read *Morning on the Lake* and model how to organize and develop ideas for a narrative. • read *Fly Away Home* and model how you weave theme into your writing through details. • read *Previously* and model how you weave passage of time into writing. • model revising writing by putting in or taking out clues about passage of time and theme. • model editing writing by checking for capitals, spelling, and punctuation.	• begin to draft a narrative, either from something in their notebooks or something new they tried out while experimenting with time. • continue writing or go back into the draft to add details that reveal theme. • continue writing or go back into the draft to add details that reveal passage of time. • revise writing by adding descriptive details to give the reader a sense of time. • edit writing by checking for capitals, spelling, and punctuation.
COMMITMENT 1 day	• create a chart of the passage through time in your favorite picture books and notice how theme is affected by time.	• celebrate completed writing: show a partner where time and theme are key story elements.
TOTAL: 10 DAYS		

SPOTLIGHT on Conventions

- Understanding Sentences in Reading
- Strengthening Sentences in Writing

As third-grade teachers, we often either dread teaching conventions because they feel so detached from the liveliness of our students' literacy experiences, or we cram in lots of instruction in concentrated periods of time, worried that we are not covering it all before they move on to the next grade. The Complete 4 approach advocates finding a middle ground. We are not going to teach conventions in isolation (although we do advocate regular word-work time for practice with patterns and strategies), nor are we going to ignore them. Instead, we are going to carefully place conventions instruction where it belongs—alongside students' authentic work. We celebrate language, punctuation, and grammar in ways that respect and give dignity to the way third graders are coming to print. The writer Eudora Welty recalled her first glimpse of the alphabet inside her storybooks as a child and how magical the swirls and curves of each letter seemed. Let us capture that magic in units on conventions. See pages 62 to 72 in *The Complete 4 for Literacy* for more guidelines on this component.

Pam Allyn

The Architecture of a Sentence

This is an integrated pair of units that takes you and your students on a journey of exploration of the parts of a sentence.

In his book *Elements of Style*, cowritten with E. B. White, William Strunk wrote: "Vigorous writing is concise. A sentence should contain no unnecessary words, for the same reason that a drawing should have no unnecessary lines and a machine no unnecessary parts." The purpose of these units is to help third graders see the elegant beauty of a well-constructed sentence. At the same time, third graders are thinking in complex ways and need to learn about the complex rules of sentence syntax—both as readers and writers. Deurelle McAfee (1981) found that explicit instruction in more complex sentence structure led to significant improvement in reading comprehension and writing complexity.

These units will help us to share with our students the extraordinary potential a well-crafted sentence has to deepen a reader's meaning and enliven an idea. E. B. White himself was the master of the "simple" sentence. These units will celebrate the beauty of the simple sentence and the magic of constructing complexity to hold more complex ideas. Just as the third grader still constructs worlds from blocks or boxes, he now learns to construct worlds from words.

Understanding Sentences in Reading   CONVENTIONS

Why Teach This?
- To help students recognize the architecture of a sentence.
- To recognize how the construction of a sentence affects its meaning.

Framing Question
- How does understanding the architecture of a sentence help us become more effective readers?

Unit Goals
- Students will identify and define nouns, verbs, adjectives, and adverbs.
- Students will identify and be able to use different forms of ending punctuation to help their fluency and understanding of a sentence.
- Students will select sentences from reading that have striking word choice and/or punctuation.

Anchor Texts
- *Charlotte's Web* by E. B. White
- *Cloud Dance* by Thomas Locker
- *Come On, Rain!* by Karen Hesse
- *Fireflies* by Julie Brinckloe
- *Hello, Harvest Moon* by Ralph Fletcher
- *Mustang Canyon* by Jonathan London
- *Pssst!* by Adam Rex

- *Shortcut* by Donald Crews
- *Thunder Cake* by Patricia Polacco
- *When I Am Old With You* by Angela Johnson

Resource Sheets

- Parent Letter for Strengthening Sentences (Resource 2.1)
- Sentences That Strike Me (Resource 2.2)
- Admiring Sentences (Resource 2.3)
- How Punctuation Affects the Sentence (Resource 2.4)

Unit Assessment Understanding Sentences in Reading			CONVENTIONS
Student name:	EMERGING	DEVELOPING	INDEPENDENT
Identifies and defines nouns, verbs, and adjectives.			
Identifies and uses different forms of ending punctuation to help their fluency and understanding of a sentence.			
Selects sentences from reading that have striking word choice and/or punctuation.			
Identifies and defines nouns, verbs, and adjectives.			
Identifies and uses different forms of ending punctuation to help their fluency and understanding of a sentence.			
Selects sentences from reading that have striking word choice and/or punctuation.			

Stage of the Unit	Focused Instruction You will	Independent Practice Students will
IMMERSION 3 days	• read aloud an excerpt from *Charlotte's Web* to find sentences that strike you with their vivid images, strong verbs, and so on. • share sentences you found in your reading and describe why they struck you. • read aloud *Hello, Harvest Moon* to notice how vivid language helps the reader better understand the story.	• collect powerful or unusual sentences found in texts during independent reading. • explore class picture books or chapter books in search of interesting sentences to record onto the class blog or sentence strips. • complete an Admiring Sentences chart.

IDENTIFICATION 2 days	• look at simple sentences to identify and define subject (noun)/predicate. • identify verbs using *Mustang Canyon* as a model; notice how special verbs can help the reader get a clearer picture in her mind as she reads; notice how strong verbs can enhance a sentence.	• record simple sentences in notebooks and on sentence strips, identifying the subjects and predicates. • collect striking verbs from their reading.
GUIDED PRACTICE 6 days	• study examples of verbs in *Fireflies* by Julie Brinckloe. • study examples of adjectives in *Thunder Cake* by Patricia Polacco. • reread *Mustang Canyon* and practice finding parts of speech, identifying subject, predicate, and adjectives. • read *Pssst!* and identify some of the ways to end a sentence; complete the How Punctuation Affects the Sentence chart. • identify how punctuation helps readers read a text.	• read independently and find sentences that they admire. • find examples of strong verbs in their independent reading. • find examples of adjective-noun combinations in their independent reading. • practice coding sentences in their independent reading. • find sentences with intriguing ending punctuation in their independent reading. • read aloud with a partner from a picture book with diverse punctuation.
COMMITMENT 1 day	• select two mentor sentences you and your class loved; name parts of these sentences with your students.	• select two mentor sentences from independent reading to share and name parts with a partner; select one mentor sentence to hang in the classroom or hall.
TOTAL: 12 DAYS		

Getting Started

Studying sentences during reading and writing time does not mean that on any given day students will be studying every sentence they read. Instead, as they read, we ask them to capture an interesting or unusual sentence in their reading by giving them a sentence strip on which they copy out the sentence. Our instructional and conferring time can be used to highlight the world of the sentence and the parts of speech. We can name the elements of a complete sentence together. Do not let the study of sentences monopolize their enjoyment of any book, though; let the study of sentences accompany their reading journeys.

Structures and Routines

Students are reading from book baggies. In the Making Choices units, they put together a nice array of books that work for them at their level. These are the books we use during this unit. When students are reading independently while you are creating big teaching points to focus on together, predictable problems may emerge. We have brainstormed some solutions for you.

Predictable Problems	Possible Solutions
The student picks up a book and can't stay with it, then tries another.	Confer with your student to help him make better choices for what goes into his "short stack." It is likely that the choices he has made for his independent reading do not match his level.
The student is not able to stay in her seat during reading time. She is wandering around the room.	Your students may need smaller increments of time with which to practice increasing her stamina. You can set personal goals for a few of your students who struggle with sitting still for longer periods of time. Establish smaller increments of time that feel doable for this student, and then allow her to stand and stretch or begin other work. Explain to the student that you are going to help her build toward the minutes of reading the others can do with a minimum of stress for her.

You also might want to consider the physical space and if it is just right for her. Are her materials comfortably arranged for her? Does she need less distraction from people around her? Would a quiet spot away from the action work best for her? Does she prefer to be in the middle of things? Ask her to take note of her own actions and what feels best for her. |
| The student is not able to talk easily to a partner about what he has read that day. | Your student may be in the wrong book—the book is too uphill for him, or it is not of high interest to him. Confer with him about alternative book selections or reading in other genres. |
| The student does not seem deeply engaged with the book she is reading and is easily distracted. | When you confer with this student, be aware that you may want to encourage her to try a downhill book for this unit, or a set of downhill books. The book may be at her level, but it requires a bit of extra work in terms of comprehension. Since this unit is about sentence awareness, it is a good idea to include some downhill books in the "short stack" to help students read smoothly and swiftly through them, working less hard on comprehension and more on pausing to admire. |

Teaching Materials

The Classroom Library

Access is a key component for success in reading. An inviting library motivates children to read and become readers. Books in the library should represent a variety of genres, including nonfiction, fiction, and poetry. Books should be placed in baskets in a way that encourages browsing and in which the covers are facing out. The baskets of books can be sorted by topic, genre, and author.

Leveled Books

A section of your library should have baskets of leveled books. In order to level a book, we look at the amount of print on a page, the number of words, the placement of the words and pictures, and the vocabulary in the book. For more information about leveling, Irene Fountas and Gay Su Pinnell have many books on this topic. They have created an A to Z system to level books.

Leveled books should comprise approximately 20 to 30 percent of your library. These books are meant for children to read independently, so you will need a nice variety. Children can choose from these books once they have learned how to make wise book choices. If you choose to use the A to Z leveling system, you may want to assign the letters a color sticker so as to minimize the issue of children feeling competitive about levels. Your third graders will quickly absorb your system. If you are positive and excited about their choices, they will not be competitive with one another.

Independent Book Bags

Your students can store their independent books in plastic bags. They need a place to keep their books that is convenient and easy for them to transport during independent reading time.

Choosing Your Teaching Texts

We recommend the texts that you choose to teach students about sentences be the same as the texts you use to focus on their writing. What are your favorite read-aloud or teaching texts? Pull them out and study them. Chances are that in addition to being wonderful models of genre, character, or theme, they are also beautifully written.

Look at *Come On, Rain* by Karen Hesse:

"It streams through our hair and down our backs. It freckles our feet, glazes our toes. We turn in circles, glistening in our rain skin."

Or notice this sentence from *When I Am Old With You* by Angela Johnson:

"When I am old with you, Granddaddy, we will play cards all day underneath that old tree by the road. We'll drink cool water from a jug and wave at all the cars that go by."

There are no perfect texts, just those you love and those that are rich in language and complexity. Don't shy away from books your students may have read already, as you will be asking them to do interesting work in these books that will be new and fresh, and the fact that they already know the story or the information will help them, not hurt them.

The following texts include strong examples of how verbs, adjectives, and varied sentence structure serve as great models for you to use in your teaching.

Text	Verbs	Adjectives	Varied Sentence Structure	Punctuation	Example
Shortcut, Donald Crews	X		X	X	"We looked… We listened… We decided to take the shortcut home."
Fireflies, Julie Brinckloe	X		X		"I forked the meat and corn and potatoes into my mouth."
Cloud Dance, Thomas Locker	X	X			"I ligh, wispy clouds race in the autumn wind."
Mustang Canyon, Jonathan London		X	X		"He screams, lashing out with his sharp hoofs like whip snaps of lightning…"
Come On, Rain!, Karen Hesse	X	X	X		"Come on, rain, I say, squinting into the endless heat."
Hello, Harvest Moon, Ralph Fletcher	X	X			"Birch trees shine as if they have been double-dipped in moonlight."
Pssst!, Adam Rex			X	X	"Great. Get two just in case."
When I Am Old With You, Angela Johnson			X	X	"In the mornings, Granddaddy, we will cook bacon for breakfast and that's all. We can eat it on the porch too."
Thunder Cake, Patricia Polacco	X	X			"Her eyes surveyed the black clouds a way off in the distance. Then she strode into the kitchen."

In many units, we need to ask our students to read from a particular genre, author, or subject area. This is a necessary part of our work. We can't feature the elements of a genre and ask our students to find examples of those elements if they aren't all reading from that genre. But this unit focuses on conventions, and as such, your students can read anything that features the form you are studying—the sentence.

For example, here is a passage from *In the Year of the Boar and Jackie Robinson* by Bette Bao Lord:

"Arms *atwirl*, she *teetered* forward. She *tottered* back. The *wicked* skates refused to obey and dumped her on the ground once more."

As your students read, they will make discoveries. The sheer magnitude of a sentence or the beauty of its repetition or a startling shift in length will signal the reader that something interesting is happening on the page.

Differentiation

It will be easy to differentiate your instruction within this unit as long as your students are matched to books at their own reading levels. In this way, every student will find something that feels and looks interesting to him or her. Your strong reader may find multiple adjectives or interesting punctuation in her book. With your vulnerable reader, it may simply be moving from a subject–object sentence to a sentence with one adornment, such as an adjective. Grammatical elements are important for every reader and writer to learn, and we believe it will resonate more deeply for your student when she learns it inside of her own chapter book, rather than on a grammar worksheet. We can use the worksheet to reinforce the learning, but her discovery should be as authentic as possible for it to be personally meaningful to her.

Reading books that are on level is the best way to build fluency and stamina. But do not dissuade a student who wants to try for an uphill book or a downhill book during this unit. The point is that whatever motivates is going to build fluency and stamina, and all books are intriguing to look at in terms of sentence construction, too.

Following is a list of possible texts for the range of readers in your class:

Vulnerable	Steady	Strong
Busybody Nora by Johanna Hurwitz	*Seven Kisses in a Row* by Patricia MacLachlan	*Smoky Night* by Eve Bunting
King Max and other books in the Max series by Dick King-Smith	26 Fairmont Avenue series by Tomie dePaola	*Andy and Tamika* by David Adler
Cam Jansen series by David Adler	Secrets of Droon series by Tony Abbott	*Mr. Popper's Penguins* by Richard Atwater and Florence Atwater
Magic Tree House series by Mary Pope Osborne	*Thimbleberry Stories* by Cynthia Rylant	*Fantastic Mr. Fox* by Roald Dahl
Marvin Redpost series by Louis Sachar	*How to Be Cool in the Third Grade* by Betsy Duffey	*The Amazing Days of Abby Hayes: Some Things Never Change* by Anne Mazer
I Love Saturdays by Alma Flor Ada	*Just Grace* by Charise Mericle Harper	*Shark Lady: True Adventures of Eugenie Clark* by Ann McGovern
George Washington's Mother by Jean Fritz	*We'll Never Forget You, Roberto Clemente* by Trudie Engel	*National Geographic Kids* and *National Geographic Explorer*
Ladybug magazine	*National Geographic Kids* and *National Geographic Explorer*	*Ask* magazine
Click magazine	*Spider* magazine	

Stages of the Unit

Immersion

As students collect sentences, help them consider the following:

What makes a sentence interesting?

- It is very different from the sentences around it—either much shorter or much longer.
- It is beautifully written.
- It is full of interesting information.
- It is unusual in the way it is written.
- I am not used to reading sentences that look like that.
- It conveys a strong feeling.
- It helped me figure out something in the text.

As your students make these discoveries, chart their observations to create a record of your learning journey. Here is an example of what this chart might look like at the end of a few days of studying the sentences in *Hello, Harvest Moon* by Ralph Fletcher.

Sentence	What We Notice
It comes up round, ripe, and huge over autumn fields of corn and wheat.	These are three specific words to describe the moon that help the reader get a picture in her mind.
If you played a nocturnal game of hide and seek and hid behind that huge pine tree, you would be almost invisible, cloaked in moonshadow.	This is a surprising verb to use here. The author might have used *covered* instead. *Cloaked* is much more specific to the moment.
Finally it starts to ease lower... —sprinkling silver coins like a careless millionaire over ponds, lakes, and seas, till all the money is spent.	Surprising language. (You might name parts of the sentence to notice the parts of speech of these words.) Different forms of punctuation.

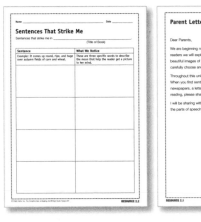

We have created a template called Sentences That Strike Me (Resource 2.2) that students may use to collect their own sentence observations.

At this time, send a letter home to your parents explaining the units (see Resource 2.1).

Identification

Students look through anchor texts, independent reading, and their own writing to notice how they and other authors build effective sentences. Guide your students to name and notice nouns, verbs, and adjectives and guide them to become aware of the impact they have on the writing in a text. Create class charts of shared definitions of parts of speech. As a class you can develop language for naming sentences. They might include names like painting a picture, strong emotion, or right-now moment. The process of closely examining a sentence to name what it does well is a central skill of writers.

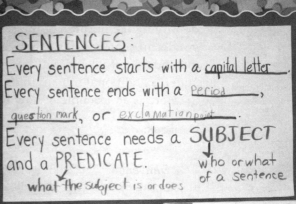

SENTENCES:
Every sentence starts with a capital letter.
Every sentence ends with a period,
question mark, or exclamation point.
Every sentence needs a SUBJECT
and a PREDICATE.
what the subject is or does
who or what of a sentence

Guided Practice

As you select texts to read aloud, it makes sense to choose texts written on your students' varied independent reading levels. This will allow you to model how to find great sentences in a variety of texts.

Surprising Sentence	Unique Noun	Unique Verb	Unique Adjective	Unique Punctuation
Mamma lifts a listless vine and sighs. "Three weeks and not a drop," she says, sagging over her parched plants. *Come On, Rain!* by Karen Hesse (anchor text)		sagging	listless parched	
He buried his nose into the stiff canvas of the material and smelled the newness. *How to Be Cool in Third Grade* by Betsy Duffey	newness	buried	stiff	
Into the corners of every room he prowled and poked and pecked with a busy thoroughness; into every closet he stared with his white-circled eyes; under and behind all the furniture he crowded his plump figure, with little subdued cries of curiosity and pleasure. *Mr. Popper's Penguins* by Richard Atwater and Florence Atwater		prowled poked pecked	white-circled plump subdued	semicolon

Students read independently in books they really like and find sentences they love. They record these sentences in their reader's notebooks, naming and identifying the purpose of the parts. For homework, too, they can search for a wonderful sentence. Since only one sentence is required, this kind of work does not and should not take away from the overall reading experience but it does give your students additional time to find, practice, and name their sentences.

Here is an example of how a student's reader's notebook might look:

Book: *Pleasing the Ghost* by Sharon Creech
Page: 1

Sentence: "I'm Dennis, your basic, ordinary nine-year-old boy, and usually I live a basic, ordinary life."	**What I noticed:** The word *ordinary* seems like it tells how normal his life is. It also makes me think that the story in the book is not going to be basic or ordinary because he says those words and it seems like it is going to be the opposite. There are a lot of commas in this sentence.

Students can use the Admiring Sentences sheet (Resource 2.3) to record their observations.

Commitment

Students have the opportunity to apply all that they have learned by selecting one of their collected sentences and naming the parts of speech—nouns, verbs, adjectives—and punctuation used in the sentence. These sentences are posted in a public place for others to see.

How to Use the Lessons in the Spotlight Units

We have scripted out the lesson—Focused Instruction, Independent Practice, and Wrap-Up—for you in each Spotlight Unit. Where you see italics, we have provided language for you as a model. You are free to use it as is, or you may prefer to adapt the language to suit your needs. For example, if we mention a book we might read aloud to our class, but you have one you like better, feel free to use that one instead. Or if we use a personal anecdote as a demonstration, you should replace it with one of your own. Where there are no italics, the lesson plan includes guidelines of what you and the students could be doing at that point in the lesson. You will notice that there is always a balance of teacher talk and suggested actions.

Day-by-Day Lessons

DAY 1 Immersion

Focused Instruction

People who love to read often pause to admire a beautiful sentence. This unit is going to help us look closely at the magic of sentences. While you will all get to continue your independent reading, we also want to notice how an author writes his or her sentences. You will spend the next several days collecting your favorite sentences and copying them onto sentence strips. I am going to read aloud to you today using the SMART Board, and I am going to stop when I get to a sentence that interests me. Be sure to let me know what you find interesting, too.

- Read aloud an excerpt from *Charlotte's Web*. Chart your and students' responses to sentences in the text.

Independent Practice

As you read today, find at least one sentence that you find interesting. Copy it onto a sentence strip.

- Students begin reading from their independent choices with the understanding that by the end of the practice period, each will have a completed sentence strip with an interesting sentence from their reading.

Wrap-Up

Let's have two students share their sentences and the reasons they chose them.

- Sentence strips are taped to the board while students share their thoughts.

DAY 2 Immersion

Focused Instruction

Today you are going to find another sentence that interests you as you read. Before we return to the meeting area, I want you to find a partner to share your sentence with. As you are reading, consider why you choose the sentence you did. What makes the sentences you selected so interesting or powerful? For example, I chose this sentence from Charlotte's Web *yesterday because it is very descriptive. I enjoyed the sound of the sentence as I read it aloud. Listen.*

- Read a sentence aloud from *Charlotte's Web*.

What do you like about my sentence? Why do you think it is a strong sentence?

- Students turn and talk to one another to discuss.

Today you may choose to read a book from our picture book collection or you can read your chapter book.

Independent Practice

- Students read independently and gather another interesting sentence by using the handout Sentences That Strike Me (Resource 2.2).

With the remaining five minutes of practice time, please meet with a partner and share why you chose your sentence. Try to name what it is about the sentence that gives it interest or power.

Wrap-Up

- Feature one student's sentence selection and ask that student to describe why he chose that sentence.

DAY 3 Immersion

Focused Instruction

One of the things that we noticed about our sentences is that we like sentences that are really descriptive or use special language. In this book, Hello, Harvest Moon, *Ralph Fletcher makes me feel like I am right there on the farm with him. Listen to how clearly he describes the setting: "The crops have been gathered. The pumpkins have been picked. The silos are filled to bursting with a million ears of corn. Tired farmers are fast asleep. But something is stirring at the edge of the world. Something is rising low in the trees." What a clear picture he paints with his sentences. I can see the farm, like it was tucked in by the farmers before they went to sleep, everything in its place. Can you see it, too? What does this author do to build his sentences so we can really see what he sees?*

- Elicit responses from students.

This author chose his words carefully and was able to create a picture that the reader could really imagine. That is what good writers and storytellers do—they think of their story and then search to find the perfect words to create a picture for the reader.

Independent Practice

Today as you read, pay attention to where a sentence just stops you with its beauty and where you notice how vivid and alive and real it feels to you. Let's name what we love about these sentences. When you find a sentence like this, you can record it in your notebook. You can set up your notebook page like this.

- Model how to fill in the Admiring Sentences chart (Resource 2.3).

Wrap-Up

- Students share the sentences they collected with a partner and say why they admire them.

DAY 4 Identification

Focused Instruction

Yesterday we looked at Ralph Fletcher's book, Hello, Harvest Moon. *We looked at some of the sentences that I found that really struck me as I was reading because they use such amazing language. There are important parts of a sentence that make it work. Every simple sentence has a subject and a predicate. The subject is what or whom the sentence is about—the noun. The predicate tells something about the subject. In the sentence, "The cat purred," the subject is* the cat, *the predicate is* purred *because that is what the subject is doing. Who found a sentence like this during your reading this week?*

- Share other examples of simple sentences identifying the subject and the predicate.

Independent Practice

- Students find examples of simple sentences in their reading, copy them onto sentence strips, and label the parts "subject" and "predicate."

Wrap-Up

- Reinforce the subject–predicate concept by taking several simple sentence strips that students recorded from their reading and cut them into "parts" using a two-column chart: subject and predicate.

DAY 5 Identification

Focused Instruction

Today we are going to think about how the words authors choose help us to create a picture in our minds. Verbs are words that authors put in their writing to show action. Authors select words that help paint a clear picture for a reader.

Let's look at this book, Mustang Canyon, *to see how Jonathan London creates a picture for the reader: "Out of the blue haze of evening comes a soft whinny as a mother mare nuzzles her foal. Less than a day old, the little pinto tries to stand. Sits. Tries again, wobbling, poking his nose beneath her, pushing for milk." Without seeing the pictures you can still get a clear image in your mind of what the horses are doing. There is a lot of action in this writing as the baby pinto tries to stand, and you can clearly see the interaction between the mother and baby just from the words, as if you were right there. Let's look at the sentence and highlight the verbs we see:* whinny, nuzzle, stand, sit, wobbling, poking—*all these verbs show the movement of the foal.*

Independent Practice

In your reading today, pay attention to the verbs you see. Begin a list of vivid verbs in your reader's notebook.

- Remind students that they are only writing down a few words that strike them—not all the verbs in their reading!

Wrap-Up

- Students share with partners the verbs they liked most.

DAY 6 Guided Practice

Focused Instruction

Verbs placed carefully in sentences and chosen well help us picture actions that occur in our stories.

Let's read Fireflies *by Julie Brinckloe. As you read, you can talk about what you see in your mind. Stop at the passage: "Blinking on, blinking off, dipping low, soaring high above my head, making white patterns in the dark."*

- Ask students to sketch what they see in their minds as you read this sentence.

Independent Practice

In our Independent Practice today, I am going to ask you to pay special attention to verbs that jump off the page.

- Students read independently, copying one striking verb they find on an index card to share at the Wrap-Up.

Wrap-Up

- Post index cards on the board to share with the class.

DAY 7 Guided Practice

Focused Instruction

We have talked about how verbs and nouns are critical to the construction of a great sentence. Now we are going to talk about the words that help verbs and nouns: adjectives and adverbs. Adjectives describe nouns and adverbs describe verbs. You can tell them apart because a verb's descriptor has the word verb in it. This is a handy trick to remember!

Let's look at some sentences with adjectives and adverbs and see how these parts of speech do their jobs.

This sentence from Thunder Cake *by Patricia Polacco shows great examples of adjectives: "The air was hot, heavy, and damp." All three words,* hot, heavy, *and* damp, *are describing the air. What part of speech is* air?

The next sentence says: "A loud clap of thunder shook the house, rattled the windows, and made me grab her clothes." Look closely at the first part of the sentence. What is the verb? Which word tells the kind of clap? Loud *is the adjective.*

Turn and talk to your neighbor about the similarities and differences between adjectives and adverbs.

Independent Practice

Use a sticky note to mark one spot in your reading where you find an adjective–noun or adverb–verb pair that strikes you.

- Students read independently, marking interesting word combinations where they pop up.

Wrap-Up

What words in your reading helped you get a picture in your mind? Share a pair of words you found in your reading today with a partner and tell why they struck you.

DAY 8 Guided Practice

Focused Instruction

Adjectives help us to build sentences that carry power. In our read-aloud, Thunder Cake, *we should find many examples of adjectives that turn the light on a noun, on the subject. With a partner today, find noun–adjective combinations you like and record them on index cards.*

- Highlight some effective adjectives from *Thunder Cake.*

Independent Practice

- Students read independently, looking for one adjective–noun combination to put on their index cards to share with a partner.

Wrap-Up

- Share adjective–noun pairs by posting index cards for all students to see.

DAY 9 Guided Practice

Focused Instruction

Today we are going to look at a piece of shared text. This is from a book we have already read together, Mustang Canyon. *Let's look together to see if we can practice finding interesting examples of the parts of speech. Together we will code parts of the sentence:* s *for* predicate, *and* adj *for* adjective.

- Code the shared document and discuss their decision making on chart paper, overhead, or SMART Board.

Now I want you to try the next sentence together with a partner.

- Students work in partnerships to practice coding one sentence in the shared document.

As you go off today, you are going to code the rest of this page with a partner.

Independent Practice

- Students work in partnerships to code the remaining sentences in the shared text.

Wrap-Up

What felt easy today about coding the sentences? Are some parts of speech easier to name than others? What felt hard?

- Select students share their reflections.

DAY 10 Guided Practice

Focused Instruction

We notice that to cap off the perfect sentence, authors do amazing things with punctuation. In the book Pssst! *by Adam Rex, we see many examples of intriguing ways to end a sentence. In addition to periods, the author uses exclamation points and ellipses.*

- Make a class chart like the one below to collect punctuation. See How Punctuation Affects the Sentence (Resource 2.4) for an extended chart.

How Punctuation Affects the Sentence			
Text	Line from text	Type of punctuation	How the punctuation affects the sentence

Independent Practice

Find sentences with ending punctuation that you admire. We will share these at our Wrap-Up and categorize them as different kinds of powerful endings.

Wrap-Up

- Chart different kinds of ending punctuation.

DAY 11 Guided Practice

Focused Instruction

Punctuation helps us know how to read a text. We use our voices in different ways depending on the form of punctuation in a text.

- Review how the different forms of punctuation affect our reading.

Independent Practice

Work with a partner to read aloud picture books that use varied forms of punctuation.

- Students read with special attention to using their voices to reflect the kind of punctuation in each sentence.

Wrap-Up

- Each student reads one line from their book to show how the punctuation affects the reading.

DAY 12 Commitment

Focused Instruction

Let's look at these two sentences that we found in our reading that we loved and see if we can figure out the parts of the sentence together.

- Name and chart parts of speech and punctuation.

Independent Practice

- Students work with a partner to select sentences they collected from their independent reading to identify parts.

Wrap-Up

- Students share their sentences and reflect on how learning about the parts of speech has helped them in their reading.

Step Forward Into the Sentence

"We want our readers to feel what we feel, experience what we see, hear, taste, and smell. That is why being specific is crucial to expressing our hearts and minds."

—Georgia Heard (2002), *The Revision Toolbox:*
Teaching Techniques That Work, pages 23–24

By third grade, our students have become more sophisticated readers with lots to say. But their writing often lags behind their thinking. The simple subject–object sentences no longer can contain the complexity of their ideas and descriptions and wonderings. As they step forward as writers we need to be there to help them name the building blocks of great sentences so they can use them effectively in their own writing.

Strengthening Sentences in Writing   CONVENTIONS

Why Teach This?

- To develop students' understanding of how the parts of speech and punctuation affect the messages they convey in their writing.
- To learn to make careful and thoughtful decisions about the words we use in our writing.
- To practice basic conventions of writing that make reading more legible.

Framing Question

- How can we build sentences with subject, predicate, and adjectives that are strong and effective?

Unit Goals

- Students will make careful decisions about the nouns, verbs, and adjectives they use in their writing.
- Students will revise sentences to select specific words that paint a picture for the reader.
- Students will pay attention to and make careful decisions about the ending punctuation of sentences to match their purpose.
- Students will write with an awareness of basic conventions, capitals, and ending punctuation.

Anchor Texts

- *Come On, Rain!* by Karen Hesse
- *Fireflies* by Julie Brinckloe
- *Hello, Harvest Moon* by Ralph Fletcher
- *Shortcut* by Donald Crews
- *Snapshots from the Wedding* by Gary Soto
- *Thunder Cake* by Patricia Polacco

Resource Sheets

- Noticing and Naming Sentences (Resource 2.5)

Unit Assessment Strengthening Sentences in Writing			CONVENTIONS
Student name:	EMERGING	DEVELOPING	INDEPENDENT
Makes careful decisions about the nouns, verbs, and adjectives used in writing.			
Revises sentences to select more specific words that paint a picture for the reader.			
Pays attention to and makes careful decisions about the ending punctuation of sentences to match the purpose of their sentence.			
Writes with an awareness of basic conventions, capitals, and ending punctuation.			

Stage of the Unit	Focused Instruction You will	Independent Practice Students will
IMMERSION 2 days	• read *Thunder Cake* and admire how Patricia Polacco conveys feelings, images, and ideas; note powerful sentences. • continue reading *Thunder Cake*, and look at how Polacco uses language to bring you into the story; give examples of when you feel you are "in" the story.	• tell a story to a partner with details and sensory imagery; talk about the sensory images. • write a piece that focuses on creating a vivid image for readers.
IDENTIFICATION 2 days	• use *Thunder Cake* to define and identify parts of speech (nouns, verbs, and adjectives) by picking specific sentences. • look at sentences to name subjects and predicates.	• pay attention to parts of speech, including nouns, verbs, and adjectives, while they write; share some particularly strong words with a partner. • find sentences in their writing that have a clear subject and predicate to copy onto sentence strips and share.
GUIDED PRACTICE 5 days	• model paying attention to word choice (verbs) while writing. Notice strong verbs used in *Fireflies* by Julie Brinckloe. • model paying attention to word choice (adjectives) while writing. Notice strong adjectives used in *Come On, Rain!* by Karen Hesse.	• write with attention to verb choice; share one special verb. • look back at any entry previously written; try to add adjectives to make it more interesting.

GUIDED PRACTICE (continued)	• discuss the importance of punctuation by revisiting anchor texts. • discuss how strong sentences are part of the author's craft; use sentences selected and name craft in chart (paint picture, strong emotion, right-now moment). • discuss and model how to use an author's technique to improve your own writing.	• revisit an entry and experiment by changing punctuation; read new sentences to a partner or the class. • read sentences from anchor texts and continue to "name craft." • revise writing using mentor sentences as models for ways to bring the reader into their writing.
COMMITMENT 1 day	• model selecting beautifully crafted sentences to publish.	• find one sentence or a short group of sentences from their writing that demonstrates a strong use of word choice and punctuation to publish on sentence strips; reflect on how this work has helped them as writers to create stronger sentences.
TOTAL: 10 DAYS		

Getting Started

Find your own sentences you love in books you are reading currently or books you have read in the past. Show your students how you find examples of great writing from your pleasure reading. This way, they can learn to do the same.

Teaching Materials

Use the anchor texts to model how authors use parts of speech and punctuation in strategic ways. Throughout both the reading and writing units, students collect examples of sentences that strike them. These examples can be used as models for writing as well. We shift our thinking from noticing individual sentences in reading to looking at the flow of sentences in a text; how the writer uses a variety of structures to make that reading more rhythmic, more interesting, and more effective in communicating her desired tone; and to writing our own entries that reflect this learning. Many of the reading charts overlap with the writing charts, creating a seamless link between your reading and writing instruction.

Setting Up Student Writing Notebooks

You will find it useful to have your students keep a simple notebook in which they can explore being writers. This might be a composition notebook or a tabbed section of a binder, but it should be a place your students can return to throughout the year, to read and reread their writing, to collect writing ideas and look for new ones, and to reflect on their growing abilities as writers. You might set aside the back of the notebook for lists of writing topics, and as students come up with new writing ideas they can add these to their lists, moving farther into the notebook as they go. Set up the first several pages for a table of contents so students can keep track of the units and the work generated in each unit. You can ask students to paginate their notebooks so that the table of contents can help them find material quickly. Or, you can establish writing "rules" for these notebooks, such as only writing on the right-hand pages, leaving the left for notes and "try-its"—attempts at new ways to write thoughts—done with you during conferences. You can ask students to skip lines so they can go back later and add missing words or phrases for clarity.

As they write their own stories, wonderings, memories, and observations in this unit, ask your students to use a mentor sentence collected during reading to help them craft a new sentence of their own. Your students revise existing sentences and chunks of writing and try out new techniques in their writing notebooks. We use the notebook as a workbench for our new efforts.

Differentiation

If you have students who are vulnerable writers who tend to use simple sentence structures, they will experiment with different kinds of simple sentences. If they are strong writers, they will be ready to take on the challenge of varying the patterns of simple, compound, and complex sentences by looking at the cumulative effect of the sentences on the page. We learn a lot about our students' understanding of sentences in reading as long as we regularly confer with our students during reading time. We should be able to roll these insights into writing time so we can help scaffold our student writers in the appropriate way.

Stages of the Unit

Immersion

Use the anchor text *Thunder Cake* by Patricia Polacco to marvel at the beauty of language and how language is the foundation for great stories. We are riveted by stories because language carries us along. Patricia Polacco is our mentor for this unit.

Identification

As a class you can develop language for the sentences you admire. It might include names like painting a picture, strong emotion, or right-now moment. The process of closely examining a sentence to name what it does well is a central skill of writers. As writers we want to use other texts to explore new ways that we can express ourselves more effectively. Looking closely at writing and naming what the writer does helps our students become more aware of these crafting techniques and the impact they have on the writing and the reader, inspiring students to want to write with the same purpose and effect. Students can use a graphic organizer like the Noticing and Naming Sentences chart (Resource 2.5) to keep track of their findings.

Noticing and Naming Sentences	
Sentence	What we call it
"It comes up round, ripe, and huge over autumn fields of corn and wheat." —Hello, Harvest Moon by Ralph Fletcher	Painting a picture
"I need them. I want them. I have to have them." —Earrings by Judith Viorst	Strong emotion
"THE TRAIN! THE TRAIN!" "GET OFF! GET OFF!" "GET OFF THE TRACKS!" —Shortcut by Donald Crews	Right-now moment
"'Catch them, catch them!' we cried, grasping at the lights." —Fireflies by Julie Brinckloe	Drawing the reader into the story

Guided Practice

Students use anchor texts to learn about how these parts of speech affect a reader's understanding of a text and then write new entries or revise old entries in their notebooks while practicing how to build similar kinds of sentences in their own writing. Demonstrate for your students how you pay attention to the parts of speech in the sentences you use in your writing; highlight words used by different authors and guide them to collect words that they admire in their notebooks. Their writing during this unit can come from all that they wonder, imagine, remember, and observe. The writing should be as genuine and authentic as ever: here they are, taking time each day to admire conventions as part of the entire writing experience.

Commitment

Students choose one sentence or a group of sentences that they feel reflects the kind of writing that creates clear sensory images for their readers through the construction of the sentences themselves. Students reflect on what they have learned about writing in this unit and how this new learning will impact future writing.

Day-by-Day Lessons

DAY 1 Immersion

Focused Instruction

In this unit, we will admire many beautiful ways writers convey feelings, images, and ideas. By building strong sentences, they are able to do all this. I am going to read aloud to you a book called Thunder Cake *by Patricia Polacco. Listen as she weaves her story together with strong sentences.*

Independent Practice

- Students tell stories to a partner with details and sensory imagery that make the listener feel like he is in the story.

Wrap-Up

- Students share stories.

DAY 2 Immersion

Focused Instruction

When writers want to make the reader feel like they are right there with them, sharing their experience, how do they do it?

- Use *Thunder Cake* to model how the author can make the reader feel like they are right there in the experience with the characters.

For example, you might say for the line, "BOOOOOM BA-BOOOOOM, crashed the thunder" that using the sounds of the thunder makes me feel like it is happening right now all around us, and crashed is such a specific word I could almost feel the thunder's crashing boom.

Independent Practice

Try writing like Patricia Polacco did in Thunder Cake *to help your reader feel like he is right there with you. If you are stuck for an idea to write about, use your brainstorm list from the Four Prompts to help you.*

- Students write a new piece in their notebooks, focusing on creating a vivid image for the reader.

Wrap-Up

Share a line from your writing today with a partner.

DAY 3 Identification

Focused Instruction

We notice that writers use certain kinds of words that help us engage with the text. They may use vivid language or specific words to help us really understand or feel a part of the events in the story. They pay attention to the parts of speech, the nouns, verbs, and the adjectives they are using and try to find the best words to describe what they are trying to say.

Let's look at this sentence and see if we can find the parts of speech used by this author.

- Name parts of this sentence from *Thunder Cake*: "The air was hot, heavy, and damp."

Independent Practice

Today as you write a story in your notebooks, pay attention to the nouns, verbs, and adjectives that you select in your writing. Consider how they help you bring your reader into your writing.

- Students write about something new or continue working on a piece from a previous day.

Wrap-Up

Meet with a partner to share a sentence that you wrote today that you think does a good job of using specific nouns, verbs, and adjectives.

- Share as a whole class some of the challenges you faced and what surprised you about your writing.

DAY 4 Identification

Focused Instruction

Yesterday we noticed many different parts of speech used in a sentence. Today I want to talk about how sentences must have certain parts to make them work. They are the subject and predicate. Every simple sentence has a subject and a predicate. The subject is what or who the sentence is about—the noun. The predicate tells something about the subject. Let's look at the sentence, "The cat purred." We noticed that the cat *is the noun and the subject, and* purred *is the verb and the predicate. When we are writing, we need to make sure that all of our sentences have these parts, too.*

- Students look with a partner at another sentence that you post for them to identify the subject and predicate and share their observations.

Independent Practice

Today I want you to look back through your writing to find an example of a simple sentence with a subject and a predicate. Copy it onto a sentence strip and we will share it at our Wrap-Up. Once you are done, if there is time, you can begin working on a new entry or continue an older one, paying attention to the subject and predicate in your sentences.

Wrap-Up

- Review the sentences that students wrote on sentence strips and notice subject and predicate.

DAY 5 Guided Practice

Focused Instruction

Today let's take a closer look at verbs. Verbs help the reader picture what is happening in a text. Let's take a closer look at Fireflies *to see how Julie Brinckloe, the author, uses verbs in her writing.*

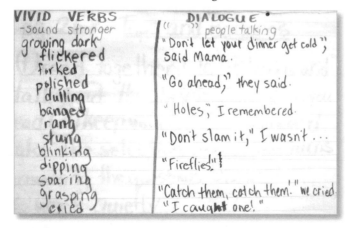

- Look at typed text of *Fireflies* together on a SMART Board or by handing out copies to students to notice verbs in her writing.

Chart student's discoveries to reinforce and celebrate learning.

Independent Practice

Write a narrative or nonfiction entry today with a special eye toward verb choice. Don't overuse special verbs, but find places to tuck them in and surprise us with your choices.

Wrap-Up

- Each student shares one special verb from their writing.

DAY 6 Guided Practice

Focused Instruction

Let's look through the book Come On, Rain! *to notice some of the adjectives that this author uses in her writing.*

- Highlight some adjectives from *Come On, Rain!* For example: "fling off their shoes, skim off their hose, tossing streamers of stockings over their shoulders. Our barelegged mammas dance down the steps and join us in the fresh, clean rain...while the music from Miz Glick's phonograph shimmies and sparkles and streaks like night lightning."

Let's look at the order of these words in the sentences we selected. Where in the sentences do the adjectives go?

Independent Practice

Revisit an entry you wrote in the past few days to look closely at the adjectives that you have used. See if you can add to or put more specific words into your writing today. Try to choose words to paint a picture for the reader.

Wrap-Up

- Create a chart of sentences from students' writing that paints a picture for the reader. Point out the position of the words in the sentences.

DAY 7 Guided Practice

Focused Instruction

As we have looked through our anchor texts, in addition to noticing words, we have also noticed that authors sometimes vary the punctuation that they use at the end of sentences. What kinds of punctuation have you noticed? What do we call these forms of punctuation?

- Use the handout How Punctuation Affects the Sentence as a Guide (Resource 2.4).

Independent Practice

As you write today, pay close attention to the kind of punctuation that you put into your writing. Consider the following: Why did you choose this form of punctuation? What does it do for your sentences?

- Students revisit an entry or begin a new one to experiment with different forms of punctuation and how they impact a sentence.

Wrap-Up

- Students read aloud a sentence that they wrote that uses punctuation in a purposeful way. Other students guess what kind of punctuation was used for this sentence and tell how they figured it out.

DAY 8 Guided Practice

Focused Instruction

We have noticed that parts of speech and punctuation are important elements to developing strong sentences. I have taken some of the sentences that we have noticed and put them into this chart. Let's work together to see if we can name the craft that the author uses and what it does for the reader.

- Give your students the opportunity to create a chart with sentences in one column and a second blank column. In the second column come up with names for these sentences (painting a picture, strong emotion, right-now moment) with your students (see Resource 2.5).

Independent Practice

- Students read anchor texts to continue to notice and name sentences using their own chart.
- Students choose one sentence from their chart that they especially admire to copy onto a sentence strip to hang in the classroom.

Wrap-Up

- Add on to your chart with sentences that students found and name the kinds of sentences together. Hang sentence strips for all students to see and use as models for writing.

DAY 9 Guided Practice

Focused Instruction

When writers notice crafting techniques that they admire in others' writing, they often try to use that technique in their own writing. Yesterday you noticed many techniques that you admired.

- Refer back to the chart.

Today you are going to use what you learned about kinds of sentences to choose a writing technique that you would like to use in your writing.

- Model for students how to do this using your writing as a model. You might say something like: "I was thinking of this funny story that happened with my dog Reggie in the park yesterday. I want to make the reader feel like they are right there with us so they will also know how funny it is. I am going to try to use really specific verbs and adjectives to create a right-now feeling."

Independent Practice

- Students write new stories from their memories, paying attention to what experience they are trying to create in their writing for the reader.

Use your brainstorm list from the Four Prompts unit to find an idea to write about.

- Students use mentor sentences as models for how to construct their sentences.

Wrap-Up

- Students share a line from their writing where they tried to create one of the feelings in the model sentences. Students name what they were trying to do as writers.

DAY 10 Commitment

Focused Instruction

We have learned so much about parts of speech, punctuation, and creating sentences to really capture an experience. You became "sentence builders"! Today we are going to reread our writing from this unit to notice what we have learned as writers. Then we are going to select one sentence that we feel really good about that shows what we learned about parts of speech, word choice, and punctuation. It might show strong verb or adjective choice or a specific crafting technique that you tried.

Once we select these sentences, we are going to write them on sentence strips and add another sentence or two explaining what these sentences show about what you learned as a writer in this unit. Let me show you what I mean.

- Model finding a sentence, then reflecting on what this sentence shows that you did well as a writer, such as finding really specific verbs, adjectives, or punctuation to use in your writing or modeling your sentence after one that you found and admired in an anchor text.

Independent Practice

- Students reread their writing to find a line to publish. They copy it onto a sentence strip and name what they did well in this sentence.

Wrap-Up

- Sentence celebration: Hang sentence strips and reflections up for others to see.
- Students read one another's sentences and reflections.

Students experiment with using descriptive language to build a strong sentence.

Inquire, Explore: The World of Information

As adults, at least 80 percent of what we read is nonfiction. Third grade is an ideal time to begin paying close attention to the skills required to read and write nonfiction texts. Your students are able to integrate lots of content, and they love to learn about the world around them. They are naturally inquisitive and eager for the facts. The note-taking unit is a precursor to the test-skills unit coming in Chapter 3 illuminating one aspect of the nonfiction process, we are able to give our students a toolbox of skills and strategies they can take with them for a lifetime of reading and learning through the genre of nonfiction.

Seeking Information: Strategies to Read Nonfiction

GENRE

Why Teach This?

• To encourage students to become more aware of the world around them.

• To learn how to access information in nonfiction texts and master research skills.

Framing Question

• What do we need to know about nonfiction texts in order to access all of the information they present?

Unit Goals

• Students will identify the genre of nonfiction.

• Students will use a variety of text features in their reading to gain understanding of the ideas in the text.

• Students will begin to distinguish between the most and least important information in a text.

• Students will share information learned from a text with others.

Anchor Texts

• *Bears: Polar Bears, Black Bears and Grizzly Bears* by Deborah Hodge

• *Big Blue Whale* by Nicola Davies

• *Can It Rain Cats and Dogs? Questions and Answers About Weather* by Melvin Berger and Gilda Berger

• *Duke Ellington: The Piano Prince and His Orchestra* by Andrea Davis Pinkney

• *Eleanor* by Barbara Cooney

• *National Geographic Explorer* and *National Geographic Kids* magazines

Unit Assessment Seeking Information: Strategies to Read Nonfiction			GENRE
Student name:	EMERGING	DEVELOPING	INDEPENDENT
Identifies genre of nonfiction.			
Uses a variety of text features in reading to gain understanding.			
Begins to distinguish between the most and least important information in a text.			
Shares information learned from a text with others.			

Stage of the Unit	Focused Instruction You will	Independent Practice Students will
IMMERSION 2 days	• read aloud a variety of nonfiction texts, including a narrative text (*Eleanor*), an informational text (*Bears*), and an article (*National Geographic Kids*). • invite students to share what they know about nonfiction.	• read nonfiction texts to notice and name features they recognize. • pick from a variety of nonfiction texts and read for enjoyment.
IDENTIFICATION 3 days	• use *Bears* to name text features, including pictures and captions, diagrams, a glossary, index and table of contents, bold words and text boxes, and fun facts. • create a chart of text features and create shared definitions of text features for students to refer to as they read. • look at different forms of writing (e.g., narrative text, informational text, article, question–answer) to notice how each type of text is written.	• read nonfiction texts to notice and name text features and their purposes in their reading. • read nonfiction texts and find two examples of the text features the class defined and identified; share with partner. • read from various examples of writing; identify form and discuss with partner.

GUIDED PRACTICE 5 days	• use *Bears* to review strategies for navigating different nonfiction texts, including reading from cover to cover versus flipping to the section you need to answer a question. • read aloud from *Duke Ellington* and model how you formulate your own questions to guide your reading—questions that come from your own wonderings about the topics. • read *Big Blue Whale*; model recording information learned on sticky notes, and organizing the sticky notes into categories in your notebook—interesting facts, questions I have about what I read, etc. • continue and revisit how to organize notes in notebook. • evaluate the information that you have collected—What is a big idea? What is a smaller idea?—modeling how to think and write about these questions.	• read from a variety of nonfiction texts and practice navigating these texts. • develop questions about a topic using the cover and title, then read on to answer questions. • use sticky notes to mark the most important information learned in a text. • use sticky notes to collect information learned and place the sticky notes in their notebooks. • think about and write the most important information and questions from notes in notebook.
COMMITMENT 1 day	• model for students how to select your most thoughtful sticky note to put in your reading response notebook and write why it is a good example of determining importance in reading; post thoughtful sticky notes on a chart for students to see.	• review sticky notes in reading and select their most important note; write reflections about what that note shows that they can do as readers of nonfiction.
TOTAL: 11 DAYS		

Naming Importance: Note-Taking Skills

Why Teach This?
- To help students become active learners through their reading by gathering new information.
- To teach students how to record information learned from a text.
- To help students learn ways to collect and record information that will be useful to them in the content areas.

Framing Question
- How can we collect the information we learn in an informational text in an organized and thoughtful manner?

Unit Goals
- Students will determine what is the most and least important information collected.
- Students will develop and use guiding questions to focus their information gathering.
- Students will record information learned in an organized and thoughtful manor.
- Students will put information learned into their own words (paraphrasing).

Anchor Texts
- *Bears: Polar Bears, Black Bears and Grizzly Bears* by Deborah Hodge
- *Big Blue Whale* by Nicola Davies
- *Big Dig* by Moish Goldish
- *Can It Rain Cats and Dogs? Questions and Answers About Weather* by Melvin Berger and Gilda Berger
- *How to Talk to Your Dog* by Jean Craighead George

Unit Assessment Naming Importance: Note-Taking Skills			PROCESS
Student name:	EMERGING	DEVELOPING	INDEPENDENT
Determines what is the most and least important information.			
Develops and uses guiding questions to focus information gathering.			
Records information learned in an organized and thoughtful manner.			
Paraphrases information learned.			

Stage of the Unit	Focused Instruction You will	Independent Practice Students will
IMMERSION 1 day	• discuss when in our lives we have to write down information to remember it. What kinds of jobs require people to take notes? Invite students to discuss what they do when they want to remember information that they learn in their reading; chart student responses.	• read and notice when something stands out to them in their reading; consider how they might record it; read and try one of the techniques listed on chart from that day to take notes.
IDENTIFICATION 4 days	• discuss how writers sometimes gather information before they begin writing and they record this information using notes; discuss the places writers may go to collect information (books, Internet, experts in a field, etc.); chart student responses; read an excerpt from *How to Talk to Your Dog* and demonstrate how you take notes. • create a list of questions you might ask someone in an interview; use these questions to conduct an interview with another adult (you can bring together two classes for teachers to interview each other) and record your findings. • select a favorite topic to investigate on the Internet; model how to read the website and record findings. • model how to look through notes review the information collected and notice how it was recorded (full sentences, bullets, quotes, etc.).	• read and collect information learned using sticky notes. • use the questions they might ask in an interview to interview a partner on their expertise, hobbies, or talents and record what they hear their partner saying. • explore a favorite author or social studies or science topic on the Internet and take notes on what they discover. • review their notes from the past three days to notice how they collected their information.
GUIDED PRACTICE 6 days	• model how note takers use questions to guide their research and use them to record their findings; model writing your question at the top of the page then recording answers to the question found through reading an excerpt from *Bears*. • use *Can it Rain Cats and Dogs?* to model using an index or table of contents to identify where in a book you might find the answer to your question.	• develop a question to guide their reading and take notes on the answers found to that question. • practice using an index or table of contents to find the part of the book that might answer their question.

GUIDED PRACTICE *(continued)*	• explain that different subjects have vocabulary that goes along with a topic (e.g. plants: photosynthesis); often these are the bolded words in the text. Talk about and model how to record this new vocabulary in your notes using the book *Big Dig* as a model. • use *Big Blue Whale* to model how to use text features in texts to collect information and record the information learned. • explore main ideas versus details; revisit a previously explored website or a new one to model taking notes focusing on main ideas. • discuss how notetakers put ideas into their own words or paraphrase; revisit notes from earlier in the unit to model for students how to paraphrase a fact found in a text (read fact, cover text, and write the information learned in your own words).	• practice taking notes on new facts or vocabulary. • take notes from information learned in text features. • revisit a book or website to take notes on the main ideas. • practice paraphrasing information collected.
COMMITMENT 2 days	• model how to select one of their note-taking sheets to make public; students will look for notes that focus on main ideas rather than details, notes that are put into their own words, and vocabulary that is specific to the subject. • post students' selected work on a bulletin board entitled We Are Learning to Take Notes on What We Read.	• evaluate their note-taking sheet and select one that they feel is the strongest. • reflect upon what they have learned about taking notes and how it has helped them as readers of nonfiction.
TOTAL: 13 DAYS		

Early Fall to Late Fall

Your routines are now firmly in place and your classroom feels like a community of readers and writers, sharing ideas and building off one another's learning. Students have been practicing new strategies that will help them make meaning of increasingly complex texts in a variety of genres. Students will begin to apply these strategies to multiple genres, sharing their thoughts about the text with others. In the coming seasons, they study character from all angles, connecting to their favorites as ways to deepen their sense of story. Their own stories unfolding, our students are invigorated by the connections to the world around them.

Chapter 3

LATE FALL

The Third Grader as Synthesizer

"'The most beautiful place in the world,' she said, 'is anyplace.'
'Anyplace?' I repeated.
'Anyplace you can be proud of who you are.'
'Yes,' I said.
But I thought, where you love somebody a whole lot, and you know that
person loves you, that's the most beautiful place in the world."

—from *The Most Beautiful Place in the World* by Ann Cameron

Your students have a wide range of experiences and are becoming keen observers.
Through the units of study in this chapter, your students will delve into the elements
of story and synthesize all their knowledge to be fully ready for the world outside.

LATE FALL UNITS

- Building Multi-Genre Reading Skills: Test Prep, *page 73*

- Building Response Skills: Writing About Reading, *page 76*

- Making Wise Book Choices, *page 79*

- Mastering Dialogue, *page 82*

- Exploring Elements of Story:
  Reading About Characters, *page 85*

- Exploring Elements of Craft:
  Writing About Characters, *page 97*

SPOTLIGHT
UNITS

Meaningful (Yes!) Test Preparation

Connections abound, and our students love to find them! E. M. Forster said, "Only connect," and no one does that better than a third grader, who is looking for all the ways the world shows its interrelatedness. He is fascinated by the night sky and sees the science of the elements, while at the same time he is the first one to be enchanted by an ancient myth telling the story of Orion's belt. He can see how science and social studies, story and poetry all go together. Nothing is separate. This is actually a test-preparation unit, important because so many state tests are asking our students to read across multiple genres and then answer questions that bring these genres together. These are good skills to learn, so we should not be too sad about test preparation if it is done well and meaningfully. If the tests are good and the tests are relevant, then test preparation should feel as rich and satisfying for us and our students as anything else we do. We mean it! Take a journey here with us into the world of meaningful test preparation.

Building Multi-Genre Reading Skills: Test Prep

GENRE

Why Teach This?

- To teach students to provide evidence to support their thoughts about a text.
- To prepare students for standardized tests, which require that students read across genres.

Framing Question

- How do we read across genres, recognizing their unique features and responding to questions that are asked in reference to the ideas about which we read?

Unit Goals

- Students will identify a genre by its title and features.
- Students will get ready to read a text by thinking about its features.
- Students will find evidence to support answers to specific questions about the text.
- Students will reread text for details, having a specific purpose or question in mind.
- Students will make connections, question, visualize, and infer to answer specific questions about a text.

Anchor Texts

- *I Dream of Trains* by Angela Johnson
- *Seymour Simon's Book of Trains* by Seymour Simon
- "Song of the Train" by David McCord (from the collection *Far and Few*)
- *Train Song* by Diane Siebert

Unit Assessment Building Multi-Genre Reading Skills: Test Prep			GENRE
Student name:	EMERGING	DEVELOPING	INDEPENDENT
Recognizes the features of poetry, nonfiction, and narrative.			
Uses the features of each genre to guide his or her thinking before and during reading.			
Identifies evidence to support thinking.			
Uses appropriate strategies to deepen understanding of text.			

Stage of the Unit	Focused Instruction You will	Independent Practice Students will
IMMERSION 2 days	• invite students to share what they know about genre; chart responses. • read aloud an excerpt from a familiar nonfiction text, poem, and narrative; discuss what students know about genre.	• read selected text with a partner; notice genre and identify features in text that show the genre. • read independently from nonfiction, poetry, or narrative texts, noticing characteristics of the genre.
IDENTIFICATION 3 days	• identify and chart the features of a poem. • identify and chart the features of a nonfiction text. • identify and chart the features of a narrative text.	• read a variety of poems, noting features. • read a variety of nonfiction text, noting features. • read narrative picture books, noting features.
GUIDED PRACTICE 8 days	• read David McCord's poem "Song of the Train" and share features of poems. • read Diane Siebert's poem book *Train Song* and discuss features of this poem picture book. • read Angela Johnson's *I Dream of Trains* and discuss features of narrative. • read Seymour Simon's *All About Trains*, noticing features of nonfiction. • give students prompted writing that relates to making connections and making inferences.	• read through a variety of poems, discussing observations of features of text with a partner. • read through a variety of nonfiction texts, discussing observations of text features with a partner. • read through a variety of narrative texts, discussing observations of text features with deeper understanding. • read multiple genres, jotting a place where an image or connection helped them to deepen their understanding.

GUIDED PRACTICE (continued)	• model how to read with a specific question in mind (use question type appropriate for your state assessment). • model how to support one's thinking by locating text evidence, whether it is a poem, a narrative, or nonfiction. • model how to reread a text, locating specific evidence/details to support focused question.	• respond to prompts given by teacher to draw connections between texts. • support their thinking by underlining evidence within the text. • reread texts to find specific evidence/details to support their thinking.
COMMITMENT 2 days	• give a practice test which has a variety of genres in it; ask students to name and notice genres. • identify and name the reasons why knowing about genres helps us on standardized tests.	• take a practice assessment. • name the reasons knowing about genres helps them understand what the test writers are looking for.
TOTAL: 15 DAYS		

Preparing for tests can be collaborative and enjoyable if the work feels truly meaningful.

Rigorous Writing

This unit also supports the work our students will do on state tests but encourages them to approach the tests with vigor and purpose and fun. Response is the key to life: how we respond to difficult times, to joyful times, to challenge, to success says a lot about us. So, too, do our responses to writing. Whether our students are responding to a poem, a nonfiction text, or a fictional piece, they must be versatile and open, bold and clear. This unit is about that kind of practice—building their capacity for flexibility and for thinking on their feet, with pencil in hand.

Building Response Skills: Writing About Reading

STRATEGY

Why Teach This?

- To help students strengthen reading responses with a clear beginning, middle, and end and supporting details.
- To help students learn how to write about their reading with both self-selected topics as well as topics that are prompted by questions.
- To help students recognize that state tests require students to write about short reading passages and make connections across texts.
- To help students recognize unique features of genres that will help them read more efficiently and effectively.

Framing Question

- How can we become skilled at responding to different genres in powerful and efficient ways?

Unit Goals

- Students will use their reading to inspire their writing.
- Students will write responses in an organized, sequential, and thoughtful way.
- Students will compare and contrast texts in writing, including evidence from the texts.
- Students will write in response to many genres, using genre characteristics to inform their responses.

Anchor Texts

- *I Dream of Trains* by Angela Johnson
- *Next Stop Grand Central* by Maira Kalman
- *Seymour Simon's Book of Trains* by Seymour Simon
- "Song of the Train" by David McCord (from the collection *Far and Few*)
- *Train Song* by Diane Siebert

Unit Assessment Building Response Skills: Writing About Reading			STRATEGY
Student name:	EMERGING	DEVELOPING	INDEPENDENT
Uses thinking in reading to generate ideas for writing.			
Writes in an organized, sequential, and thoughtful way.			
Uses paragraphs, full sentences, and examples from the text to explain thinking in writing.			
Recognizes genre elements and uses them to help inform writing.			

Stage of the Unit	Focused Instruction You will	Independent Practice Students will
IMMERSION 2 days	• read aloud excerpts from anchor texts on trains (*I Dream of Trains*, *Seymour Simon's Book of Trains*, "Song of the Train"); discuss how readers make connections across texts and across genres. • model writing a brief reading response to the different genres with sticky notes.	• write responses to one of the genre types—poetry, narrative, nonfiction—using one of the anchor texts (give the students a packet with excerpts from each anchor text they can use throughout this unit, and let them select one). • write a reading response to a genre of their choice with a sticky note; with a partner, discuss responses to the different genres.
IDENTIFICATION 3 days	• name and chart why we write responses to what we read (to share our thinking about reading with others, to compare/contrast ideas, to respond to a question, to record evidence of our thinking). • name what students noticed in their own writing and discuss how they might identify the kinds of responses they wrote, adding to the list you are creating, as an anchor chart. • look at examples of student writing from their notebooks, naming and charting the characteristics of writing about reading that are important, including: compare/contrast, using evidence from the text, drawing knowledge about genre into the writing response, writing in response to a question or prompt.	• read independently and record their thinking in a notebook, noticing what they write about in response to each genre. • continue to read independently and record their thinking in their notebook; mark places they think their responses are strong. • read text excerpts from the multigenre packet, incorporating the important characteristics discussed as a class.

GUIDED PRACTICE 8 days	• read aloud "Train Song" and *I Dream of Trains*; briefly compare and contrast the genres; model writing a compare and contrast response to the texts. • read aloud excerpts from *Next Stop Grand Central* and *A Book of Trains*; briefly compare and contrast the genres; model writing a compare and contrast response to the texts. • reflect on your compare and contract model responses; model revising your writing from notes to a more organized paragraph, including beginning, middle, and end. • reread excerpts from *Seymour Simon's Book of Trains*; model drawing important evidence from the text; model writing a brief response to the text including evidence. • reread "Song of the Train"; model drawing evidence from the text; model writing a brief response to the text including evidence. • reflect on your evidence-writing responses; model revising your writing from notes to a more organized paragraph, including beginning, middle, and end. • reread excerpt from *Next Stop Grand Central*; discuss how the genre will affect the writing response; model writing a response including genre characteristics in the response. • choose an exemplary sample of student writing from a student notebook; work with the class to add genre characteristics to the response, using them to inform your writing.	• read independently; find ways to compare/contrast to other texts they've read; write a brief compare and contrast response in their notebooks. • read independently from two different genres; based on those readings, write a brief compare and contrast response in their notebooks. • choose one of their compare/contrast notebook entries to revise; rewrite their entry from notes to organized paragraph. • read independently and write in response to their own reading, including evidence (quotes, key phrases, ideas, or information) from a text. • read independently from two different genres; write in response to their own reading, including evidence from their texts; notice how their evidence changes depending on the genre. • choose one of their evidence-gathering notebook entries to revise; rewrite their entry from notes to organized paragraph. • read independently; write in response to their reading; include genre characteristics in their responses. • read independently; write in response to their reading; including genre characteristics to inform their responses.
COMMITMENT 2 days	• create a chart that shows several things a reader can do to write in response to reading (e.g., compare and contrast, share evidence-based connections, use knowledge of genres to read and respond to texts). • choose a favorite writing response from the unit; revise and publish the writing response.	• share favorite writing responses from this unit with a partner. • choose a favorite writing response from the unit; revise and publish the writing response; share their response with a partner.
TOTAL: 15 DAYS		

Decision Makers

Third graders are changing so much as readers. Every day brings new growth and new possibility. But they need our support now more than ever before. They will appear as though they have it all figured out, when in fact they may still struggle to figure out who they are as readers and what book choices make the most sense for them. This is all the more reason to tuck in a brief unit on reading choices at this time of the year, when we can explicitly share suggestions on how we make choices and why we make them. There are many wonderful independent book selections for third graders, books that will enchant and hook readers of all levels. Use this unit to expose your students to new titles and reread some old favorites. By teaching about choice, we give both our students and ourselves the gift of growing independence.

Teachers often wonder what books to offer students as choices for independent reading. Third graders bridge from primary to upper-grade students: their levels in this grade are hugely varied. Here are some suggestions for you in terms of what you are stocking in your classroom libraries or helping students to find in their local libraries as well.

For your more vulnerable students: *Mixed-Up Max* by Dick King-Smith, *A to Z Mysteries* by Ron Roy, *Weird Planet* by Dan Greenberg, *Cobble Street Cousins* by Cynthia Rylant, *Gooney Bird Greene* by Lois Lowery, and DK Eye Know series

For your steadier students: Stink series by Megan McDonald and Peter H. Reynolds, *Ivy and Bean* by Annie Barrows, Judy Moody series by Megan McDonald, Clementine series by Sara Pennypacker, Tashi series by Anna Fienberg and Barbara Fienberg, Wayside School series by Louis Sachar, *Who Was Eleanor Roosevelt?* by Gare Thompson, and other books in this biographical series.

For your stronger students: *A Mouse Called Wolf* and other books by Dick King-Smith, Igraine the Brave and Ghosthunters series by Cornelia Funke, *The Spiderwick Chronicles* by Holly Black, Winning Season series by Rich Wallace, and *Harriet Tubman* by George Sullivan and other books in the series.

These are just some suggestions. You and your students will find many more to add to this list as the year goes on.

Making Wise Book Choices

PROCESS

Why Teach This?

• To revisit the idea of making independent book choices.

• To give students time to read in areas of high interest.

• To add to students' "book stacks" (books they plan to read this year.).

Framing Question

• How can we make smart book choices for our independent reading lives?

Unit Goals

- Students will review the ways to make strong book choices, including finding books that interest them, choosing books written on a comfortable reading level, and choosing books about topics, by authors, or in a series with which they are familiar.
- Students will create a list of books they would like to read this year to add to their "stack."
- Students will practice their reading strategies and share thinking with a partner.

Anchor Text

- *Library Mouse* by Daniel Kirk

Unit Assessment Making Wise Book Choices			PROCESS
Student name:	EMERGING	DEVELOPING	INDEPENDENT
Makes strong book choices, including choosing books that interest them, are written on a comfortable reading level, and are about topics, by authors, or in a series with which they are familiar.			
Creates a list of books to add to his/her "stack" they would like to read this year.			
Practices reading strategies independently.			
Shares thinking with a partner.			

Stage of the Unit	Focused Instruction You will	Independent Practice Students will
IMMERSION 1 day	• read aloud *Library Mouse*; discuss how readers select books to read; chart student responses; share books from your own reading life.	• review books they've read so far this year to think about how and why they selected them.
IDENTIFICATION 1 day	• teach the ways readers select books, including finding books that interest them; finding books that are comfortable for them as readers; finding books that they have some familiarity with from the author, series, or subject; use the following books as examples for different kinds of readers to try: • for a gentle read try *Mercy Watson Goes for a Ride* and other books in the series by Kate DiCamillo, or *Franny K. Stein Mad Scientist* by Jim Benton	• look through class library to identify books that interest them; find books that are comfortable for them as readers; find books that they have some familiarity with from the author, series, or subject.

IDENTIFICATION *(continued)*	• for a more challenging read try The Cobble Street Cousins series by Cynthia Rylant or *Clementine* by Sara Pennypacker • for a challenging read try *Andy and Tamika* by David Adler or *Zebra Wall* by Kevin Henkes	
GUIDED PRACTICE 2 days	• discuss how readers feel like reading different kinds of texts at different times and how their stack of books reflects that variety; show the diversity of reading materials that are in your stack of books, including magazines, newspapers, poetry, nonfiction, and fiction texts. • discuss how readers sometimes challenge themselves with harder texts and sometimes need gentler reads; model reviewing texts in your stack to identify the different kind of texts you have selected and when you might read each type (e.g., before bed, when you want to learn new information, etc.)	• find different kinds of texts to add to their stack of books, including magazines, poetry, picture books, chapter books, fiction, and nonfiction texts. • review texts in stack of books to evaluate when they might read each text; meet with a partner to share when they plan to read each text and why they made that decision.
COMMITMENT 1 day	• review how readers make wise book selections and bring variety to their reading.	• commit to making book choices that feel wise and effective; celebrate their stack of books by posting a list of the books in their stack in a public place.
TOTAL: 5 DAYS		

Characters Talking and Talking

There are a few things that can really get in the way for your third graders. One of these is the complex punctuation required to write dialogue. So rather than write it, your students will shy away from it, and their writing looks like straight narrative. Even a bit of well-chosen dialogue can enliven and energize a piece of writing. This is a great year to take some time to practice writing using dialogue. Your third graders are incredibly tuned in to the social worlds around them. They are paying close attention to adult conversations as well as those of their friends. Before we enter into a longer character unit in writing, let's take a week to explore with our students what it takes to write dialogue and what tools we need to write it well.

Mastering Dialogue   CONVENTIONS

Why Teach This?

• To help students use dialogue in their writing and become aware of the conventions that allow it to be used effectively.

Framing Question

• What punctuation do we need to know in order to write dialogue?

Unit Goals

• Students will recognize the punctuation that contains dialogue.
• Students will use punctuation appropriately when their characters are speaking.

Anchor Texts

• *Cowboy & Octopus* by Jon Scieszka
• *I Will Never Not Ever Eat a Tomato* by Lauren Child
• *Little Night* by Yuyi Morales
• *My Dadima Wears a Sari* by Kashmira Sheth
• *The Stories Julian Tells* by Ann Cameron

Unit Assessment Mastering Dialogue			CONVENTIONS
Student name:	**EMERGING**	**DEVELOPING**	**INDEPENDENT**
Uses quotation marks correctly.			
Uses ending punctuation correctly inside and outside quotation marks.			
Uses dialogue effectively in stories.			

Stage of the Unit	Focused Instruction You will	Independent Practice Students will
IMMERSION 1 day	• read aloud *Cowboy & Octopus* by Jon Scieszka, noting punctuation for dialogue after you read (going back and pointing it out).	• read independently, noting punctuation for dialogue if it comes up in their reading.
IDENTIFICATION 1 day	• identify and chart the ingredients for dialogue (quotation marks, commas, periods, capital letters).	• write about someone in their life who matters to them, noting where dialogue might improve writing.
GUIDED PRACTICE 2 days	• read aloud *I Will Never Not Ever Eat a Tomato* and discuss how writers use dialogue to convey a character's voice. • read aloud an excerpt from *The Stories Julian Tells* by Ann Cameron and discuss how dialogue can affect your understanding of a character.	• write dialogue for their character. • revise and edit their piece, checking for all punctuation that is needed for dialogue.
COMMITMENT 1 day	• read aloud *Little Night* and demonstrate how to read aloud when dialogue is used—with inflection!	• read aloud with inflection where dialogue is used.
TOTAL: 5 DAYS		

SPOTLIGHT on Strategy

- Exploring Elements of Story: Reading About Characters
- Exploring Elements of Craft: Writing About Characters

Strategy is thinking about what tools (physical or cognitive) we need and have available to understand and solve a problem, create a plan, and put the plan into action to solve the problem. The effective reader, writer, and thinker asks: What are the ways of looking at this problem that others have successfully employed, and what are the tricks of the trade I can use? We often spend time teaching different strategies separately (making connections and asking questions, for example) when the real challenge is helping our children understand what type of strategy would best be used to solve a particular problem, and then identifying the particular strategy to solve it. The strategies we use as readers and writers depend on our intuitive understanding of what is happening at that time, in that moment, as we read and write, and how that relates to the goal we are trying to achieve. By properly identifying the problem, we can use the right strategy to fix it.

In *Strategies That Work*, Stephanie Harvey and Anne Goudvis (2000) write:

"The term *strategic reading* refers to thinking about reading in ways that enhance learning and understanding. Researchers who explicitly taught students strategies for determining important ideas (Gallagher, 1986), drawing inferences (Hansen, 1981), and asking questions (Gavelek & Raphael, 1985) found that teaching these thinking/reading strategies improved students' overall comprehension of text. Research by Palincsar and Brown (1984) and Paris, Lipson, and Wixon (1983), however, suggests that it isn't enough for students to simply understand a given strategy. They must know when, why, and how to use it."

Watching a third grader elaborately plan out how recess will go with best friends, or organize a complex play at lunch, or read across an entire series of books, we know how strategic he can be. Strategy units are about helping our students build these powers of concentration, connections, and inquiry as they explore new or complex information in their literacy work.

Building knowledge of story elements is the frame for all strategy work in the reading of fiction and narrative text. In third grade, our students are developing deep connections to a multitude of characters who guide them through text plots and keep them engaged in series books as they build stamina. In these next units, we will take a close look at how we can help our students become more strategic in thinking about characters as they relate to story elements across the pages of multiple texts. For more information on strategy units for your primary readers and writers, see pages 73–79 in my book *The Complete 4 for Literacy*.

Pam Allyn

Characters Move and Delight Us

Up until now your third graders have been practicing using a wide range of reading strategies and written responses to make meaning of what they have read throughout the first half of the year. They are ready to move on to the next level of analysis in their thinking. An author study builds upon the concept that reading is thinking by asking children to spend some time reading multiple books written by an author and looking for commonalities between these books. They can use their developing knowledge to analyze and interpret texts to deepen their thinking. Researching an author to take a closer look at the development of one of the characters and how that author brings that character to life is a natural focus for this unit.

Exploring Elements of Story: Reading About Characters

STRATEGY

Why Teach This?

- To make connections between prior learning about story elements in the fiction reading unit.
- To focus on character development in order to develop a deeper understanding of the text.
- To take a closer look at a character in a story and to research how an author makes that character come to life.
- To write thoughtfully about what they are reading to show their understanding and thinking about a text.

Framing Question

- How does reading multiple books by one author help us learn about how authors create characters and bring them to life?

Unit Goals

- Students will recognize and identify the elements in a story.
- Students will look across texts by the same author to find similarities and differences.
- Students will analyze and trace a character through multiple books.
- Students will recognize patterns that occur in the different writing techniques the author uses to bring the characters to life.
- Students will write about the characters they research and write through the lenses of those characters.
- Students will collaborate with others to research an author and character through multiple texts.

Anchor Texts

- *Children's Books and Their Creators*, edited by Anita Silvey
- *The Stories Julian Tells*, *More Stories Julian Tells*, and *Julian's Glorious Summer* by Ann Cameron

Resource Sheets

- Parent Letter for Character Study (Resource 3.1)
- Tracing a Character (Resource 3.2)

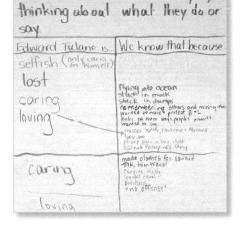

Unit Assessment Exploring Elements of Story: Reading About Characters			STRATEGY
Student name:	EMERGING	DEVELOPING	INDEPENDENT
Recognizes and identifies the elements of a story.			
Identifies similarities and differences across texts by the same author to think more deeply about one element.			
Makes connections between texts about a character by analyzing and tracing him or her through a book.			
Recognizes the ways in which the author brings the character to life.			
Understands how to write through the lens of the character.			
Engages in productive and conversational book talk.			
Works cooperatively with others.			

Stage of the Unit	Focused Instruction You will	Independent Practice Students will
IMMERSION 4 days	• introduce the author Ann Cameron by sharing biographical information and the texts that will serve as anchors for the unit; discuss how reading multiple books by an author allows readers to take a closer look at how an author brings a character to life. • read aloud from *The Stories Julian Tells*; pose questions to guide students to think about the characters' physical and personality traits. • read aloud from *More Stories Julian Tells*, having students think about the characters' physical and personality traits. • read aloud from *Julian's Glorious Summer* and discuss story elements and how they affect the character.	• reflect in their notebooks what they have learned about the author and predict what kind of characters this author might portray in her books now that they have learned more about her. • reread *The Stories Julian Tells* with a partner and create a list in their notebooks of the main characters' traits; write a reflective statement about the character. • read from *More Stories Julian Tells* and add more character traits to their list. • reread *Julian's Glorious Summer* with a partner and note characters' changes and any new information.

IDENTIFICATION 3 days	• reread one of the anchor texts aloud and introduce the Tracing a Character organizer (Resource 3.2), on which they will collect information about a character. • model how to trace a character across multiple texts by using the words of the author to identify the physical and personality traits of the character. • model how to look at the dialogue and the interactions the character has with others and how the characters solve problems.	• work with a partner to reread the anchor texts and fill in the organizer. • find examples of physical and personality traits of a character and write down the textual evidence to support these findings. • reflect and record on the organizer what they further notice about the character.
GUIDED PRACTICE 7 days	• model how to analyze the information gathered. • model with two students how to have a conversation as if they were Julian and a friend having a conversation. • model how to take information researched to create a character profile. • place students into small groups and model how to decide on an author and character to study. • model how to research a character and how to complete a Tracing a Character chart. • model how to begin writing a character profile. • review student work and plan for celebrating.	• talk in small groups about Julian and write about how he might solve problems. • with a partner, pretend to be Julian and one of his friends engaging in a conversation. • create a character profile, including information about their character and how the author brings this character to life. • research biographical information about their author's life; fill in the Tracing a Character chart and write a reflective statement about their character in their reader's notebook. • continue to read their books and complete the Tracing a Character chart. • begin to write a character profile using the information from the chart. • complete the character profile.
COMMITMENT 1 day	• instruct students to share profiles with another group and reflect on their learning.	• share these profiles with other groups and reflect on what they have learned about their author and the way this author brings the character to life.
TOTAL: 15 DAYS		

Getting Started

These reading and writing units are designed to allow students to take a closer look at story elements and to better understand the characters they come across in reading so that they will be able to create richer characters in their writing.

Structures and Routines

This unit is divided into two parts: a whole-class study of an author and character and small-group studies of an author and character of their choice. The whole-class study allows you to lead students through the process of learning about an author and his or her way of bringing a character to life.

Partnerships

The shared reading of these texts allows students to support one another's thinking in authentic and purposeful ways. For the first part of the unit, students participate in partnerships in which they can solidify their understanding of the text. In the second half of the unit, rather than having many different authors and characters studied at once, create small groups based on the students' reading levels and match them to texts written by authors at their reading level. This will also help with the management of the groups and allow you to support different groups at different times.

Teaching Materials

Anchor Texts

The best choices for anchor texts are those stories that have a main character that recur in at least three books written by the same author. Some of our favorite titles with characters who reappear in other books include *The Stories Julian Tells* by Ann Cameron, *Peter's Chair* by Ezra Jack Keats, and *A Chair for My Mother* by Vera B. Williams.

Choosing the Texts for Students to Read

Matching books to readers is an essential component of the success of this study and further enables differentiation. Richard Allington (2005), in his book *What Really Matters for Struggling Readers: Designing Research-Based Programs,* cites studies that show that "frustration-level reading accuracy below 95 percent, word-by-word reading, and comprehension below 75 percent was to be avoided because of the negative impact such experience had on both learning and attitude." When we match students to books, we use this information to guide our students toward wise book choices.

Differentiation

Place your students into groups by their reading level. We want to make sure the texts to which we match our students fall into the 95 percent readability level for each student. In order for students to make comparisons and form observations across books, each group should read at least three books by the author they are studying. For groups that are reading chapter books, the expectation is that some of the reading will be done as homework.

Below, we have categorized picture and chapter books that feel appropriate for each category of reader.

Vulnerable	Steady	Strong
Picture Books: *Peter's Chair, The Snowy Day, Whistle for Willie* by Ezra Jack Keats	**Picture Books:** *Something Special for Me, A Chair for My Mother, Music, Music for Everyone* by Vera B. Williams	**Picture Books:** *Zen Shorts* and *Zen Ties* by Jon Muth
Chapter Books: *Otto Undercover #1: Born to Drive, Otto Undercover #2: Water Balloon Doom, Otto Undercover #6: Brain Freeze* by Rhea Pearlman and Dan Santat *Busybody Nora, Nora and Mrs.-Mind-Your-Own-Business, New Neighbors for Nora* by Johanna Hurwitz *Marvin Redpost Kidnapped at Birth?, Marvin Redpost Alone in His Teacher's House, Marvin Redpost Class President* by Louis Sachar	**Chapter Books:** *Jake Drake Know-It-All, Jake Drake Teacher's Pet, Jake Drake Bully Buster* by Andrew Clements *Ivy and Bean, Ivy and Bean and the Ghost That Had to Go, Ivy and Bean Take Care of the Babysitter* by Annie Barrows *The Stories Julian Tells, More Stories Julian Tells, Julian's Glorious Summer* by Ann Cameron	**Chapter Books:** *Half Magic, The Time Garden, Knight's Castle* by Edward Eager *Henry Huggins, Henry and the Clubhouse, Henry and Beezus* by Beverly Cleary *Midnight for Charlie Bone, Charlie Bone and the Time Twister, Charlie Bone and the Shadow* by Jenny Nimmo

Stages of the Unit

Immersion

We start by reading multiple texts by an author with a recurring main character. Engage students in a discussion of what they observe by having them activate their prior knowledge of story elements. Students discuss what they notice about the character's physical and personality traits and get an initial sense of who this character is. See Parent Letter for Character Study (Resource 3.1), at right.

Identification

As students follow a character through multiple texts, they identify the textual evidence to support their findings of the character's physical and personality traits. Class charts are created to keep track of their thinking to further identify the character's distinguishing characteristics.

Guided Practice

Students practice using their new thinking about character understanding by writing as if they are that character. Sharing their work with partners helps them clarify their thinking. As the whole-class study is wrapping up, the small-group work is just

Students come together to share their observations about the characters in their books.

starting. The nice thing about doing this same kind of thinking twice in a row is that the students' first experience is fresh in their minds, so when they apply these skills in the texts that are on their reading level, they have their previous experiences to support their work. Students analyze information to have a better understanding of their character. Students create character profiles that introduce others to how an author creates and brings life to a character.

Commitment

Students have the opportunity to read and celebrate one another's character profiles while learning about the different authors. They also have a chance to reflect upon the learning they did in this unit.

Day-by-Day Lessons

DAY 1 Immersion

Focused Instruction

We are going to do a class study of an author, Ann Cameron. This means we will read a few books written by her and spend some time researching and looking deeper at one of her characters.

Here is background information on Ann Cameron. You can go to childrensbestbooks. com for great information on Cameron's life. She loved nature as a child, she loved to make up pretend games, and she was very, very close to an older sister she idolized.

Independent Practice

In your reader's notebooks, reflect on what you have learned about Ann Cameron and predict what kind of characters she might portray in her books.

- In their reader's notebooks, students should predict what kind of characters Cameron might portray in her books based on what they know of her life.

Wrap-Up

- Invite children to share their reflections. Chart their predictions to see whether there are any patterns that emerge among their thinking about the characters that might be portrayed in Cameron's books.

DAY 2 Immersion

Focused Instruction

Today we are going to begin our author study of Ann Cameron by reading aloud two chapters from the book The Stories Julian Tells. *We will take a closer look at Julian. When I stop reading, remember to turn and talk to your partner about what's happening in the story and what we are learning about this character.*

- Explain to students the difference between physical and personality traits.

Independent Practice

With a copy of the text and a partner, reread the chapters that we read aloud yesterday. As you read, create a list in your reader's notebook of what you notice about Julian. Write down any of Julian's physical or personality traits that Cameron described. Then discuss and write a reflective statement about Julian.

- As students reread the text with a partner, they write down both the physical and personality traits of Julian.
- After discussing how Cameron describes Julian, students write a reflective statement about Julian.

Wrap-Up

What did we find out about Julian today?

- Begin a class chart listing the descriptive traits of Julian.

DAY 3 Immersion

Focused Instruction

Today we are going to continue to learn about Julian in another book called More Stories Julian Tells. *Just like in the books we read yesterday, we will hear more about Julian, his brother Huey, and his good friend Gloria. When I stop reading, talk about the story. Focus on any connections you notice about Julian between the different books.*

Independent Practice

Just like yesterday, you are going to reread the text that we read aloud. Then you will add to the chart in your reader's notebook that you began about the physical and personality traits of Julian. After you and your partner have discussed the text, write another reflective statement about Julian, incorporating any new information you learned about him.

Wrap-Up

What did you notice about the two books? What new information did we learn about Julian?

DAY 4 Immersion

Focused Instruction

So far, we have read two books by Ann Cameron and we are starting to notice connections between her books. Today we are going to read another one of her books called Julian's Glorious Summer. *When you turn and talk today, continue to discuss what's happening in the story and what you notice about this book in comparison to the other two books we have read. Think about Julian and what connections we can make about him between the books and what new facts we are learning about him.*

- Students talk about how Cameron depicts Julian in each of the three books and about what connections Cameron makes among the three books.

Independent Practice

- Students reread the sections from *The Stories Julian Tells, More Stories Julian Tells,* and *Julian's Glorious Summer.*

- In their reader's notebooks, students should write the new facts they learned about Julian and any connections they noticed among the three books.

Wrap-Up

What are some of the connections you were able to make across the different books? What did you notice about Julian across the different stories?

- Students share their thinking and continue to add on to the chart about Julian's physical and personality traits.

DAY 5 Identification

Focused Instruction

We have read three books by Ann Cameron and have started to notice some connections that arise among her books. Today we are going to reread The Stories Julian Tells *and start moving our notes from our reader's notebook onto this chart (Tracing a Character). This chart will help us organize the information we gather on Julian across the different books. As we gather our observations on Julian's physical and personality traits, we are going to take a closer look at how Ann Cameron creates these images for us by writing down our observations on the other side of the chart.*

- Model how to complete the Physical Traits of a Character and Personality Traits of a Character sections of the Tracing a Character chart (Resource 3.2).

Independent Practice

- Students work with a partner to reread the texts and complete the Physical Traits of a Character and Personality Traits of a Character sections of the Tracing a Character chart.

Wrap-Up

- Students share their charts with one another and discuss any patterns in Julian's physical and personality traits that are starting to emerge.

DAY 6 Identification

Focused Instruction

Yesterday we started filling in our chart using The Stories Julian Tells. *Today we are going to reread* More Stories Julian Tells *and continue to fill in our chart. Since we have spent some time getting to know Julian, we are going to take a closer look at the interactions he has with other characters by studying the conversations he has with the other characters in the story. What do we learn about Julian through these conversations?*

- Choose a conversation in the book and read it aloud to the children.

- Students turn and talk and discuss what they observe about the conversation between Julian and the other characters.

- Model how to complete the Dialogue Evidence From Story and Interactions With Other Characters sections of the Tracing a Character chart.

Independent Practice

- With a partner, students continue to reread the texts from both days and fill in the Dialogue Evidence From Story and Interactions With Other Characters sections of the Tracing a Character chart.

Wrap-Up

How does Ann Cameron give us more insight into Julian by using dialogue?

- Students turn and talk and discuss the question by using the information gathered on their charts.
- Add to the class chart the information students share.

DAY 7 Identification

Focused Instruction

Today we are going to reread Julian's Glorious Summer *and continue to fill in the chart. What have we learned so far about the way Julian solves problems?*

- Spotlight a section of the book that indicates how Julian solves problems.
- Model how to complete the Problem-Solving Strategies of the Character section of the Tracing a Character chart with their recent observations.

Independent Practice

- With a partner, students should reread all three texts and complete the chart.

Wrap-Up

- Students share the information they have gathered.
- Add the new information to the class chart.

DAY 8 Guided Practice

Focused Instruction

Today we are going to start analyzing all of the information we have gathered on the chart. What have we learned about Julian? Who is he?

- Invite students to think about the chart and how it can help them look across the three books and draw conclusions about Julian.
- Students work in small groups to discuss what they can say about Julian from their observations.
- Guide a whole-class discussion by helping students use the chart to support their thinking.

Independent Practice

In your small groups, discuss how Julian is a problem solver. What would he do if he were faced with a problem? How would he go about solving it? Use the information from your chart to think about the following problem.

- Pose a problem for the small groups to discuss.
- Students write in their readers' notebooks how Julian would solve the problem.

Wrap-Up

- Students share what they have written.
- Create a class chart of the conclusions they are starting to draw.

DAY 9 Guided Practice

Focused Instruction

We have started to think about what we can learn about Julian from the chart we have filled in. Today I am going to invite some students to join me in a conversation as if they were Julian talking to his friend Gloria and his brother Huey. You are going to sit in a circle around us and notice what we do in our conversation and what we say. You might notice whether we refer back to a book. You might also notice how we show one another we are listening. Or you might notice whether the conversation truly portrays how Julian would interact with Gloria and Huey. When we are done, we will talk about what you saw.

- The idea of this "fishbowl" activity is that a small group participates in a discussion that everyone else can observe and learn from. You create two circles, one on the outside of students observing the conversation and a smaller one in the middle of students having the conversation. The students on the outside take notes on what they see the speakers do and what they hear them say. The group in the middle models a conversation, bringing with them all of the materials they need, including the text and chart.
- Students share what they noticed during the conversation and reflect on how accurately Julian was portrayed.

Independent Practice

- In pairs, students pretend to be Julian and one of his friends engaging in a conversation. Each student writes down the conversation in his or her reader's notebook.

Wrap-Up

- Students share what they have written and get feedback from their classmates.

DAY 10 Guided Practice

Focused Instruction

We are going to take all of the information from our chart and the learning that we have done about Julian to create a character profile. This profile will share information on who he is as a person and how Ann Cameron brings him to life for us. We want to introduce Julian to other readers.

- Model for students how to organize the information to write a profile of Julian. Also model how to use the information from the chart to bring in the writing techniques (such as developing personality and physical traits) used by Ann Cameron to create Julian.

Independent Practice

- Students work with a partner to create the profile.

Wrap-Up

- Students share their profiles with one another.

DAY 11 Guided Practice

Focused Instruction

Today you are going to be given the chance to work in small groups to decide on an author and character of your choice that you would like to study. Before you start reading the books by one author, find out some biographical information on him or her.

- Place students into small groups by reading level. Each group is given a few author choices at their level.
- Students decide in their small groups the author they would like to read and the character they will trace.

Independent Practice

- Students research their author to get some biographical information, using books about authors' lives, including *Children's Books and Their Creators*, edited by Anita Silvey, as well as Scholastic's Authors and Illustrators series.
- Students start reading the books in small groups and filling in a new Tracing a Character chart like the one they created for the whole-class study.
- Students follow the same structure as the whole-class study by writing a reflective statement about their character in their reader's notebook.

Wrap-Up

- Students share what author and character they are studying as well as any information they have learned so far.

DAY 12 Guided Practice

Focused Instruction

We are going to continue to meet in our small groups to research our character. What have you noticed about the friendships your character has? What kind of friend is your character?

- Students talk with a partner to get ready to add information to their Tracing a Character chart.

Independent Practice

- In their small groups, students continue to read their books and fill out their Tracing a Character charts.
- Students begin to draw conclusions about their character.

Wrap-Up

- Students share how the process is going.

DAY 13 Guided Practice

Focused Instruction

Today we are going to finish reading the books and filling in the chart in anticipation of the character profiles we are going to write. What are some of the conclusions your group is starting to make?

- Students talk in their small groups and then share some of their thinking.

Independent Practice

- Students finish reading and completing the Tracing a Character chart.
- Students analyze the information from the chart and organize it to write a character profile.

Wrap-Up

- Students share which part of this author study has been challenging so far and which part has been easy to handle.

DAY 14 Guided Practice

Focused Instruction

Admire your students' work and plan for a celebration in which students will share their profiles.

Independent Practice

- Students complete their character profiles.

Wrap-Up

- Students share any connections they can make with their new author and character to Ann Cameron and Julian.

DAY 15 Commitment

Focused Instruction

We are going to celebrate how we have grown as readers during this month. We have learned a lot about two different authors and two different characters. What have you learned about yourself as researchers of an author and character?

Independent Practice

- Students write a reflective statement in their reader's notebook, sharing their thinking on what they have learned about themselves as readers through this unit.
- Students share their character profiles with other groups.

Wrap-Up

- Students share one thing they learned about themselves as readers that they will take away from this unit to apply to the rest of their reading lives.

Mentors Show Us How to Write

Many third graders come into school knowing who their favorite authors are and why. We can help our students take one of these authors and use them as a mentor to polish their writing. Children learn from example; whether it is how to hit a baseball, be a team player, or how to knit, they are always watching and observing others. Giving students the opportunity to find writing mentors allows them to practice writing in similarly joyous and playful ways.

Exploring Elements of Craft: Writing About Characters

STRATEGY

Why Teach This?

- To model how writers are inspired by mentor authors.
- To make connections between their prior learning about story elements and their study of character development.
- To help students develop their own characters.

Framing Question

- What can we learn about the development of a character from a mentor author to improve our own writing?

Unit Goals

- Students will be able to identify and use the story elements in their writing.
- Students will learn how to use a mentor author to guide their writing.
- Students will recognize patterns that occur in the different writing techniques the mentor author uses to bring the character to life.
- Students will be able to use the mentor author to create a character that's as well developed as the one they are researching.

Anchor Texts

- *The Stories Julian Tells*, *More Stories Julian Tells*, and *Julian's Glorious Summer* by Ann Cameron

Resource Sheets

- Tracing a Character (Resource 3.2)
- Pre-Draft Organizer (Resource 3.3)
- Character Development Organizer (Resource 3.4)
- End-of-Unit Reflection (Resource 3.5)

Unit Assessment Exploring Elements of Craft: Writing About Characters			STRATEGY
Student name:	EMERGING	DEVELOPING	INDEPENDENT
Rereads notebook to pick a topic that can be developed using the story elements.			
Recognizes and uses the story elements in their writing.			
Recognizes and uses the different writing techniques the mentor author uses to bring a character to life.			
Creates a well-developed character that reflects the style of the mentor author.			
Uses the mentor author's text to revise their writing.			
Works cooperatively with others.			

Stage of the Unit	Focused Instruction You will	Independent Practice Students will
IMMERSION 2 days	• explain how students will use an author as a mentor to help them with writing; discuss concept of a mentor author; reflect on a time when you took on the role of mentor or a time when you were mentored to learn something new or to get better at something. • model how to reread your writing in search of really compelling ideas.	• reflect in writing about a time they took on the role of mentor or a time when they were mentored (admiring someone or being someone who is emulated). • reread their writer's notebook, reflect on entries written, and share with a partner.
IDENTIFICATION 5 days	• model how author Ann Cameron uses story elements (character, setting, plot) in her series about Julian. • model choosing a topic and writing an entry using the story elements. • model how to use Ann Cameron as a mentor to develop a character (character traits and profile). • use mentor author and text to discuss how dialogue is used. • refer to mentor text and discuss the problems Julian faces and how he manages them.	• reread their entries to create a list of possible writing topics that lend themselves to the use of story elements. • practice adding story elements to their selected topics. • using mentor author/texts guide their writing about characters. • practice adding dialogue to their pieces. • write about a problem their character will face and how he/she will respond to it.

GUIDED PRACTICE 7 days	• model how to take a chosen topic and use the writing techniques of Ann Cameron, your mentor author, as your guide to bring a character to life. • discuss how writers plan ahead by preplanning their drafts; model how to fill in a Pre-Draft Organizer. • model and guide students through some more writing about their character in their writer's notebook by using the information from the reading unit to develop character's actions and motivations. • discuss the relationship between characters and model how to complete the Character Development Organizer. • model how to use the organizers and your writer's notebook to write a draft. • model how to revise a draft using a mentor author's text. • model how to edit with a focus on dialogue.	• use the writing techniques of their mentor author to bring a character to life. • fill in the Pre-Draft Organizer. • write in their writer's notebook to continue developing their characters' actions and motivations. • fill in the Character Development Organizer and share with a partner for feedback. • write a draft. • revise their drafts with attention to story elements and dialogue. • edit drafts with a focus on dialogue.
COMMITMENT 1 day	• celebrate and share students' published pieces and reflect on what was learned from Ann Cameron's writing.	• share their writing with family and friends and reflect on how a mentor author helped improve their writing.
TOTAL: 15 DAYS		

Getting Started

Helping students improve their writing by studying characters and the authors who create them is tremendously exciting. Characters come to life; authors feel like real people. Share with your students books you have read and characters who have affected you. Share with them a time when an author really made a difference to you. Do not underestimate yourself as a mentor to your students: if they see you falling in love with characters and the authors who created them, they are going to follow you on this journey.

Structures and Routines

Partnerships

Partnerships in this unit are fluid and change as often as needed, depending on the focus of the instruction. Students can be matched to help support each other as writers by matching one child's writing strength with one child's writing weakness. For all of the writers to learn from each other, matching students of the same writing level gives these writers a chance to push their own thinking and allows those students who always serve as mentors an opportunity to learn from a classmate. Having fluid and changing partnerships helps with the management of supporting writers who need more guidance. This also allows the teacher to support different students at different times.

Teaching Materials

Although we recommend three of Ann Cameron's most famous books, she has written many others. Dip into these and have them available for your students in an Ann Cameron basket in the room.

Stages of the Unit

Immersion

Students spend some time rereading their notebooks to find possible topics they can write more about. They narrow down their list to topics that lend themselves to a narrative structure with strong story elements.

Identification

As students try out different topics, they are beginning their character development work by experimenting with the writing techniques of the mentor author they researched in the reading unit. At the end of this stage, students will pick a topic to create a published piece.

Guided Practice

The modeling that is done daily supports the students as they practice the writing techniques of their mentor author. Students preplan their drafts to ensure that the writing style of the mentor author is present.

Commitment

Students have the opportunity to share their writing with one another and the community and to celebrate all of the hard work they have done as writers. They also reflect on their learning they did in this unit by filling out the End-of-Unit Reflection.

Day-by-Day Lessons

DAY 1 Immersion

Focused Instruction

We are going to analyze how the author Ann Cameron creates a character who has feelings, opinions, and a personality that we can trace. We are going to use Ann Cameron as a mentor to help us with our writing. A mentor is someone from whom we can learn new things or how to become better at something. When have you been a mentor for someone?

- Students turn and talk and discuss a time when they took on the role of a mentor.

When have you been mentored?

- Students turn and talk and discuss a time when they were mentored.

Independent Practice

In your writer's notebook, write about a time when you were mentored or a time when you took on the role of a mentor. Think about what you learned from the experience and what it felt like.

- Students record an example of mentoring another person or being mentored.

Wrap-Up

- Students share experiences being mentored or mentoring someone else.

DAY 2 Immersion

Focused Instruction

Today I am going to show you how I reread the entries in my writer's notebook and think about what I have written and whether there is something I would like to revise and publish.

- Model how to reread and reflect on entries.
- Show how to mark an entry with a sticky note if you think more writing can be done.

Independent Practice

I write best when I find a comfortable place to write. Where is your favorite place to sit when you write? Today you are going to find a comfortable place in the room to sit while you reread your writer's notebook. As you read, remember to reflect on your entries and decide whether you can add even more writing. When you find a place where you think that you could add a few more ideas, mark the page with a sticky note.

- Students reread and mark spots that have potential.

Wrap-Up

- Students share with a partner.

DAY 3 Identification

Focused Instruction

Ann Cameron writes with a strong sense of story elements. She writes strong characters, strong sense of place (setting), strong plot, strong sense of movement through time.

- Students find possible topics that would lend themselves to work on strong story elements.

Independent Practice

- Students reread and reflect on their entries to create a list of at least four possible writing topics.

Wrap-Up

- Invite students to share some of the topics they have on their list.

DAY 4 Identification

Focused Instruction

Today I am going to take a topic from my list and write an entry using the story elements.

- Model writing an entry that incorporates the story elements. (Or read an excerpt from one of the Julian stories that reflects the story elements.)

Independent Practice

Consider story elements in your writing today.

- Students work on adding story elements to the topic they have selected.

Wrap-Up

- Students read their draft aloud to a partner.

DAY 5 Identification

Focused Instruction

Today I am going to pick a new topic to write about. I am still going to use the story elements in my writing, but this time I am going to spend more time on developing my character by using the kind of language Ann Cameron uses in The Stories Julian Tells. *The words she uses as a writer allow me to clearly picture what Julian looks like and what his personality is like. I am going to use Ann Cameron as a mentor today to help guide me with my writing.*

- Model how to use *The Stories Julian Tells* as a mentor text by highlighting and naming how information gathered on their Tracing a Character organizer (Resource 3.2) can be used to create a character with distinct physical and personality traits.

Independent Practice

- Students turn and talk to a partner to share their writing plans.
- Students write, using Ann Cameron's books as mentor texts.

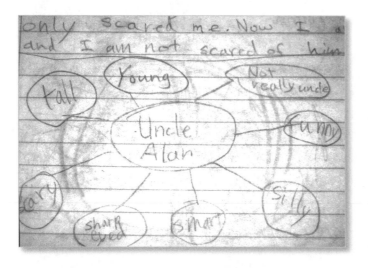

Students collect details about their characters to prepare for writing.

Wrap-Up

- Students read their writing aloud to a partner and get feedback about their character.
- Invite students to share how they used Ann Cameron as a mentor in their writing.

DAY 6 Identification

Focused Instruction

I am going to continue developing a character by using Ann Cameron as a mentor. Today I am going to use More Stories Julian Tells *to look at how Ann Cameron uses the conversations Julian has with other characters to give readers more information about how he interacts with others. What can my readers learn about my character through conversations they have with others?*

- Discuss how dialogue is used to show the character's relationship with another character.

Independent Practice

- Students use dialogue in their writing.

Wrap-Up

- Students read aloud their entries to a partner and get feedback about their character.

DAY 7 Identification

Focused Instruction

Today I am going to pick another topic to write about, using the story elements. I am going to use Julian's Glorious Summer *to see how Ann Cameron creates a character who is a problem solver. I want to take a closer look at the problems Ann Cameron has Julian deal with and the problem-solving techniques he uses.*

- Use *Julian's Glorious Summer* as a mentor text by naming the problem the character will face and the problem-solving techniques the character will use.

Independent Practice

Share the problem your character will face and what problem-solving techniques he or she will use.

- Students write about the problem their character faces, just like Ann Cameron did.

We have spent the last few days trying out different topics. Let's take some time today to read over our entries and decide on a topic we would like to use to create a published piece of writing.

Wrap-Up

- Invite students to share their topics and how they chose them.

DAY 8 Guided Practice

Focused Instruction

Today I am going to show you how I am going to add on to the entry that I wrote on this topic a few days ago. I am going to first reread it and then add on to it by focusing on my character. I want to make sure that I develop one character using the writing techniques of Ann Cameron.

Independent Practice

- Students write, using Ann Cameron as an inspiration.

Wrap-Up

- Students share what they have written and get quick feedback from their classmates.

DAY 9 Guided Practice

Focused Instruction

Before writers move on to writing their draft, they spend some time planning. Today I will share with you some tools we can use to help us get our ideas organized. We are going to spend some time thinking about our draft and filling in the Pre-Draft Organizer.

- Model how to fill in the Pre-Draft Organizer (Resource 3.3).

Independent Practice

- Students complete the Pre-Draft Organizer.

Wrap-Up

- Students get feedback from a partner.

DAY 10 Guided Practice

Focused Instruction

Let us spend some time thinking about our characters. What kinds of actions do they take? Why do they do what they do? In Ann Cameron's books, Julian often gets advice from his father in order to solve a problem. What do your characters do to solve problems?

Independent Practice

- Students develop character actions and motivations.

Let's do some pre-draft planning on our characters by filling in the Character Development Organizer.

- Model how to fill in the Character Development Organizer (Resource 3.4), using ideas from students' notebooks and adding in new ideas. Spend time explaining that the right-hand side of the organizer is for phrases they may want to use in their draft. These phrases reflect the words and writing techniques Ann Cameron uses.

Independent Practice
- Students fill in the Character Development Organizer.

Wrap-Up
- Students share how the process is going.

DAY 11 Guided Practice

Focused Instruction
Today we are going to spend some time developing the relationships our character has with others. After we do some writing, we are going to finish filling in the Character Development Organizer by transferring over some of the writing we did today and adding any new ideas.

Independent Practice
- Students continue to fill and finish the Character Development Organizer.

Wrap-Up
- Students share their organizers with a partner and get feedback.

DAY 12 Guided Practice

Focused Instruction
Today we are going to use our organizers, writers' notebooks, and everything we have learned about Ann Cameron's writing techniques to write our drafts.
- Model how to use the information from the organizers and writer's notebooks to write a draft that includes the story elements and a developed character that reflects the style of the mentor author.

Independent Practice
- Students draft their writing.

Wrap-Up
- Students share how their character reflects the style of Ann Cameron.

DAY 13 Guided Practice

Focused Instruction
Now that we have finished writing our drafts, we are going to spend today revising them. We are going to use this text that we are very familiar with to help us guide our revising today so that our characters reflect the writing techniques of Ann Cameron. The characters in Ann Cameron's books speak to one another in very deep ways that convey emotion. The dialogue conveys insight into the minds and feelings of the characters.
- Model adding dialogue and emotion to your writing.

Independent Practice
- Students revise their drafts with attention to dialogue that conveys insight into the minds and feelings of characters.
- Students meet in partnerships to get feedback from each other.

Wrap-Up

- Students share how the mentor text helped them with revising.

DAY 14 Guided Practice

Focused Instruction

We used dialogue in our writing to share with our reader more information on who our characters are. Today we are going to edit our writing by learning how to write dialogue using the correct punctuation marks. We are going to add on to the list of things we already do when we edit a piece of writing.

- Model how to edit for dialogue.

Independent Practice

- Students edit their writing.

Now that we have finished editing, we are ready to write our final drafts.

- Students write their final draft.

Wrap-Up

- Students share what they have learned about themselves as writers.

DAY 15 Commitment

Focused Instruction

We are going to celebrate how we have grown as writers during this unit. We have learned a lot about Ann Cameron and how she creates and develops characters in her stories. We also learned how to use her as a mentor author to help make our writing better.

Independent Practice

- Students reflect on the learning they did in this unit by filling out the form titled End-of-Unit Reflection (Resource 3.5).

Wrap-Up

- Students will share one way using a mentor author helped make their writing better.

Late Fall to Winter

As winter approaches, a noticeable shift in your third graders' thinking begins to take place. Students are beginning to think and work independently in dramatically new ways. Our conventions units have fostered their growing strength in their use of language. As the winter deepens, their friendships and understandings of one another deepen, too. Students engage in social activities that involve group work, independence, and integration of content into their reading and writing.

This learning community continues to flourish, with new learning to come.

Chapter 4

WINTER

The Third Grader as Social Thinker and Collaborator

"I sure am glad you came to visit again this summer. It makes me happy that you like to hear your grandfather's stories."
—from *The Blues Singers: Ten Who Rocked the World* by Julius Lester

The units of study in this chapter will foster your third graders' insatiable curiosity and offer them access to the genre of nonfiction and the unique way in which these texts tell a different kind of story. Join us as we learn about how readers and writers talk and listen, too.

WINTER UNITS

SPOTLIGHT UNITS

EARLY FALL

LATE FALL

WINTER

SPRING

Invigorate the Content Areas

In the winter, as students become increasingly complex thinkers, we teach them to take their new skills and apply them to the content they are learning in their science and social studies units through nonfiction reading and writing units. These units allow our students to apply what they have learned about reading and writing nonfiction in authentic ways. They also allow us to integrate the curriculum in ways that will invigorate our students and inspire our community.

Becoming Scientists and Historians: Reading Nonfiction

GENRE

Why Teach This?

- To teach students how to read for a specific purpose.
- To teach students how to gather information from multiple sources around a specific topic.
- To teach students how to determine the most important information in reading.

Framing Question

- How do we navigate, understand, and use features of nonfiction to gather information about a specific topic?

Unit Goals

- Students will use graphic aids and text features to guide their reading and enhance their understanding.
- Students will choose texts that are relevant to the topic they are researching.
- Students will ask questions before, during, and after reading to gather and clarify information learned.
- Students will take notes while they are reading and use these notes to determine the most important information in what they have read.

Create a bins of social studies or science books that invite students to explore subjects independently.

Anchor Texts

- *Duckling,* Watch Me Grow series, DK
- FOSSWeb Science Kit
- *Gandhi* by Demi
- Historic Communities series, and other books by Bobbie Kalman
- *...If You Lived With the Iroquois* by Ellen Levine, and other books in the series
- *Time for Kids*, *National Geographic Kids*
- True Book series by Stefanie Takacs
- *Vote* by Eileen Christenlow
- *The Wright Brothers (In Their Own Words)* by George Sullivan, and other books in the series

Unit Assessment Becoming Scientists and Historians: Reading Nonfiction			GENRE
Student name:	EMERGING	DEVELOPING	INDEPENDENT
Recognizes the uses of nonfiction features to enhance understanding of text.			
Uses note-taking to record understanding.			
Chooses appropriate texts to support research content.			
Determines the most important information in reading.			

Stage of the Unit	Focused Instruction You will	Independent Practice Students will
IMMERSION 2 days	• highlight the features noticed using a variety of nonfiction texts. • create a nonfiction features chart.	• browse through nonfiction texts, identifying features from the texts; share findings with partners and add to the class chart.
IDENTIFICATION 3 days	• flip through a variety of nonfiction texts, including *Gandhi*, *True Book*, and *Duckling,* to highlight the features on that page and the information we can obtain from each feature. • highlight how certain nonfiction features help a reader decide whether or not a text will give them the information they need (table of contents, headings, index). • focus on graphic aids found in nonfiction (charts, time lines, graphs) and how to interpret each; review the purpose of bold and italics.	• continue browsing through nonfiction text with partners, discussing what information they are gathering from the features. • choose a text they would like to read more about based on the title, table of contents, headings, and index. • look specifically at graphic aids in text, describing to a partner what they are learning from them.

GUIDED PRACTICE 8 days	• introduce topic for content research; use …*If You Lived With the Iroquois* to model the types of questions you have before reading. • read from …*If You Lived With the Iroquois* to model the types of questions you have during reading. • finish …*If You Lived With the Iroquois* and model the types of questions you have after reading the text. • model how to take notes while reading. • reinforce note-taking skills using student work as models. • model rereading notes. • model how to organize notes into big ideas or categories. • summarize the notes in order to determine the most important part of the text.	• choose a text to begin learning about their topic. • write down questions they have before reading. • write down questions they have while reading. • write down questions they have after reading the text. • continue researching their topic and begin taking notes. • reread notes. • organize their notes into big ideas. • summarize the notes they have taken to determine the most important part of what they have read.
COMMITMENT 2 days	• model how to share information learned with a partner.	• share the information they have learned with a partner. • reflect upon their learning.
TOTAL: 15 DAYS		

Becoming Scientists and Historians: Writing Nonfiction

Why Teach This?

- To teach students how to gather and present information from multiple sources around a specific topic.
- To encourage students to enhance their writing by using text features in a purposeful way.
- To expose students to different forms of nonfiction (main idea with details, compare and contrast).

Framing Question

- How do we use our questions, notes, and the craft of writing nonfiction to present written information about a specific topic?

Unit Goals

- Students will use the notes and information learned from the reading unit as a basis for a writing topic.
- Students will choose a format of nonfiction in which to present their work.
- Students will use text features in their writing, including table of contents, index, glossary, bold words, headings, italics, and graphic aids.
- Students will paraphrase what they have read to make it their original writing.

Anchor Texts

- *Can It Rain Cats and Dogs? Questions and Answers About Weather* by Melvin Berger and Gilda Berger
- *A Child's Day* and other books in the Historic Communities series by Bobbie Kalman
- FOSSWeb Science Kit reading materials and websites
- *...If You Lived with the Iroquois* by Ellen Levine, and other books in the series
- *Journey Around Boston from A to Z,* and other books in the series by Martha Zschock and Heather Zschock
- *Martin's Big Words* by Doreen Rappaport
- True Book series by Stefanie Takacs
- *What Do Animals Do in Winter? How Animals Survive the Cold* by Melvin Berger and Gilda Berger

Unit Assessment Becoming Scientists and Historians: Writing Nonfiction			GENRE
Student name:	EMERGING	DEVELOPING	INDEPENDENT
Uses nonfiction features appropriately.			
Stays within the format chosen for writing.			
Writes learned information in his or her own way (paraphrasing).			
Presents important parts of what has been learned.			
Appropriately uses text features in writing to support ideas being conveyed.			

Stage of the Unit	Focused Instruction You will	Independent Practice Students will
IMMERSION/ IDENTIFICATION 1 days	• preview *Can It Rain Cats and Dogs?*, *Martin's Big Words*, and *Journey Around Boston from A to Z from A to Z* to notice how you know that these books are nonfiction and the type of text it is (all about, question/answer, etc.).	• read through nonfiction texts to notice how they know that they are nonfiction and how the texts are organized.
GUIDED PRACTICE 10 days	• model how to get started on one's book; ask: How do you want to begin your text? How will you grab your readers' attention? Use *Journey Around Boston from A to Z* to see how these authors grab their readers' attention. • use a Historic Communities text to demonstrate how to include main ideas and details in a text. • use your writing to model how to include main ideas and details in writing. • model how to write a text using the structure of compare and contrast. • model how to plan research: How does a writer find out more information? Model how to add new research into a draft. • model paraphrasing; read short excerpts from *What do Animals Do in Winter?* and retell the information in your own words. • demonstrate how to paraphrase with student writing (show where information was copied, then model how to write it in the student's own words or have the students explain how he or she did it). • model how to write a conclusion by looking at *Martin's Big Words*. • model how text features and graphic aids support one's writing; use *Can It Rain Cats and Dogs?* • base these editing/revision lessons on student writing.	• begin drafting their texts, using the web they created as their guide. • continue drafting their texts, focusing on a main idea and supporting details for each topic included in their texts. • continue drafting their texts, comparing and contrasting one topic included in their projects (e.g., graphic aid of Iroquois vs. Algonquin housing). • research their topics further to gather more information (students may need to do this one or two additional times, especially in the revision phase; base this on conferences). • continue their drafts, focusing on writing learned information in their own words (this should continue to be a focus for students throughout the rest of the unit, especially in the revision phase). • incorporate new research into their drafts, focusing on writing learned information in their own words. • begin writing their conclusions. • continue writing their conclusions. • begin adding text features and graphic aids to their projects. • revise/edit their writing.

COMMITMENT 3 days	• read a completed section of students' projects, highlighting required components that are included. • reflect on student learning. • model your own reflective thinking: What have I learned? How have I changed as a writer? How has my writing improved?	• publish their writing. • share their nonfiction pieces with partners, parents, or a buddy in class. • reflect on their own learning, orally or in writing.
TOTAL: 14 DAYS		

Build Ideas With Clarity

Third graders are resourceful, purposeful, and playful. They love to build things, to create intricate block structures, to put together shows and worlds of their imaginations and games that go on forever. They know better than anyone else how important building is to the construction of ideas; they are in a constant state of invention. Because they are now 8 and nearly 9, their building takes on a new dimension, a more sophisticated air. They can build their worlds from what they see and what is real and also what they can only imagine. What is not there is as important as what is there.

Creating a paragraph requires both an understanding of what is there and what is not there. Great writers use white space as purposefully as they use words themselves, and paragraphing is all about the deep understanding of when to take a breath.

These units are all about the study of what is there and what is not there. They're about building a world of ideas from a toolbox of both words and white space. And for our third graders, who build worlds upon worlds, building a world of words can be a joyous pleasure.

Paragraphing Power: Reading
CONVENTIONS

Why Teach This?

- To learn the purpose of the "chunks" in texts and name them as paragraphs.
- To use awareness of paragraphs to help foster students' fluency and comprehension of a text.

Framing Question

- How do paragraphs help us better understand the information presented in a text?

Unit Goals

- Students will understand that a paragraph is a convention that writers use to separate ideas in a longer text.
- Students will recognize paragraphs in independent reading books.
- Students will notice how paragraphs chunk ideas in a text.
- Students will use paragraphs to guide them in their reading fluency.
- Students will read aloud to a partner, paying attention to how the paragraph influences how they use their voices.

Anchor Texts

- "The Lightwell" by Lawrence Yep in *Home: A Collaboration of Thirty Distinguished Authors and Illustrators of Children's Books to Aid the Homeless*, edited by Michael J. Rosen
- *National Geographic Explorer*
- "Puffballs," in *Katya's Book of Mushrooms* by Katya Arnold

Unit Assessment Paragraphing Power: Reading	CONVENTIONS		
Student name:	EMERGING	DEVELOPING	INDEPENDENT
Identifies a paragraph as a convention that writers use to separate ideas in a longer text.			
Recognizes paragraphs in independent reading books.			
Identifies how paragraphs chunk ideas in a text.			
Uses paragraphs to guide reading fluency.			
Reads aloud to a partner, paying attention to how the paragraph influences how the voice is used.			

Stage of the Unit	Focused Instruction You will	Independent Practice Students will
IMMERSION 1 day	• conduct a shared reading of "The Lightwell"; notice how the piece is organized and invite students to share what conventions they notice.	• read from chapter books and notice how the writing is structured.
IDENTIFICATION 2 days	• show and define a paragraph; look at "Puffballs" and invite students to explain why sentences are divided into separate groups. • notice that paragraphs chunk ideas in a text; model how to identify the chunks of ideas in a text.	• notice paragraphs in their independent reading and explain why the author created these paragraphs in the writing. • notice paragraphs and identify the big idea in one or two main paragraphs.
GUIDED PRACTICE 3 days	• model reading a passage without paragraphs and one that is divided into paragraphs; reinforce that paragraphs help us understand what we are reading by organizing the writing so the reader can better understand the message. • model how paragraphs help readers know how to use their voices as they read by pausing at the end of a paragraph. • model reading using the paragraph to guide inflection.	• notice the different types of paragraphs in their reading. • read texts aloud with partners to practice using paragraphs to read fluently; students may stop periodically to discuss big ideas in a "chunk" or paragraph. • read independently, paying attention to how paragraphs effect how they read the text.
COMMITMENT 2 days	• model looking through reading to find a paragraph(s) that stands out to you as a reader; identify the big idea in one chunk.	• find a paragraph in their independent reading to share with a partner and notice the big idea in that paragraph.
TOTAL: 8 DAYS		

Paragraphing Power: Writing

Why Teach This?

- To teach students how to organize their ideas in writing.
- To learn the structure of paragraphing.

Framing Question

- How can paragraphing help us organize our writing clearly?

Unit Goals

- Students will identify a paragraph as a convention that writers use to separate ideas in a longer text.
- Students will recognize a paragraph in a text.
- Students will chunk ideas in a text.
- Students will create paragraphs using the format of indenting and lining the following sentences up with the margin line.
- Students will write a piece using one or more paragraphs to organize their thinking.

Anchor Texts

- "The Lightwell" by Lawrence Yep in *Home: A Collaboration of Thirty Distinguished Authors and Illustrators of Children's Books to Aid the Homeless*, edited by Michael J. Rosen
- "Puffballs," in *Katya's Book of Mushrooms* by Katya Arnold
- *Time for Kids*, *Scholastic News*

Unit Assessment Paragraphing Power: Writing			CONVENTIONS
Student name:	EMERGING	DEVELOPING	INDEPENDENT
Identifies a paragraph as a convention that writers use to separate ideas in a longer text.			
Recognizes a paragraph.			
Chunks ideas in a text.			
Creates paragraphs using the format of indenting the first sentence and lining the following sentences up with the margin line.			
Writes a piece using one or more paragraphs to organize thinking.			

Stage of the Unit	Focused Instruction You will	Independent Practice Students will
IMMERSION 1 day	• read "The Lightwell" by Laurence Yep; ask students how the sentences are organized on the page; ask students what we notice about these chunks of writing.	• read with a partner, noticing paragraphs in a text; note size, shape, transitions, and so on.
IDENTIFICATION 1 day	• define a paragraph as a group of sentences that are all written on the same topic.	• look through their own writing to see where a paragraph might begin and end.
GUIDED PRACTICE 4 days	• share a piece of writing from which you have removed all paragraphing, and discuss. • model writing a paragraph that is disorganized, with sentences on different topics; work together to rewrite the paragraph with a clear focus. • model rereading your writing to make sure that you broke it up in the correct places. • look at a *Time for Kids* or *Scholastic News* feature article to notice multiple paragraphs in the piece; note that class conversation should focus on when a paragraph ends and a new one begins.	• rewrite a piece using different paragraphing. • look through writing for a "chunk" of writing on one topic and highlight; take that chunk and rewrite on a new page as a paragraph. • share with a partner where they decided a new paragraph should begin; the partner will give feedback to help the pair assess each other's work. • look through their writing to notice entries that could be broken into two or more paragraphs; use editing marks to indicate when a new paragraph will begin.
COMMITMENT 1 day	• model how to select a piece of writing to quickly publish with one or more paragraphs (quick publishing should only take one day and include formatting, writing into paragraph form, and basic editing for spelling, punctuation, and capitals).	• select a piece with paragraphs to publish quickly; share writing with a partner; discuss what they learned about writing a paragraph from this unit.
TOTAL: 7 DAYS		

SPOTLIGHT on Process

- Building Conversations: Reading Clubs
- Nurturing Collaborations: Writing Clubs

In my book *The Complete 4 for Literacy*, I explain in detail how process units are designed to build identity, capacity, collaboration, and responsibility. Although these form the foundations upon which readers and writers grow, because they are so intangible they often take a backseat in our instructional plans. A student's understanding of herself and the actions that move her forward as a reader and writer are all such important parts of her growth as a third grader. Establishing a strong understanding of processes now will help us move forward smoothly, rather than having to grapple with management issues later on in the year. Our explicit instructions for working with a partner give our students a structure for growing ideas and supporting one another. Lessons on building community will create a spirit of joy and collaboration that is indispensable in sustaining the atmosphere of safety and trust in your room. In these units, students learn how to develop the essential process skills of reading and writing stamina. These capacities are critical to establishing lifelong independence as readers and writers, and so we have created lessons that take our students through the experience of choice in a supported, layered approach.

For more information on process units, see pages 37–47 of my book *The Complete 4 for Literacy*.

Pam Allyn

Conversations That Matter

Third graders love to talk. They love to share what they know about any and all topics, and they love to help their classmates understand a new idea or concept. As their reading skills grow, they love to read aloud from a beloved picture book or share a funny illustration with a friend. They are becoming social beings, building and strengthening their interpersonal skills. In this unit, we use students' hunger for social interaction as a way to move their reading forward. Conversations enhance students' understanding of a topic, expand their thinking, and build conversational skills. Clubs provide an authentic way for students to practice and develop these skills.

Working together in collaborative clubs is an effective method for strengthening comprehension. As Douglas Kaufman (2000) says in *Conferences and Conversations: Listening to the Literate Classroom*, "When students talk honestly about their work, they hear themselves and are often able to solve their own problems. They learn, perhaps for the first time, what they know."

To know is to be empowered, and to see reading as an essentially social act is also empowering. It means we are never truly alone and our ideas are going to be heard. We will be changed, and we have the potential to change others.

Building Conversations: Reading Clubs   PROCESS

Why Teach This?

- To teach book conversation as a lively, engaged part of a reader's life.
- To learn the skills of engaging in thoughtful conversation.
- To develop a social outlet for sharing thoughts and questions about texts.

Framing Question

- How do readers have energetic, thoughtful conversations about books?

Unit Goals

- Students will engage in lively, active conversations with a partner or book club.
- Students will jot down notes and questions about texts that spark conversation.
- Students will use conversational language with a partner or club.
- Students will work collaboratively in a group to make decisions.
- Students will build on conversations by asking questions.

Anchor Texts

- *Ashley Bryan's African Tales, Uh-Huh* by Ashley Bryan
- *The Big Big Big Book of Tashi* by Anna Fienberg and Barbara Fienberg
- *Frog and Toad Together* by Arnold Lobel
- *Home: A Collaboration of Thirty Distinguished Authors and Illustrators of Children's Books to Aid the Homeless*, edited by Michael J. Rosen
- "The Rider" by Naomi Shihab Nye, in *Fuel: Poems by Naomi Shihab Nye*
- *Time for Kids*, *Scholastic News*, and *National Geographic Kids*

Resource Sheets

- Parent Letter for Reading Clubs (Resource 4.1)
- Noticing Conversations (Resource 4.2)
- Preparing for Reading Talks (Resource 4.3)
- Reading Club Reflection (Resource 4.4)

Unit Assessment Building Conversations: Reading Clubs			PROCESS
Student name:	EMERGING	DEVELOPING	INDEPENDENT
Engages in lively, active conversation with a reading club.			
Jots notes and questions about a text that spark conversation with others.			
Uses conversational language with a partner or club.			
Works collaboratively in a group to make decisions.			
Builds on conversations by asking questions.			

Stage of the Unit	Focused Instruction You will	Independent Practice Students will
IMMERSION 3 days	• discuss the purpose of clubs and why people join them. • discuss the characteristics of a successful conversation. • model a short conversation about a book; using *Frog and Toad Together*, ask students what they noticed about the conversation.	• discuss the qualities of a successful club. • jot down one thing that tells them when people are having a lively conversation. • jot down a great question about a book on a sticky note that can start a fun or lively conversation.
IDENTIFICATION 5 days	• create a two-column chart (T-chart) to identify what good conversations look and sound like. • read "The List" from *Frog and Toad Together* and model jotting down a quick note when reading to remember something you want to share with your book club.	• meet with a partner to have a lively conversation on a topic; jot down one note while reading something they want to share with their book club. • discuss the class questions from "The Dream" from *Frog and Toad Together* with a partner.

IDENTIFICATION (continued)	• read "The Dream" from *Frog and Toad Together* and model jotting down two great questions that will start lively conversation in a reading club. • discuss what readers do when their conversation gets stuck; model using the conversational language chart; read from "The Rider." • model writing questions that begin with if, how, and why; read from a newspaper.	• write big ideas or questions on sticky notes. • meet with book clubs to discuss "The Rider," using the conversational language chart if they get stuck. • discuss an article from a newspaper, using if, how, and why if they get stuck.
GUIDED PRACTICE 5 days	• introduce the routines for reading club meetings; break students into their clubs. • introduce the methods for reading clubs' choosing their texts and setting reading goals. • model adding on to a partner's ideas in a conversation. • chart strategies to use when the conversation goes off topic. • discuss how club members include everyone in the conversation.	• independently read their club's short text; jot down two notes or questions on sticky notes, and then meet to discuss their club's text. • meet with their club to choose a short text to read and to discuss and set reading goals. • meet with their club, focusing on listening during conversation. • meet with their club, using strategies to keep conversation on track. • work to include all club members in their conversation for the day.
COMMITMENT 2 days	• introduce the Reading Club Reflection form. • model how to reflect on talks by answering the following questions: How did my club do in the conversation? How did I do as a participant in the conversation?	• complete a group evaluation form. • reflect on their experience as a club member by answering the following questions: How did my group do in the conversation? How did I do as a participant in the conversation?
TOTAL: 15 DAYS		

Getting Started

When students come together to talk about a text, they are creating new meaning and enhancing one another's understanding. The purpose of collaboration is to inspire one another and also to create the kind of energy that motivates people. Learning to have trusting, positive, and fruitful disagreement is as important as learning how to build consensus. Our students learn that conversation leads to new ideas, ideas they never would have thought of alone.

Structures and Routines

There are predictable problems that do arise when running clubs. Here are some of our solutions.

Predictable Problems	Possible Solutions
A club member has not read the assigned pages or is not prepared for the talk.	• The club will create (with your help) really good routines and structures that are predictable so that each member is fully prepared regarding homework. • You may need to talk privately with the club member, asking if he needs help catching up or if there is anything you can do to support his keeping up so that he can maintain his dignity in the club and continue to be a part of the club even if the reading is a bit more challenging for him.
Some members' voices and ideas are heard more often than others.	• Some groups work well when members are given a specific role/job for the discussion. It focuses them on the discussion and allows voices that are not heard as often to be heard. Harvey Daniels's book *Literature Circles: Voice and Choice in Book Clubs and Reading Groups* gives ideas for different roles that can facilitate a discussion in which all members participate. • Practice with your students how to bring out the quieter voices. Have students partner even in their club meetings to support bringing out one another's voices. Give them tips such as helping them to use one another's names in eliciting ideas: "Sarah, would you share more?" • Help students become more self-aware about the kind of club member they are. If they track their talk and realize they are talking a lot in such a way that may prevent others from talking, help them to jot notes when a new idea comes to them, wait until more members have had a turn, and then look to their notes to recall their idea.
Conversations are very brief and students run out of things to say very quickly.	• Model how to stay with one topic in a conversation for a long time. Strategize together about ways to expand the conversation, including referring to the text, asking questions about what the speaker is saying, and inviting other members of the group to share their thoughts on the topic. Invite students to practice talking about one topic for increasing lengths of time.
A student is not happy about being grouped with one or more of the students in the group.	• Spend time building a learning community. This means that all students in a class support one another in their learning and that everyone works together at different times throughout the year. Help students feel comfortable sharing concerns and being open with one another. • Speak privately with this club member about her concerns. She may have very valid concerns about one or more members of the club, and prior social experiences that made her uncomfortable. Either make a quiet, quick change, respecting her need, or ask her to give it a go and say that you will be by her side to support her however you can. Also assure her that you will make a quick change if it does not feel comfortable after two trial days.

Teaching Materials

Choosing Student Texts

For all whole-group work in this unit, use short texts. This will allow you to model and invite conversations between students. It is nice to use texts from a variety of genres including fables, narratives, current events articles, and poetry, all of which encourage different kinds of thinking and discussion. When selecting a shared text consider the range of students in your room and select a text that is accessible to the most students on an independent reading level.

In these circumstances, where you are asking students to develop thinking together, it also makes sense to read the text aloud to your students once as they follow along and then invite them to do their own reading so they can take notes as they read. By reading the text aloud first, you are helping all students access a shared text that may be slightly above their independent reading level.

Genre	Book or Text Titles
Narrative	*Home: A Collaboration of Thirty Distinguished Authors and Illustrators of Children's Books to Aid the Homeless*
Poetry	"The Rider" by Naomi Shihab Nye
Fables	*Fables* by Arnold Lobel Teaching tip: If you delete the moral at the end, students' discussion can center around working together to find the moral or theme in the piece.
Nonfiction/Current Events	*Time for Kids*, *Scholastic News*, *National Geographic Kids*

Student Texts and Groups

Because this unit is centered around students reading a shared text independently, all students must be able to access the text equally. For this reason, you will want to group your students by similar reading levels. When we talk about reading levels, we are talking about texts that a reader can both decode and comprehend independently with 90 to 95 percent accuracy.

Select a variety of short texts in different genres, from *Scholastic News* to poems, for clubs. The more involved the students are in the selection process, the more they will be engaged in the reading and excited about the club discussion.

Stages of the Unit

Immersion

Introduce students to the unit by having them share what they already know about book clubs, book talks, and lively conversation. This reinforces understanding of why we do this unit and where it fits into our own reading lives, rather than thinking about book conversation as something we do only in school. Our third graders are riveted by our lives outside of school! This unit is the perfect opportunity to share your own talks about books with your students and even to bring in a friend or colleague to model that talk. Introduce parents to clubs through a parent letter (Resource 4.1) so that they can support their child's learning.

Identification

Invite students to think about and notice what makes a strong conversation. We suggest you create a two-column chart of students' observations titled What a Great Conversation Looks Like/What a Great Conversation Sounds Like (see Resource 4.2, Noticing Conversations). This chart, which you may add on to as the unit progresses, will become an anchor chart for the unit, helping students to remember what they need to do as participants in conversations. A model chart is shown below.

What a Great Conversation Looks Like	What a Great Conversation Sounds Like
• People are sitting in a group looking at one another. • Everyone has his or her book, notes, reading response notebook, and a pencil available. • People look at the speaker when he or she is talking. • Everyone opens to the page in the book when someone wants to share a passage. • People lean in to indicate interest and engagement in the discussion.	• One person talks at a time, although sometimes people get excited and jump in quickly. • Everyone is actively listening to the person who is talking and demonstrates this with eye contact, note-taking, and nodding. • The conversation is about the text that everyone has read. • People use conversation language to talk about the text and to add on to one another's ideas. • Everyone tries to stay on the same topic for a while before moving on to a new topic.

Guided Practice

Provide students with tips and techniques to practice and learn in order to have productive, long-lasting conversations. Students practice reading club routines, including making choices about what they will read and creating assignments as a club.

Commitment

In this final stage of the unit, we ask students to reflect upon their experience with reading clubs. Students think about what they have learned about conversation and how they will use these skills to enhance future discussions.

Students use their books to bring examples to the discussion.

Day-by-Day Lessons

DAY 1 Immersion

Focused Instruction

Let's talk about clubs. What kind of clubs do you like? Why do you like them?

- Students share their thoughts on clubs.

Independent Practice

Today I want you to think about the qualities of a successful club. What are they like when they really work well?

- Students record ideas about clubs when they go well.

Wrap-Up

- Students share ideas about successful clubs.

DAY 2 Immersion

Focused Instruction

Now we are going to begin a unit on reading clubs. The most important thing we practice in reading clubs is really not the reading; it is the conversation. What is a conversation? Why do people have them? How do you know when people are having a successful conversation?

- Students share their thoughts about what a conversation is, why people have them, and how they identify when people are having a successful conversation.

Independent Practice

Today I want you to jot down one thing you observe when people are having a conversation. Think back to different times you've seen people having a conversation. What kinds of things do they do when the conversation feels great?

- Students jot down one thing that tells them when people are having a great conversation (e.g., they are looking at each other, they are responding to each other, they look happy).

Wrap-Up

Who can share their observation of people having a conversation? What do people do when they have a great conversation?

DAY 3 Immersion

Focused Instruction

Yesterday we began thinking about conversations, and we each wrote something we observe when people are having a great conversation. Today I want you to observe a conversation.

- Read aloud a story from Arnold Lobel's book *Frog and Toad Together* and then model a short conversation with another teacher (bring classes together to watch this demo) or an assistant about the text. The conversation should be full of great clarifying questions that keep the talk lively and energized.

What did you notice about our conversation?

- Students briefly share what they noticed.

Did you see how many questions we asked in our conversation? We started out with great questions for each other about the book, but we didn't stop there! If we didn't understand something our partner said, we asked even more questions until we did. That's something that great readers do—they ask a lot of questions that make a conversation energized and full of life.

Independent Practice

Today you are going to jot down a great question on a sticky note. Choose a book from your independent reading collection and think about a great question that would start a lively or fun conversation.

- Students jot down a question about a book on a sticky note.

Wrap-Up

I noticed many of you wrote great questions that would start really fun conversations. I will chose two students to share their questions with the class today.

- Two students you chose during Independent Practice share their sticky-note questions with the class.

DAY 4 Identification

Focused Instruction

Today we're going to use the sticky notes we wrote about things you observe when people are having a conversation. We're going to make a big chart of what great conversations look and sound like.

- Students share their observations from their sticky notes to create a two-column chart titled What a Great Conversation Looks Like and What a Great Conversation Sounds Like (e.g., facing each other, taking turns talking, asking each other questions, looking at each other, using conversational language such as "I agree" and "I disagree"). (See Noticing Conversations, Resource 4.2.)

Independent Practice

Today you are going to meet with a partner to have a lively conversation. You're going to draw a topic out of a hat that you will talk about. Remember to use our chart to remind yourselves what great conversations look and sound like.

- Students meet with a partner and draw a topic to discuss out of a hat. Possible topics include:
  - What is your greatest wish?
  - What is your dream job?
  - If you could have one superpower, what would it be?
  - What have you heard about in the news lately that affected you?

Wrap-Up

I saw some great conversations happening today! I chose one partnership that was having a really lively conversation to model for us today. Watch what they do when they talk with each other.

- Choose one partnership that demonstrated excellent conversation skills to model for the class.

DAY 5 Identification

Focused Instruction

When I first started meeting with my reading club, I found that I couldn't remember things from the book. I had to find ways to help me remember things while I was reading that I wanted to talk about with my club. One way readers can remember things is by using a sticky note to quickly jot down a few points you want to remember.

- Model reading a page from "The List" from *Frog and Toad Together* by Arnold Lobel. Jot down a quick note inspired by the page (e.g., "just like the lists I make" or "very silly things to do").

Did you notice how I didn't write a whole sentence? I just wrote enough to remind me to mention that part when I meet in my club.

Independent Practice

Today during independent reading, you're going to make one note on a part of the book you want to be sure to mention with your reading club. Jot down some words that will remind you why this part was memorable.

Wrap-Up

- Selected students share the notes they jotted.
- For homework, students use Preparing for Reading Talks (Resource 4.3) to gather ideas for their conversations based on one of the sticky notes they wrote.

DAY 6 Identification

Focused Instruction

Yesterday we jotted down notes about parts of books we wanted to discuss with our clubs. Today we're going to practice discussing great questions with a partner. These are the kinds of questions that will start lively conversation when we meet with our groups.

- Read "The Dream" from *Frog and Toad Together*. Jot down two questions on a sticky note inspired from the story during reading (e.g., "Why did Toad have such a strange dream?" or "Why did Frog get smaller and smaller in Toad's dream?").

I think I could talk a lot about either of those questions with my book club. What do you notice about the questions I wrote?

Independent Practice

Today during independent reading, you're going to discuss the questions I wrote about "The Dream" with a partner.

Wrap-Up

I noticed some great conversation happening today! I asked one partnership to share with us. They're going to model some of the conversation they had about the questions.

DAY 7 Identification

Focused Instruction

We've been talking a lot about great conversations. Today I want to share something that also happens at my reading club meetings. Sometimes we get stuck. We don't have that much to say about the book. We run out of questions to talk about. Today we're going to talk about how readers keep conversations going. There are some sentences that great readers use to keep thinking about the book, rather than getting stuck. One of the ways that we can do this is by using our special conversation language to continue thinking about an idea.

- Introduce a conversational language chart:

> I agree with _____ because...
> I disagree with _____ because...
> I want to add on to _____...
> I didn't understand completely. Can you explain your thought?
> Can you show me where in the text you found that idea?
> I liked what you said, and want to add on _____.

Today you're going to discuss a poem in your club. We'll read the poem together, I'll give you a moment to think about it, then you'll meet to have a conversation.

- Read "The Rider." Pause after reading to give students a moment to reflect, then reread.

Before you meet with your clubs, I want you to think of one idea or question you will share with your club members. Jot it down on a sticky note.

Independent Practice

If you and your club get stuck in your conversation today, don't get worried. It's completely natural and it happens to adults all the time. Just remember to look at the conversational chart to see if there's something you could use to get the conversation started again.

- Students meet with a club (four to five students total) to discuss "The Rider."

Wrap-Up

- Students share what went well in their conversations and what was challenging.

DAY 8 Identification

Focused Instruction

When we bring thoughts to a conversation we want them to be big ideas or questions that get other people excited to talk. We want to bring ideas or questions that get everyone involved. We might ask our club to respond to an opinion we have about a character or event in our books, or pose a question that invites other people to share their opinions. Questions that invite discussion often begin with a few key words: if, how, and why.

- Model writing questions that begin with if, how, and why. ("If you were the character, what might you have done in that situation?" "How do you think it felt to be in that situation? Why?" "Why do you think the character chose to do that?")

I'm going to read an article from the newspaper. Think of big ideas or questions you could ask your club about the article. Remember, the questions should get people excited to talk.

- Read a short article from the newspaper. Pause after reading to give students a moment to reflect, then reread.

Independent Practice

- Students write big ideas or questions on sticky notes.
- Students meet with their clubs to discuss their questions.

Wrap-Up

- Students share their big ideas or questions.
- Students discuss how the conversation went in their clubs.

DAY 9 Guided Practice

Focused Instruction

Today you're going to meet with your clubs. Each member of your club will read the same story, poem, or article before you meet to talk. You'll each be responsible for writing two notes or questions that will create conversation with your group. Remember, the notes or questions you write should start a lively conversation. Use our chart to keep your conversation going.

- Break students up into their clubs (four to five students) and hand out their short texts. In every club, each student will read the same short story, poem, or article independently and jot down two notes or questions about the text. Students should be able to finish reading the texts in five to ten minutes so there is time for them to meet with their club.

Independent Practice

- Students independently read their club's short story, article, or poem. Each student jots down two notes or questions on sticky notes.
- Students meet to discuss their club's text.

Wrap-Up

- Discuss students' experiences working in clubs.

DAY 10 Guided Practice

Focused Instruction

Yesterday I assigned you texts to read. Some clubs read short stories, some read poems, and some read articles. Today you are going to practice making decisions as a club. You will choose what kind of text you want to read and what each member of the club will bring to the conversation. Yesterday I assigned you each two notes or questions to discuss. Maybe your club wants to do more or less than that.

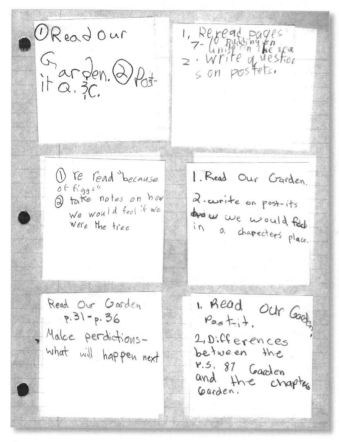

Student sticky notes from reading clubs.

Independent Practice

Your club has two decisions to make today: What will you read? What will each member bring? Once you make those decisions, you will each read independently, just like you did yesterday. When everyone in the club is finished, you will meet and have a conversation.

- Students decide which text they will read.
- Students decide what each club member is responsible for bringing.
- Students read short texts independently and complete the work agreed upon.
- Students meet in their clubs to have a conversation.

(Note: All clubs may not make it through this process in one day. They may continue the process on Day 11.)

Wrap-Up

- Students share which text each club selected and why.

How did the conversations go in your club? Did you get stuck? How did you keep the conversation going?

DAY 11 Guided Practice

Focused Instruction

Sometimes when readers get really excited about a conversation, it is hard to listen closely to what other club members are saying. But let's practice building upon others' ideas in conversation.

- Model building off a partner in conversation, either with another adult (teacher or aide) or with students. Emphasize how really listening well and responding sparks deeper conversation.

Independent Practice

Today you are going to meet with your reading clubs to continue the work you started yesterday. Think about how to listen closely to what your club members are saying. Maybe something they say will spark another thought or question you want to share.

- Students continue club work from Day 10.

Wrap-Up

- Students discuss active listening and share thoughts or questions that were sparked by another club member's topic.

DAY 12 Guided Practice

Focused Instruction

One thing that sometimes happens in clubs is that we get off topic in our conversation. Suddenly my book club will be talking about our weekend plans or what movies we've seen—things that are not related to our book! Effective book clubs stay focused on the topic and keep the conversation going. Here are some things that readers do to stay on topic:

- *Go back to the text.*
- *Ask questions building onto the first question.*
- *Listen to one another's ideas.*
- *Change opinions based on one another's thoughts.*
- *Take one idea written on a sticky note and put it in the middle of the table. Talk about it as long as you can.*

Independent Practice

Today you will continue work with your club. If your club already finished discussing the short text you were reading, go through the process again: pick a short text, decide reader responsibilities, read independently, and meet with your club to discuss. Remember, if your group gets off topic, use one of the strategies we discussed to get back to the book.

- Clubs continue working together.

Wrap-Up

- Clubs share thoughts on their work for the day.

DAY 13 Guided Practice

Focused Instruction

One of our jobs in a club is to make sure that everyone knows what is happening in the discussion and understands the ideas being discussed. It is important that our conversations are balanced and that everyone has equal time to talk. This might mean that a different person begins the conversation each time you meet and you also might invite the quieter club members into the conversation. You can do this by asking someone what they think about what you are talking about. By checking in with everyone throughout the meeting time, you are showing them that you care about their thoughts and want them to be part of the discussion, too.

Independent Practice

- Students read club texts, prepare for conversation with sticky notes, and meet with their clubs.

Wrap-Up

Today I noticed one club that really worked to involve each club member in the conversation.

- Share an observation of a club that included all members in the conversation.

DAY 14 Commitment

Focused Instruction

Today I want to give you a chance to reflect on how your conversations are going.

- Introduce the Reading Club Reflection (Resource 4.4) to assess performance as a club member. Show students how to answer the questions on the form and talk about the importance of being honest with yourself to help your learning grow.

Independent Practice

- Students complete the Reading Club Reflection (Resource 4.4).

Wrap-Up

What did you notice about your work and your club's work from filling out the evaluation form?

DAY 15 Commitment

Focused Instruction

We have completed our reading club activity and now we have a chance to reflect upon our experience. Let's spend some time thinking together about clubs. What went well for your club?

How do we have thoughtful conversations about reading? How do these conversations help deepen our thinking about what we read?

Independent Practice

- Students reflect upon the questions and write their responses.

Wrap-Up

What do you want to change in your conversation for next time? How did reading clubs change you as a reader?

Talk That Warms the World

Writing clubs develop organically from the work that you and your students have been doing all year. Students are beginning to develop preferences as writers. They have been exposed to a broad variety of writing that exists in the world, and they have developed new skills that enable them to explore new types of writing with greater ease. In addition, students have experienced group work and have a strong sense of their role in a group. This unit provides a great opportunity for your students to demonstrate both their independence and also their warm capacity to support one another as writers.

Nurturing Collaborations: Writing Clubs

PROCESS

Why Teach This?

- To give students the freedom to direct their learning in a fun and structured way.
- To reinforce the use of mentor authors and/or texts to guide writing within a genre.
- To give students an opportunity to work with a group to develop their skills as writers.

Framing Questions

- How do writers create pieces that reflect their interests, personalities, and writing styles?
- How can writers with similar interests help us achieve our writing goals?

Unit Goals

- Students will work in clubs to explore a shared genre of interest.
- Students will meet with club members to share what they have learned about their genre.
- Students will select mentor texts to guide their writing.
- Students will produce an original piece of writing that reflects their interests, writing styles, and voices.
- Students will collaborate with club members to provide and receive feedback for revision and editing of pieces.

Anchor Texts

- *The Best Pet of All* by David LaRochelle (narrative)
- *Big Blue Whale* by Nicola Davies (nonfiction)
- *Dumpling Soup* by Jama Kim Rattigan (narrative)
- *Next Stop Grand Central* by Maira Kalman (nonfiction)
- *Sports Illustrated for Kids* (magazine/sports writing)
- *Winter Poems* by Barbara Rogasky (poetry)
- *Yoshi's Feast* by Kimiko Kajikawa (narrative)

Resource Sheets

- Parent Letter for Writing Clubs (Resource 4.5)
- Finding Mentor Texts (Resource 4.6)
- Noticing Text Features in Mentor Texts (Resource 4.7)
- Writing Clubs Homework: Researching My Topics (Resource 4.8)
- Editing Checklist for Writing Clubs (Resource 4.9)

Unit Assessment Nurturing Collaborations: Writing Clubs			PROCESS
Student name:	EMERGING	DEVELOPING	INDEPENDENT
Works in a club to explore a shared topic or genre of interest.			
Meets with club members to share what he or she has learned about the topic or genre.			
Selects a mentor text to guide his or her writing.			
Produces an original piece of writing that reflects his or her interest, writing style, and voice.			
Collaborates with club members to provide and receive feedback for revision and editing of pieces.			

Stage of the Unit	Focused Instruction You will	Independent Practice Students will
IMMERSION 3 days	• guide students to think about being a member of a club: What is it like? Why do we join clubs? • define writing clubs and create a list of clubs for the unit (based on students' interests as writers). • read *Yoshi's Feast* and *Sports Illustrated for Kids*; think aloud, making observations and learning about your genre.	• write a letter about what kind of writing club they would like to be in and why. • read books from club-themed bins and share their observations about the writing with club members. • begin to create a list of genre characteristics with their group.
IDENTIFICATION 1 day	• demonstrate how writers look at different elements of a text to notice how features affect the text; model collecting information on a genre using Noticing Text Features in Mentor Texts (Resource 4.7).	• work in partnerships to collect information on their genre.

GUIDED PRACTICE 10 days	• identify characteristics of each club's genre; chart these responses. • model rereading your writing to choose a topic to write about; emphasize choosing a topic about which you have a lot to say. • model how to find a mentor author or text; emphasize that writers use mentors as guides for their writing. • model giving constructive feedback to a partner. • model how writers use mentor texts to help guide their writing. • model rereading your writing to look for anything that doesn't make sense. • discuss revising leads and endings. • model revising your writing with a focus on leads and endings. • discuss various narrative structures, with attention to form. • model using an editing checklist.	• experiment with features they noticed about their genre in their writing. • look through their writing and create a list of possible topic choices; choose a topic to work toward publishing. • choose a mentor author or text for their writing. • practice giving feedback to a partner in their clubs. • choose one element of their mentor text to try in their writing. • reread their writing before adding on to their pieces; use sticky notes or additional paper to add anything they notice is missing. • rethink their pieces, noting teacher's and their own questions as guides. • reread their leads and endings and revise. • revise pieces according to their genre. • complete their editing checklist.
COMMITMENT 1 day	• remind students of publishing party protocol, including reading one another's writing and writing positive comments to their classmates.	• read each other's writing and write constructive comments; reflect on how it felt to write within a genre and with a club.
TOTAL: 15 DAYS		

Getting Started

Because writing clubs require a great amount of self-motivation and independence, there are structures that are helpful to have in place before beginning this unit. Students should be familiar with the writing process, be able to work independently for longer periods of time, and be able to work effectively and cooperatively with peers. These skills have increased throughout the year to ensure students will be successful working in clubs.

Structures and Routines

Allow students to choose club genres that appeal most to them, submitting their choices in letters to you. From these letters, you can assemble your class into clubs of four to five students. Students should have their bins of mentor texts with them at all times so they can easily access their texts as they work. Conferences in this unit can be with writing clubs or with individual students, depending on students' needs. Your observations may also affect the order and speed of our suggested lessons.

Teaching Materials

In this unit, students select mentor texts within their club genre. These texts serve as guides for their writing, with students using them as models for both text features and text components. Here are some suggested texts.

Genre	Mentor Texts
Nonfiction Expert Books	*Big Blue Whale* by Nicola Davies *Can It Rain Cats and Dogs? Questions and Answers About Weather* by Melvin Berger and Gilda Berger *What Do You Do With a Tail Like This?* by Robin Page and Steve Jenkins *Pumpkins* by Ken Robbins
Poetry	*Winter Poems* by Barbara Rogasky *Candy Corn* by James Stevenson *Insectlopedia* and *Winter Eyes* by Douglas Florian *Joyful Noise: Poems for Two Voices* by Paul Fleischman *A Kick in the Head* by Paul B. Janeczko *Creatures of Earth, Sea and Sky* by Georgia Heard *If I Were in Charge of the World and Other Worries* by Judith Viorst *In Daddy's Arms I Am Tall* by Javaka Steptoe
Realistic Narrative	*My Rotten Redheaded Older Brother* by Patricia Polacco *All the Places to Love* by Patricia MacLachlan *Come On, Rain!* by Karen Hesse *Birthday Presents* by Cynthia Rylant *When I Was Five* by Arthur Howard
Fictional Narrative	*The Best Pet of All* by David LaRochelle *The Flying Dragon Room* by Audrey Wood *Kidogo* by Anik McGrory *The Rainbow Goblins* by Ul De Rico *Weslandia* by Paul Fleischman
Sports Writing	*Sports Illustrated for Kids* *USA Today's* sports section *Hoops* by Robert Burleigh

Stages of the Unit

Immersion

Students consider purposes of writing clubs and how being a member of a club can help them improve their writing skills. We also ask students to begin to explore texts in their selected topic or genre so that they begin to develop a deeper understanding of how these texts are written. Send home the Parent Letter for Writing Clubs (Resource 4.5).

Identification

Students are in their clubs and are beginning to think about how writers start a new project and the role of the club in helping to develop an understanding of their genre. Students work in their clubs and independently to look through texts within their selected genre, noticing and naming characteristics of the writing.

Guided Practice

Students research and write about their topics. This will help them develop a sense of how to write within their genre. They will ultimately focus on one writing piece of their choice to develop through the writing process.

Students have the opportunity to make decisions about the format, text features, and presentation style of their piece and savor their preferred genre.

Commitment

Students enjoy reading one another's pieces and providing constructive feedback. Students will love to read what their classmates wrote to them and use these comments to improve their writing in the future.

Finally, we ask the students to think about how this experience has changed them as writers. Many times, students form their own writing clubs and continue them throughout the summer because they like the structure so much.

Day-by-Day Lessons

DAY 1 Immersion

Focused Instruction

Writing clubs bring writers with similar interests together. If I want to learn more about writing poetry, I might join a poetry club to meet with other poets. What kinds of writing clubs might you want to be in?

- Brainstorm and chart the kinds of clubs that students might explore in your classroom.

Independent Practice

Today, please write me a special letter. Let me know what kind of writing you would like to learn more about during this unit and how you would like a writing club to go if it were to really, really help you with your writing.

- Students write a letter explaining the writing club they might want to join and why.

Wrap-Up

Share with us what kinds of writing you are thinking you might like to do in a club.

DAY 2 Immersion

Focused Instruction

From your letters and the list we created yesterday it seems like there are a few big topics that people are interested in exploring. These topics are: poetry, sports writing, realistic narratives, fictional narratives, and nonfiction. These five topics are going to be the names of the writing clubs that we have in our class. I have assigned you to a club based on what you said in your letter and what I know about you as a writer. Your names are written below the club's name on this chart. Today we are going to begin exploring our topic by reading books in this genre.

- Remind students how reading books through a writer's lens helps us learn about that kind of writing.

Independent Practice

- Students read books from club-themed bins and share their observations about the writing with club members.

Wrap-Up

- Students share what they noticed about their genre.

DAY 3 Immersion

Focused Instruction

Yesterday we began reading texts in our genre and forming observations about how they are written. We learn from other writers by noticing how they use words and share information. We might look at Come On, Rain! *if we want to think more about how a writer uses vivid and precise language to make the reader feel like she is right there in the book, or* Next Stop Grand Central *if we want to see how we write about a nonfiction topic in a fun and unique way.*

Independent Practice

- Students continue exploring texts in their genre. Students read through the books in their club-themed bins, noticing features or elements of their genre.
- Students meet with their group members to begin to create a list of characteristics that they have noticed in their genre.

Wrap-Up

- Students share how exploring these texts helped them better understand their genre.
- Have students complete the organizer Finding Mentor Texts (Resource 4.6).

For the next few days I would like you to be on a hunt for more mentor texts that you and your club members can read and learn from. You may find these books at home, at the bookstore, or in the school or public library. Please bring these texts in to share with your club members. You can even put a sticky note on them saying why you choose to include it in your club-themed bin.

DAY 4 Identification

Focused Instruction

We have been making many observations about our genre as we read. When we are reading our texts, there are certain parts of the writing that we might want to focus on. We can examine how the writing begins, how it ends, and how the author shares information. We can ask ourselves some important questions: Who is telling the story?

Does the book have any special text features? What do you notice about the language the author uses?

- Create a chart of what students should look for as they read (see the chart from Resource 4.7).

As you read, notice how these features affect the text. Writers pay attention to these elements of a text as they read because they help them learn new strategies to use in their own writing.

Noticing Text Features in Mentor Texts				
Text Features	Leads (beginnings)	Endings	Language or Text Features That Strike Me	Special Text Features I Would Like to Try
Text example: *Big Blue Whale* by Nicola Davies	Makes comparisons to show how big the big blue whale is, and the text gets bigger with each comparison to echo the large size of the whale.	The words get smaller to end the book to show how small a whale is in comparison to the ocean.	Fun facts about the big blue whale are included next to illustrations. Uses onomatopoeia.	Add fun facts and make comparisons to paint a picture for the reader.

Independent Practice

- Students work in partnerships to collect information on their genre using the graphic organizer Noticing Text Features in Mentor Texts (Resource 4.7) to identify strategies they can use in their own writing.

Wrap-Up

- Students meet in their groups to share what they have learned from reading their texts.

DAY 5 Guided Practice

Focused Instruction

When we write, we want to make sure that our writing matches our genre. What are the characteristics that let you know whether something is fiction, nonfiction, sports writing, and so on? Let's chart how you know the writing is specific to your genre.

- Go through each writing club and have students name characteristics of their genre that are identifiable. For example, students in the nonfiction club might say their genre uses nonfiction text features like bold words, pictures, and captions, and is about something true in our world. Chart these responses. This will become a checklist for their writing later in the unit.

Independent Practice

- Students experiment with features they noticed about their genre in their writing.

Wrap-Up

How did you choose the feature you used? How did it fit into your writing?

- First students share with a partner from their group, then students share as a whole class.

- As homework, students reflect upon what they have learned from their mentor texts using the Writing Clubs Homework: Researching My Topics sheet (Resource 4.8).

DAY 6 Guided Practice

Focused Instruction

We have been collecting so much writing in our genre! Today it is time to make some decisions about what you want to focus on for your publishing. You have been writing a lot and trying out different topics and craft strategies in your notebook entries. Now you have to commit to one idea to develop into a full piece of writing. In order to make this selection, you can choose from one of the topics you have already started to write about, or begin a new topic either from your brainstorm list or a different one that you have been thinking about.

- Model rereading your writing to choose a topic to write about. Emphasize choosing a topic about which you have a lot to say.

Independent Practice

- Students look through their writing and create a list of possible topic choices. They then choose a topic to work toward publishing. Make sure that the topics students choose match the club's focus.

Wrap-Up

What topic did you choose to write about and why did you select it?

- Students share with their club.

DAY 7 Guided Practice

Focused Instruction

Writers often use mentor texts to help them craft their writing. I want to show you how I find a mentor text to guide my writing.

- Remind students that you are looking for a mentor text in writing style, not necessarily one about a specific topic.

If you are writing all that you know about plants, you don't have to choose a plant book; you can choose a science book that is written in a way that you like and you think lends itself to your topic. If you are writing a family story, you can choose a fiction book that has the shape or kind of language you would like to try in your writing.

Independent Practice

- Students look through texts in their bins to find a mentor author for their writing.

Wrap-Up

- Students share their mentor text with a partner and explain why they chose it.

DAY 8 Guided Practice

Focused Instruction

Today I want to show you how I might use my text to help me in my writing. I am going to look through my text for the kinds of crafting techniques on our chart. I will notice leads and endings, language that strikes me, or something that I would like to try as a writer. As I write, I will keep the book next to me and look at parts of it to notice how my mentor author writes. Let me show you what I mean.

- Model using a mentor text to guide writing.

Independent Practice

- Students choose one element of the mentor text to try in their writing.

Wrap-Up

- Students share writing that is modeled after their mentor text with a partner, then meet as a whole class to talk about how our mentors help us as writers.

DAY 9 Guided Practice

Focused Instruction

One of the great things about working in a club is that you have lots of people to help you with your work. When we work in clubs or partnerships as writers, we can use each other to help us evaluate our writing. Today we are going to meet with our club members to share our writing and give one another feedback about what we are doing well and what needs work. Before we do, let's remind ourselves what it means to give feedback and how we can give feedback in a kind and constructive way.

- Review how to begin with a positive comment and then give suggestions based on the writing only. You may have students use mentor texts to help them explain what they are describing to other writers.

Independent Practice

- Students meet in clubs to share writing that they have done so far. Invite them to explore the questions: What do you notice about my writing? What is working? What isn't?

Wrap-Up

- Students share how their club members helped them think about their writing in a new way.

DAY 10 Guided Practice

Focused Instruction

Effective writers reread as they write. They don't always just write through until they're finished. They go back to reread what they have read, make sure it makes sense, and figure out what would make sense to add to the writing. I want to show you what I mean.

- Model rereading your writing to notice any of the following:
  - places where more information can be added
  - information is irrelevant
  - sequencing is out of order

Independent Practice

- Students reread writing before adding on to their pieces and use sticky notes or more paper to add anything they notice is missing. Students can also use editing marks to delete and edit as needed.

What did you notice about your writing? Did you leave anything out?

Wrap-Up

- Students share how rereading helped improve their writing.

DAY 11 Guided Practice

Focused Instruction

Today I want to talk about how you know when you are ready to revise. When does a draft feel complete?

- Invite responses from students explaining how they determine whether their draft feels complete.

There are a few ways I know I'm finished with my writing. One is to reread my writing to see if it has a clear beginning, middle, and end. Another way to know is to ask myself: Is there anything else that I wanted to say that isn't in the writing yet? A third way is to look at my mentor text to see if there are any features or crafting techniques that I wanted to include but didn't.

- Chart questions, reinforcing what writers do for each question.

I am going to reread my writing now and think about each of these elements so I can better decide whether I am done drafting and am ready to revise.

Independent Practice

- Students decide whether their draft is ready for revision by rereading and thinking about each of the questions listed on the chart.

Wrap-Up

- Students share where they are in the writing process.

How did you decide what you need to work on?

DAY 12 Guided Practice

Focused Instruction

I'm so happy that all of you are ready for revision. Today we're going to talk about one way that writers revise their work—by examining the beginnings, or leads, and ends of their pieces. Writers want to make sure that the writing begins in a way that draws the reader in and ends leaving the reader satisfied and wanting to continue thinking about the text. We looked at strong leads and endings together as a class and noticed how different writers do this. You then worked with your group to notice strong leads and endings in your genre mentor texts. Today I want you to go back to the leads and endings that you liked in the books you read and think about what the authors did to create such powerful ways to begin and end their writing. Then you are going to revisit your lead and ending to make it more interesting.

Independent Practice

- Students revisit texts from club-themed bins to notice leads and endings. They reread their own lead and ending, deciding whether they need to revise them to make them more interesting.

Wrap-Up

- Students share their leads and endings with their writing clubs.

DAY 13 Guided Practice

Focused Instruction

Today we need to think about how our writing is going to look on the page. Each genre's writing looks different. If you are writing poetry, remember that you need to think about how the words will look on the page and how you will use the space around the poem to help share your message. We need to think about the words on the page for all of the genres in which we are writing because each genre looks different. For nonfiction, for example, you will decide where you will add text features to support your writing; for narrative you will need to think about page breaks and where the text will go on the page; and for sports writing you may think about picture or chart placement and whether you want your writing to look like an article or a narrative. There are many decisions that writers need to make about how their writing will look, and they can use mentor texts to help them make these decisions.

Independent Practice

- Students explore different structures (narrative, picture book, article, poetry, etc.) within the genre to decide what their published piece will look like.
- Students revise their pieces to fit the genre in which they are writing.

Wrap-Up

What are you thinking about including in your published piece?

- Students share their pieces with their writing clubs. Students give one another feedback on how their work is developing.

DAY 14 Guided Practice

Focused Instruction

I want to review using our editing checklist to make sure that we are checking our work for editing issues before we are completely finished. Watch me as I use the Editing Checklist for Writing Clubs (Resource 4.9) to reread and fix my work.

Independent Practice

- Students continue working on their writing, using the editing checklist to guide their final revisions.

Wrap-Up

- Students share writing progress with their writing clubs.

The winner is ....
Arena football

Awards

Scarsdale, NY. By, Spencer Serling. Arena football is one of my favorite sports. It is like regular football except it is played inside an arena. There are boards around the field so it hurts more when you check. Like in hockey. After the other team kicks from the end zone they have different rules than pro football. Here are a few examples: there is checking on the boards, touchdowns sometimes cost less points, when you take a field goal not after a touchdown it sometimes cost less points, and there is no goal posts. An arena football field is 50 yards long.

Finals

The finals are at the end of the season and they are played between the best teams who survived through the playoffs. One of the most exciting final games was a fierce game between Grand Rapids vs. Nashville on August 19ᵗʰ ,2001.T he game was. The game was held at the Van Andel Arena in Grand Rapids Michigan. The attendance at the Van Andel .

quarter the sco
score was 37-2:
51-35. The gam
electrifying tea
record in the le
please GRAND
the arena. The
touchdowns. I
finals next yea

Awards

Awards are given out to a few of the best players during the league. The first award is the Tinacton Iron-man Award. The award goes to Dameon Porter on Chicago. The award is the offensive award goes to Aaron Garcia on New York! The defensive award goes to, Kenny McEntyre, on Orlando. The rookie man of the year goes to Kal Truluck, from Detroit. The coaches need a award. So we made one up for them. The award goes to the coach Michael Trigg!!!!!!!! We hope to se you next time!!!!!

Published writing reflects the genre of the piece.

DAY 15 Commitment

Focused Instruction

Today is our celebration! You have done an amazing job in your writing.

- Remind students that during a celebration students read one another's writing and write comments to their classmates about what they did well in their writing.

Independent Practice

- Students read one another's pieces and write constructive comments.

Wrap-Up

- Clubs meet one last time to thank one another for their support.

From Winter to Spring

As late winter melts into spring, students are having fun with their learning and developing important reading, writing, and collaborative skills that stretch across all the subject areas. Our third graders are literally blooming by the minute—they suddenly look like fourth graders! Their legs are long and the hint of something new is in the air. What a perfect time it is to study all the enchanting aspects of language with a unit on poetry and, in other units, through a close look at the comma. Like your third graders, language itself is fascinating, quite magical, and also very, very practical. We end the year with more collaboration, and then our reflection units, echoing back to the ARCH. We celebrate a year of reading and writing, and at the same time continue to help our students set goals for their next steps—readers and writers in the world.

Chapter 5

SPRING

The Third Grader as Explorer of Language

" 'Are you looking for a home?" the preacher asked, real soft, to Winn-Dixie. Winn-Dixie wagged his tail. 'Well,' the preacher said. 'I guess you've found one.'"
—from *Because of Winn-Dixie* by Kate DiCamillo

Let your classroom be a place where your children find a sense of home, even as they explore the world around them. These seasonal units focus on the power and beauty of language through poetry and through the conventions of text. Here, we share with you units of study that will open new worlds for your students.

EARLY FALL

LATE FALL

WINTER

SPRING

SPOTLIGHT on Genre

- Exploring Poetry Connections Through Reading
- Exploring Poetry Connections Through Writing

There are a few great writers who have been able to write across several genres. E. B. White comes to mind. He wrote the classic children's books *Charlotte's Web*, *The Trumpet of the Swan*, and *Stuart Little*. He wrote small humorous snippets for *The New Yorker* in the "Talk of the Town" column. And he cowrote the seminal "how to" guide to grammar: *The Elements of Style*. White was the rare genius who could accommodate all genres, fitting his observations, his wonderings, his memory, and his imagination into a wide variety of "containers." Great ideas are like water, flowing clear: a stream. Genre is a container we use to hold these ideas. The ideas are the same, but they look different depending on the container that holds them. Loneliness inside a poem, for example, looks different from loneliness inside a science fiction novel. Courage inside a biography looks different from courage inside a letter. A clear idea, held inside the right container, can change someone's mind, even someone's life. See Pages 47 to 61 in my book *The Complete 4 for Literacy* for a more detailed description of the elements and categories of genre and the importance of these studies to the lives of our students. They are seeking to clarify, extend, and share from their own stream of ideas.

Pam Allyn

Spring Awakens, Poetry Blooms

Why poetry? The great poet Billy Collins was asked this question after September 11, 2001, when shock and despair resonated around the world. Thousands of poems traveled around the Internet, shared by strangers and friends. He said, "Poetry tells the history of the human heart." Third graders understand this. Loving, open, kind, and curious, the students experience all of these emotions in their school community through poetry. Reading together, laughing, acting silly or serious, talking about big themes and small observations brings us closer to one another and also gives us the chance to linger with the beauty of language.

The poet and editor Paul Janeczko (1999) wrote:

"Sometimes when you write a poem, you may think you know what that poem is going to be. But as you write and tinker your way through several drafts, you find that the poem wants to be something else. Maybe you thought you wanted to write a poem about a party, but the poem wound up being about friendship. As a writer, you must learn to trust your intuition. When a poem wants to go its own way, let it. See where it takes you."

Exploring Poetry Connections Through Reading

GENRE

Why Teach This?
- To inspire students to become more fluent readers through the rhythm, rhyme, and repetition in poetry.
- To help students learn how to interpret poetry.

Framing Questions
- How do we read poetry and develop our own interpretations?
- How will we learn to recognize types of poetry and their characteristics?

Unit Goals
- Students will identify what poets write about—observations of the world around them and questions they have.
- Students will recognize three types of poetry.
- Students will use context clues to find the meaning of unknown words.
- Students will use phrasing with awareness of repetition and white space in poetry to build fluency.
- Students will form interpretations about poetry.
- Students will recognize how sensory images relate to theme.

Anchor Texts
- *Baseball, Snakes, and Summer Squash: Poems About Growing Up* by Donald Graves
- *The Dream Keeper and Other Poems* by Langston Hughes
- *The Flag of Childhood: Poems From the Middle East*, edited by Naomi Shihab Nye
- *From the Bellybutton of the Moon and Other Summer Poems* by Francisco Alarcón
- *Honey, I Love* by Eloise Greenfield

- *Moon, Have You Met My Mother?* by Karla Kuskin
- "Ode to My Socks" by Pablo Neruda (in various collections)
- *The Place My Words Are Looking For* ("Yellow Sonnet"), edited by Paul Janeczko
- *Poetry for Young People: Carl Sandburg* ("Ars Poetica"), edited by Frances Schoonmaker Bolin
- *Spring: A Haiku Story* by George Shannon
- *Sweet Corn: Poems* (particularly "Old Dog") by James Stevenson

Resource Sheets

- Parent Letter for Exploring Poetry Connections Through Reading (Resource 5.1)
- Sensory Images in Poetry (Resource 5.2)
- Interpretation (Resource 5.3)

Unit Assessment Exploring Poetry Connections Through Reading			GENRE
Student name:	**EMERGING**	**DEVELOPING**	**INDEPENDENT**
Recognizes at least three types of poetry (free verse, haiku, and ode).			
Recognizes that sensory images in poetry connect to ideas and themes.			
Develops interpretations about poems through drama, art, and writing.			
Supports opinions/interpretations with lines from the poem.			
Recognizes use of repetition and white space in poetry as a key function to meaning.			

Stage of the Unit	Focused Instruction You will	Independent Practice Students will
IMMERSION 4 days	• read aloud quotes by poets on poetry. For example: • "Poetry is the report of a nuance between two moments when people say: 'Listen!' and 'Did you see it?' 'Did you hear it?' 'What was it?'" (Carl Sandburg) • "A good poem celebrates life and quickens us to it." (John Ciardi) • identify sensory images in the poems "April Rain Song" and "The Train of Stars." • read aloud from *Honey, I Love* or "April Rain Song" and discuss how poets celebrate love in their poems.	• begin to put sticky notes on poetry in poetry books where they find something that is particularly meaningful or exciting. • read through the classroom collection of poems and identify where poets create images and sounds or capture moments in time though their choice of words. • read poetry with a partner; begin to collect favorites in a poetry folder.

IMMERSION (continued)	• begin chart: how do poets find ideas (observations, wonderings, memories, imagination)?	• complete Sensory Images in Poetry (Resource 5.2).
IDENTIFICATION 1 day	• identify the qualities of poetry: repetition, white space, rhyme, sensory images; create a chart of the characteristics of poems.	• mark with a star in the margin the different qualities of poetry they find in their own favorite poems.
GUIDED PRACTICE 9 days	• read aloud for rhythm and repetition using "Honey, I Love" and "Jumprope Rhymes"; as a whole class, set the poems to music. • define interpretation and read aloud from "The Dream Keeper" by Langston Hughes. • Read aloud from "Yellow Sonnet" by Paul Zimmer. • read aloud for sensory image using *Moon, Have You Met My Mother?* • read aloud with attention to how we read poetry aloud—attention to white space and how we pause and why we think pausing is important—in the poems "Roadside Stand" and "Old Dog" by James Stevenson. • read aloud from *Spring: A Haiku Story* by George Shannon to introduce haiku as close observation and the importance of "quiet" and perfect word choice in poetry. • read aloud from "Ode to My Socks" by Pablo Neruda; define odes as poems about appreciation and admiration. • model for students how to compile a poetry anthology. • model for students how to write a reflection of a poem.	• put one of the two poems, "Honey, I Love" or "Jumprope Rhymes," to a song or beat with the help of a partner. • create an interpretation of Langston Hughes's poem "The Dream Keeper." • record their interpretations of their favorite poems. • illustrate their interpretations of *Moon, Have You Met My Mother?* • identify the characteristics of a free-verse poem and understand the purpose of white space in a poem. • identify the characteristics of a haiku. • identify the characteristics of an ode. • create an anthology of his or her favorite poems. • write reflections for three of the poems in his or her poetry anthology.
COMMITMENT 2 days	• name the qualities of poetry (repetition, white space, word choice). • name ways sensory images affect our understanding of theme (feelings, emotions) connected to image.	• share dramatic interpretations or songs from poems. • share poetry anthologies.
TOTAL: 16 DAYS		

Getting Started

Create a hum of poetry in your room! Bring in lots of poems and let your students spread them out and pore over them. Poetry is best read on the stomach with feet waving in the air! Or standing true and tall and reciting it in a loud voice! Have fun with the silliness of poetry, as well as the awesome seriousness of it.

Structures and Routines

This unit should involve many opportunities to work with a variety of partners. Your students can work across reading levels in this unit, as poems are often short and easily accessible even to the most struggling readers in your classroom. Allow for opportunities to mix and match your students for the different interpretation activities, so that they can all enjoy one another's company as much as possible and get to know one another as poets and readers of poetry.

Teaching Materials

Anchor Texts

When selecting poetry to use for instructional purposes there are a few helpful guidelines to consider as you search for the right ones. Do not be afraid to read poems that seem a bit mysterious or "over the heads" of your kids. Poetry is meant to be enjoyed slowly. Let your students help you find beautiful and wonderful poems. Poems speak to people in different ways, and therefore your students will become your best hunters for poems that speak to your entire community.

Favorite collections include:

- *Baseball, Snakes, and Summer Squash: Poems About Growing Up* by Donald Graves
- *Creatures of Earth, Sea, and Sky* by Georgia Heard
- *The Flag of Childhood: Poems From the Middle East*, edited by Naomi Shihab Nye
- *Hoops* by Robert Burleigh
- *If I Were in Charge of the World and Other Worries* by Judith Viorst
- *In Daddy's Arms I Am Tall* by Javaka Steptoe
- *Insectlopedia* by Douglas Florian
- *A Kick in the Head* by Paul Janeczko
- *Pass the Poetry, Please!* by Lee Bennett Hopkins
- *The Place My Words Are Looking For*, edited by Paul Janeczko
- *Poem Stew*, selected by William Cole
- *Rainbows Are Made: Poems by Carl Sandburg*, selected by Lee Bennett Hopkins
- *Sweet Corn* by James Stevenson
- *Winter Eyes* by Douglas Florian

Organizing Your Materials

Create theme baskets for your poetry books and for individual poems. Let students help you name them. You can laminate poems that you explore in depth so that students can return to the text during their independent or partner reading time. Keep sticky notes and pens close to your poetry collections so students can jot their initials onto sticky notes and place them alongside a poem they love. This way, they can see who else has "dropped by" that page.

Stages of the Unit

Immersion

Here you will immerse your students in the beautiful sounds and structures of poetry. Give them plentiful time to roam through books of poetry and to read to one another aloud. The room will feel lively with exploration. Hang lines and snippets of poems all around your classroom. Let your students help you do that. Read aloud, read aloud, read aloud! Tuck a poem into every corner of your day, throughout this unit and all units to come. Send home the Parent Letter for Exploring Poetry Connections Through Reading (Resource 5.1).

Parent Letter for Exploring Poetry Connections Through Reading

Identification

Read aloud, listening to the rhythm and thinking about what causes rhythm: repetition, sound, size of words, and white space. Students will name these elements as they read poems with partners. Read aloud, focusing on sensory images and their connection to theme. Become aware of and name three kinds of poems: odes, haiku, and free verse. These forms are accessible to students and become wonderful fun to write during the writing portion of this unit.

Guided Practice

Your students are interpreting poetry; drama, song, and art are all ways for them to respond to poetry. At this time they are also creating a poetry anthology, savoring their favorites and marveling over how different their favorites might be from their best friends'. They are deepening their understanding of how sensory images in poetry connect to larger themes. Give them time to talk to one another about their artistic interpretations and to share them with the class. They will love to see how the images a poet creates appear differently in the minds of each and every reader.

Commitment

Alongside this unit, your students are writing poetry, too. The commitments they make as readers will be visible as we watch them explore their own growing sense of themselves as poets. The anthologies are also a way to make a commitment to the study of poetry and the lifelong love of it. They will work with you to create a chart that lists the qualities of poetry and the types of poetry they have learned about.

Day-by-Day Lessons

DAY 1 Immersion

Focused Instruction

The poet John Ciardi said, "A good poem celebrates life and quickens us to it." Today we are going to pore over poems and think about what John Ciardi means. See if you can find a poem that "celebrates life."

- Model for students how to choose a poem that celebrates life. Read the poem and explain how it speaks to you. Possible poems might be "Honey, I Love" by Eloise Greenfield or "April Rain Song" by Langston Hughes.

Independent Practice

- Students read through a variety of poetry and identify a poem that celebrates life. Add a sticky note with student's name onto the poem.
- Begin to collect these poems by rewriting or photocopying the selected poems and putting them into a folder titled Poems That Celebrate Life.

Wrap-Up

- Students share poems they have found and why they feel the poems they like celebrate life.

DAY 2 Immersion

Focused Instruction

Carl Sandburg said, "Poetry is the report of a nuance between two moments when people say: 'Listen!' and 'Did you see it?' 'Did you hear it?' 'What was it?'" Poetry captures moments in time, images, and sounds. Today, look through our collections of poetry and find where poets have captured moments in time, images, or sounds.

- Read through *Sweet Corn* and identify for the students how James Stevenson captures moments in time. Describe how he uses sound and images to create the moment.

Independent Practice

- As students read through the classroom collection of poetry, they should again mark the pages they love and where they see how a poet captured a moment in time, an image, or a sound.
- Again, students should write down or photocopy the poem they selected to add to their collection.

Wrap-Up

- Students should share the poems they selected and add them to a folder titled Poems That Capture Moments, Images, and Sounds.

DAY 3 Immersion

Focused Instruction

Langston Hughes and Naomi Shihab Nye are two poets who create sensory images on the page. Sensory images are the images that poets evoke in their poems through the five senses. Look for poems today that capture a sensory image.

- Read "April Rain Song" by Langston Hughes and "The Train of Stars" from *The Flag of Childhood*, edited by Naomi Shihab Nye.
- With students, compile a list of sensory images that these two poems evoke.

Independent Practice

- With a partner, students look for poems that create strong visual images.
- Students illustrate the images they get in their mind when they read the poems using the chart Sensory Images in Poetry (Resource 5.2).

Wrap-Up

- Students share poems they found that contain sensory images and their illustrations.
- Display these illustrations for future reference.

DAY 4 Immersion

Focused Instruction

How do poets find ideas that inspire them to write? We have discovered that poets are really good at making the ordinary sound extraordinary. Like scientists, poets have to be good at observing the world around them. Poets have to be good at wondering about the world around them. Poets have to be good at remembering what they observed and wondered. Poets have to have a good imagination. Earlier this year we talked about the Four Prompts (I remember, I wonder, I observe, I imagine, and we have been using them ever since to look for writing ideas. Poets use the Four Prompts, too. As you read and browse through poems today, take time to muse over one poem; where do you think that poet got his or her idea?

- Reread "April Rain Song" by Langston Hughes and "The Train of Stars" from *The Flag of Childhood*, edited by Naomi Shihab Nye. Discuss what might have inspired them to write their poems.

Independent Practice

- With a partner, students should divide a sheet of paper in half. On one side, they should write the name of the poem and on the other side they should write the possible inspiration.

Wrap-Up

- Students share poems they love and how a writer might have gotten his ideas.

DAY 5 Identification

Focused Instruction

Today we are going to identify the characteristics of a poem and record them together. Look at the poems that we have gathered into our folders. Find a poem that has repetition in it. Find a poem that rhymes. Find a poem that creates sensory images. Find a poem that has white space or blank space put in by the author for a purpose.

- Read to students from *Moon, Have You Met My Mother?* by Karla Kuskin and discuss why the poet chose to rhyme.

Independent Practice

- Students read through the poems in their collection and put a star in the margin next to the poem where they see examples of rhymes or repetition or white space or sensory images.

Wrap-Up

- Together, create a chart titled Characteristics of Poems: What Makes a Poem a Poem?

DAY 6 Guided Practice

Focused Instruction

Today we are going to read poems together called "Honey, I Love" and "Jumprope Rhymes," both by Eloise Greenfield. Let's see if we hear music in the poems. Clap out a beat as we go. All poems have rhythm. Sometimes rhythm comes from the way the words are on the page and sometimes the beat comes from the repetition of words. Today we are going to practice finding the music in poems.

- Read "Honey, I Love" and "Jumprope Rhymes" aloud. Have students clap out the beat as you read the poem.

Independent Practice

- With a partner, students should put either "Honey, I Love" or "Jumprope Rhymes" to a beat or a song.

Wrap-Up

Students share their interpretations of the two poems.

DAY 7 Guided Practice

Focused Instruction

The next poem we're going to hear is "The Dream Keeper" by Langston Hughes. Let's see if we can interpret this poem by acting it out or finding a way to tell the story of this poem through movement. Interpretation is when a reader has a reaction to a text and then creates an idea around that reaction. By acting out poems or singing them, we are engaged in a kind of interpretation.

- Point out the white space and images that Langston Hughes creates in his poem "The Dream Keeper" as you read it aloud.

- Ask students to identify the purpose of the white space and the images they see when they hear the poem read aloud.

Independent Practice

- With a partner, students should interpret the poem through movement. They come up with a short dance or set of hand signals that shows their interpretation of the poem.

Wrap-Up

- In a whole-group discussion, students should show their own interpretations of the poem.

DAY 8 Guided Practice

Focused Instruction

Yesterday you interpreted a poem through drama, and the day before we interpreted poems through music. How can we learn to interpret what poets are trying to say in their poems? Today we are going to try and understand what your favorite poet is saying in one of his or her poems.

- Read "Yellow Sonnet" by Paul Zimmer, from *The Place My Words Are Looking For*, edited by Paul Janeczko.

Independent Practice

- With a partner, students record interpretations of their favorite poems on the Interpretation sheet (Resource 5.3).

Wrap-Up

- Students share their written interpretations.
- Discuss the difference between musical interpretations, dance interpretations, and written interpretations.

DAY 9 Guided Practice

Focused Instruction

Sensory images are very important to poetry. The image is not just about describing, it is about feeling. Today we are going to hear a poem called "Moon, Have You Met My Mother?" by Karla Kuskin. Close your eyes as I read this poem. You will draw an interpretation of this poem.

- Read the poem "Moon, Have You Met My Mother?"
- Discus the images that the poem evokes.

Independent Practice

- Students draw their interpretations of Kuskin's poem.

Wrap-Up

- Students should share their interpretations of "Moon, Have You Met My Mother?"

DAY 10 Guided Practice

Focused Instruction

Poets use white space—blank areas in their poems so that readers will take a breath and think about the poem. The two poems we are about to hear are called free verse. There is no rhyming in these poems, but the white space gives us clues about how to read them.

- Read "Roadside Stand" and "Old Dog" by James Stevenson.
- Identify why "Roadside Stand" and "Old Dog" are examples of free-verse poems.
- Indicate where the poets added white space. Discuss what is supposed to happen at each place where there is white space.

Independent Practice

- Students look closely at one or more of the poems in their collection and describe to a partner the importance of white space in that poem. They address why the poet left white space where he or she did.

Wrap-Up

- In a whole-group discussion, create a chart titled The Purpose of White Space.

DAY 11 Guided Practice

Focused Instruction

In Japan, haiku poets would wander the country telling poems to different communities. They were the eyes of the world.

- Read aloud from the collection *Spring: a Haiku Story* by George Shannon.

Independent Practice

- Students should find a haiku they love to add to their collection of poems.
- Students should rewrite or photocopy their favorite haiku to add to a folder titled Haikus.

Wrap-Up

- Students share their haiku and explain why they loved it.
- Together, create a chart titled Characteristics of a Haiku.

DAY 12 Guided Practice

Focused Instruction

An ode is a famous kind of poem that is all about appreciation and admiration. Many years ago, when people wanted to describe something to someone and really convey it visually, they would write an ode to it. Many poems are really about admiration and appreciation of something or someone. Can you find some in your collection that are about that?

- Read aloud from "Ode to My Socks" by Pablo Neruda.
- Discuss poems from students' collections that are also about admiration or appreciation for someone or something.

Independent Practice

- With a partner, students should identify a favorite ode and rewrite or photocopy it to add to their collection.

Wrap-Up

- Students share their odes and explain why they loved their ode.
- Create a chart titled Characteristics of an Ode.

DAY 13 Guided Practice

Focused Instruction

We have been collecting poems and looking at them to find the qualities of great poetry. Now I would like you to take some time create an anthology of your favorite poems. Gather all of the poems that you have copied and put them together into a book, leaving space for you to write your reflections on each poem tomorrow.

- Model for students how to compile a poetry anthology by collecting all of the poems you have read aloud and placing them together with an illustrated cover page.

Independent Practice

- Students gather their poems and put them into a poetry anthology.
- Make sure to include the written and drawn interpretations of the poems in the anthology.

Wrap-Up

- Students share their anthologies with the class.

DAY 14 Guided Practice

Focused Instruction

Throughout this unit, you have been reading, interpreting, and studying many different poems. For three of your favorite poems that you gathered into your poetry anthology yesterday, you will write reflections.

- Model for students how to write a reflection of a poem by writing a reflection of one of the poems you have read aloud to the class.

Independent Practice

- Students should write reflections for three of the poems they have compiled for their anthologies.

Wrap-Up

- Share completed poetry anthologies.

DAY 15 Commitment

Focused Instruction

Let's name the qualities of poetry we explored together: white space, repetition, rhythm, sensory image, and word choice. We found that sensory image is connected to the feeling or emotion of the poem. Today let's return to some of our dramatic interpretations or songs and see whether our interpretations have changed now that we have studied so much poetry.

- Revisit the charts of all the characteristics of poetry.

Independent Practice

- Students revisit their interpretations and revise with their partners.

Wrap-Up

- Students share their new and rewritten interpretations.

DAY 16 Commitment

Focused Instruction

When we write poetry, let's remember all the ways poets have of communicating. It is a poetic tradition that poets would write about poems to demonstrate what they know about poetry. It can be a way for you to share your passion for poems and your new understandings about this art form. There is a tradition that every poet at least once in his or her life is obligated to write an Ars Poetica. We'll end this unit by writing a poem about poetry, called Ars Poetica. Ars Poetica means "the art of poetry." What is the art of poetry?

- Together, create a chart titled Poetry Is...

Independent Practice

- With a partner, students discuss characteristics of the art of poetry.

Wrap-Up

- Complete the Poetry Is... chart.

Poets Create Songs of Words

"After hearing many poems, students begin to know what different kinds of poetry sound like, and they come to their own understanding of what makes a poem a poem...which is crucial preparation for writing their own."

—from *For the Good of the Earth and Sun* by Georgia Heard

The study of poetry brings with it special gifts. When we invite students to experiment with words, shapes of poems, and white space, we may give a certain kind of freedom to our most struggling writers, too. The freedom, creativity, and sanction for brevity in poetry allow our most vulnerable students to experiment with language without the anxieties they bring to longer, more structured texts and the gulf of a blank page.

For your strongest students, poetry has a sophistication that is extremely alluring. It is a way for them to immerse themselves in language that is deeply intuitive and also highly structured. Poetry creates bridges wherever it goes.

Exploring Poetry Connections Through Writing

GENRE

Why Teach This?
- To teach students to use qualities of poetry to create their own poems.
- To develop in students a love of poetic forms.
- To build fluency through the reading of and writing of poetry.
- To help students use imagery, repetition, and white space to convey meaning.

Framing Question
- How can we learn about the forms of poetry and write poems that convey our ideas and feelings?

Unit Goals
- Students will develop ideas independently.
- Students will write poems inspired by an anchor poem or poet.
- Students will write poems with awareness of word placement.
- Students will revise a poem.
- Students will read their own poems aloud with fluency and confidence.

Anchor Texts
- *Baseball, Snakes, and Summer Squash: Poems About Growing Up* by Donald Graves
- *Beach Stones* by Lillian Moore
- "dog" by Valerie Worth
- *Color Me a Rhyme* by Jane Yolen
- *The Dream Keeper and Other Poems* by Langston Hughes
- *From the Bellybutton of the Moon and Other Summer Poems* by Francisco Alarcón
- *Honey, I Love* by Eloise Greenfield

- *Horizons* by Jane Yolen
- *If I Were in Charge of the World* by Judith Viorst
- *Insectlopedia* by Douglas Florian
- "Old Dog," in *Sweet Corn* by James Stevenson
- "The Sidewalk Racer" by Lillian Morrison
- "Valentine for Ernest Mann," in *Red Suitcase* by Naomi Shihab Nye
- "We Could Be Friends," in *The Place My Words Are Looking For* by Myra Cohn Livingston
- *Winter Poems* by Barbara Rogasky
- "Write About a Radish" by Karla Kuskin

Resource Sheets

- Parent Letter for Exploring Poetry Connections Through Writing (Resource 5.4)
- Poetry Homework: Learning About Poets Through Their Words (Resource 5.5)
- The Mood of Poetry (Resource 5.6)
- Noticing White Space (Resource 5.7)
- Poetry Checklist (Resource 5.8)
- A Poet's Editing Checklist (Resource 5.9)
- Poetry Celebrations (Resource 5.10)
- Comments for the Poet (Resource 5.11)
- Ways to Celebrate Our Writing (Resource 5.12)

Unit Assessment Exploring Poetry Connections Through Writing			GENRE
Student name:	EMERGING	DEVELOPING	INDEPENDENT
Develops ideas independently, using observation, wondering, memory, and imagination to spark ideas.			
Writes with strong images.			
Writes with awareness of white space.			
Writes with awareness of rhythm.			

Stage of the Unit	Focused Instruction You will	Independent Practice Students will
IMMERSION 1 day	• read aloud "Valentine for Ernest Mann" by Naomi Shihab Nye; ask your students to think about where Nye might have found inspiration for her poem.	• partners discuss where they might find inspiration for their poems.
IDENTIFICATION 5 days	• identify poems that demonstrate observation; read aloud from anchor poems by Pablo Neruda, Valerie Worth, or Douglas Florian, which model for students how to write poems about observations, and begin a Poetry Ideas chart.	• write poems about observations.

| IDENTIFICATION (continued) | • identify that poets use their writing to wonder about something; read aloud from the anchor poet James Stevenson's "Old Dog" to model for students how to write poems about wonderings.

• identify poems about memory; read aloud from anchor poets such as Donald Graves or Paul Zimmer ("Yellow Sonnet") to model how poets write about memory.

• identify poems in which poets reveal parts of themselves (fears, likes, feelings); read "Honey, I Love" by Eloise Greenfield, Valerie Worth poems, and the poems of author Judith Viorst such as "Fifteen, Maybe Sixteen Things to Worry About" to model how these poets revealed aspects of themselves in their poems.

• identify poems about imagination; read aloud anchor poems such as "If I Were in Charge of the World" by Judith Viorst and "Write About a Radish" by Karla Kuskin, which model how to write "Imagine if…" poems. | • share and record wonderings.
• write poems about a memory or an image.
• write poems about topics that interest them.
• write poems about imagination ("Imagine if…") and share the poems they have written with a partner. |
| GUIDED PRACTICE 7 days | • read aloud poems from anchor poets such as James Stevenson, Judith Viorst, or Langston Hughes to model for students how poets convey a mood through their word choice, use of white space, and rhythm; create a chart that identifies poems, the mood the poet conveys, and how the poet conveys the mood.

• read aloud poems that demonstrate sensory images, such as "Beach Stones" by Lilian Moore; "dog" by Valerie Worth; and "Winter Eyes" by Douglas Florian. | • write a poem that conveys a mood like loneliness, happiness, stillness.
• reread collected poems to find strong images. |

GUIDED PRACTICE (continued)	• read aloud poems from anchor poets, such as "The Sidewalk Racer" by Lillian Morrison and "We Could Be Friends" by Myra Cohn Livingston, that demonstrate how poets use white space to convey an idea or feeling. • identify how haikus use white space to convey images. • identify how poets write to make the ordinary seem extraordinary; use odes to model for students how Pablo Neruda does this. • model for students how to create a poetry checklist. • model using a poetry editing checklist.	• write poems that evoke images about their five senses. • rewrite a poem two different ways that shows how white space can be used. • write haikus based on observations. • write an ode. • revise and edit writing using a poetry checklist.
COMMITMENT 3 days	• create your own poetry anthology. • create a Poetry Café. • reflect on what you have learned about poetry.	• celebrate a selection of poems and create a poetry anthology. • have a poetry celebration! • reflect on what they have learned about poetry.
TOTAL: 16 DAYS		

Getting Started

Even if you are not a poetry lover, let yourself enjoy this unit. By following the passions of your students, you can't go wrong. Let their enthusiasm and energy guide you in this unit. Allow yourself to be flexible; if a day comes when the snow is falling outside your window, or the sun is shining just that beautiful way across the tree outside your classroom, don't follow our script. Do what poets over the centuries have instructed us to do: lay down your worries and go out and find yourselves a poem.

Structures and Routines

This unit should involve many opportunities to work with a variety of partners. Your students can work across reading levels in this unit, as poems are often short and easily accessible even to the most struggling readers in your classroom. Allow for opportunities to mix and match your students for the different interpretation activities, so that they can all enjoy one another's company as much as possible and get to know one another as readers and writers of poetry.

Teaching Materials

The texts that you will use to model and teach students about writing poetry overlap with the poetry from the reading unit. The following books are also excellent resources for this unit in that they discuss where poets find their ideas and also the structure and uniqueness of the poetic form:

- *A Kick in the Head,* edited by Paul Janeczko
- *Knock at a Star: A Child's Introduction to Poetry* by X. J. Kennedy and Dorothy M. Kennedy
- *Pass the Poetry, Please!* by Lee Bennett Hopkins
- *The Place My Words Are Looking For,* edited by Paul Janeczko

Stages of the Unit

Immersion

You and your students have been poring over collections of poems during your reading time. In writing time, have students revisit their notebooks and highlight lines that feel like they could be used in a poem. Inspire your students by reading more poems aloud. Let students take their poetry notebooks and tour around the school with you, looking for places where poetry might be hiding. Send a letter home to parents about the writing poetry unit (Resource 5.4).

Parent Letter for Exploring Poetry Connections Through Writing

Identification

As you and your students read through the pieces you are selecting as anchor texts, allow students to notice similarities and differences between the pieces and to name these writing characteristics. For example, students might say that the poet uses sounds in his writing. We can call those sounds sensory imagery or onomatopoeia. Other features they might notice include repeating words, rhyming or rhythm, varied positioning of text, and use of capitals and punctuation.

It's a good idea to put these texts on SMART Boards or a document camera and to give students a copy to analyze. This way they can work with a partner to learn more about the writing and mark places in the text. When you share observations as a class, you can mark them on your chart or overhead and keep them in a public place for students to refer back to while they are working.

Guided Practice

During the Guided Practice stage, students select topics and techniques to use that support their writing. You will provide support as it is needed. Through conferences you may encounter a topic that you think needs to be shared with the whole class. If the teaching point is a small one or something you want to highlight, you might stop the whole class and tell them what happened in the conference: "Let's pause in our writing for a moment so you can hear what I just learned about John's writing while we were having a conference. He saw a poet using repetition in her writing and tried in on his own. Look at what he did! Isn't that great?" When a teaching point is bigger, something you need for the whole class to learn, you can plan that as a Focused Instruction for later in the week. You always have the option to add more time to the unit if necessary.

Guide students through the revision process. You have given them the opportunity to look closely at qualities of a poem. Now you are going to ask students to select poems, which they will revise using all of the skills that they have learned about writing poetry. They will look at how to create sensory images and to use white space in ways that feel profound and beautifully connected to their big ideas.

Commitment

At the end of this unit, celebrate students' learning and hard work. Invite parents or students from another class to come visit a poetry museum, or host a Poetry Café for other classes.

Day-by-Day Lessons

DAY 1 Immersion

Focused Instruction

Naomi Shihab Nye writes about how we can find poems anywhere if we really look, sometimes in the most surprising places. While we read lots of poetry, we are also going to write lots of poetry. And so we have to be very alert for the poems that are tucked into our lives everywhere we go. In this unit, we will carry our notebooks with us nearly everywhere we go so that we are ready at a moment's notice for the magic of poetry. I will be asking you to do some Poetry Homework (Resource 5.5) to "find" poems in your own life and write them down.

- Locate and read aloud "Valentine for Ernest Mann" by Naomi Shihab Nye.

Where do you think Nye found her inspiration for her poem?

Independent Practice

- Students should brainstorm with a partner for poems that they could "find" from any object or person in the room.

Wrap-Up

- Students share their findings.

DAY 2 Identification

Focused Instruction

Poets observe the world very closely. That is how they are able to convey such strong sensory images. They notice things that other people might not even see. And sometimes, the way they see these things is truly unique and special. Let's look at some poets who are close observers of the world to see how they describe what they see.

- Read aloud a variety of poetry relating to close observation ("Ode to My Socks" by Pablo Neruda; selections from *Horizons* by Jane Yolen, *All the Small Poems and Fourteen More* by Valerie Worth, and *Insectlopedia* by Douglas Florian).

- Create a chart called "Where Poets Get Ideas" and write "Poets observe the world."

Independent Practice

- Students take something they have already written in their notebooks that felt strong in terms of sensory image and recreate it as a poem, or they write something based on close observation.

Wrap-Up

- Students write about something in their world. You can take a nature walk and write outside or students can choose items in the classroom or look out the window to write about what they see.

DAY 3 Identification

Focused Instruction

Poets wonder about the world. The haiku poets were walking through the countryside both observing AND wondering about the world. Modern-day poets do the same. James Stevenson has a very short poem called "Old Dog" in which he wonders where a dog might be going. Even the shortest poems can be about a very big wondering and convey an essence of loneliness or of the passing of time.

- Add to the Where Poets Get Ideas chart a section titled Poets Wonder About the World… and record some wonderings of famous poets.
- Brainstorm about what wonderings the class could record.

Independent Practice

- Students share wonderings with one another and then record them in their poetry journals, either as poems or as entries for later poems.

Wrap-Up

- Students share their own wonderings and poems.

DAY 4 Identification

Focused Instruction

Poets often write about what they remember. Today we are going to look at two poets who wrote poems about a time that they remember. Then you are going to write about a moment that you remember. For example, I wrote a poem once about my first day in the third grade. It was about how excited I felt, but also how I was a little bit nervous about meeting new friends and my new teacher.

- Read some of Donald Graves's poems from *Baseball, Snakes, and Summer Squash: Poems About Growing Up*. Read "Yellow Sonnet" by Paul Zimmer from *The Places My Words Are Looking For*.
- Add to the Where Poets Get Ideas chart a section called Poets Write Their Memories and record some of the memories famous poets included in their poems.

- Brainstorm what memories students could write a poem about.

Independent Practice

- Students remember an image or a moment and write about it as a poem.

Wrap-Up

- Students share their memory poems.

DAY 5 Identification

Focused Instruction

We have noticed that poets also use their poetry to reveal a piece of themselves in their writing. They might talk about their likes, dislikes, feelings, interests, ideas, opinions, and even information that they know really well and want to talk about through poetry. Let's look at some of the poems we are reading together to see how these poems tell us something about the poet. Today we are going to write poems about ourselves as poets.

- Look at "Honey, I Love" by Eloise Greenfield, Valerie Worth's poems, and the poems of author Judith Viorst, such as "Fifteen, Maybe Sixteen Things to Worry About."
- Add to the "Where Poets Get Ideas" chart a section called "Poets Reveal a Piece of Themselves" and write what famous poets have revealed about themselves in poems.
- Brainstorm ideas that could be included in our poems about ourselves.

Independent Practice

- Students write about topics of interest or preoccupation, anything that matters to them. Or you can use a prompt based on Judith Viorst's poem "Fifteen, Maybe Sixteen Things to Worry About."

Wrap-Up

- Students share how their poetry reflects something about them.

DAY 6 Identification

Focused Instruction

Poets imagine worlds. They use their imaginations to create things that do not exist. That is one other way they find ideas.

- Read "If I Were in Charge of the World" by Judith Viorst and "Write About a Radish" by Karla Kuskin.

Independent Practice

- Students write "Imagine if..." in their notebooks and write poems from that prompt.

Wrap-Up

- Students read their "Imagine if..." poems to partners. They then trade off partners around the room, so they can hear other students' poems.

DAY 7 Guided Practice

Focused Instruction

Poets hear the sounds of language; the white space and the kinds of words they choose affect how they say the poem. The poem is not just words on the page; it is also the order and flow of the words on the page. We had fun putting some poems to music. Today in your own writing, you have lots of ideas you have been putting on the page: wonderings, imagination, memory, and observations. Take one of these and imagine music is playing with them. How would you write your words differently? Make the way you write the words match the mood of what you are trying to say. Look at "Old Dog" by James Stevenson. He puts very few words on the page. It matches the loneliness of that dog. Look at Judith Viorst. She uses lots of words and a good rhythm so you can get into her idea. Look at "The Dream Keeper" by Langston Hughes. He wants you to flow into his big idea, so there is repetition to his words. Let's make a chart to represent all of these ideas.

Mood of Poetry		
Poems We Like	Mood the Poet Conveys	How the Poet Conveys It
"Old Dog"	Loneliness	Few words, white space
"If I Were in Charge of the World"	Bold, different	Lots of words, repetition of key words
"The Dream Keeper"	Sadness, hope	Patterns of two or three words on a line, and then longer lines; repetition of key words.

(See Resource 5.6 for an extended chart.)

Independent Practice

- Students take one idea (wondering, remembering, observing, or imagining) and try to write a poem where the mood is impacted by how they choose to write and place the words on the page.

Wrap-Up

- Add students' own poems to the chart you created above.

EARLY FALL LATE FALL WINTER SPRING

DAY 8 Guided Practice

Focused Instruction

Poets are masterful at painting a picture with words. Because they use fewer words than in narrative writing, they need to choose their words carefully and find the best words so they can to say what they are thinking. They use language purposefully to share their ideas.

- Read "Beach Stones" by Lilian Moore, "dog" by Valerie Worth, and "Winter Eyes" by Douglas Florian.
- Look at the language the poets choose to use in their poems and discuss how poets build images through language.

Orange

A cold orange ball
with a gray mountain top
dotted white with snow.
A dream world
or hand held wonder.

A student poet uses his powers of observation to create a beautiful image.

Independent Practice

- Students read through poems they collected and find places where poets build strong images.

Wrap-Up

- Share a line from the poems students revised to show where the student changed the words to include language that builds images.

DAY 9 Guided Practice

Focused Instruction

We have five senses: hearing, smelling, seeing, touching, and tasting. Have you ever smelled something that has made you remember something from your past? Whenever I smell apple pie, I think of my grandma, because she used to cook apple pie whenever I went to visit her. Let's look at Douglas Florian's poem "Winter Eyes" to learn how poets use all their senses to capture images. After we read Douglas Florian's poem, we are going to create images.

- Read "Winter Eyes" by Douglas Florian and identify where in the poem he uses senses (sight, touch, smell, taste, and sound) to create an image.

Independent Practice

- Students create five boxes to write about their senses—hearing, smelling, seeing, touching, and tasting—and write a memory based on the senses.
- They then take the information in the boxes and reshape it as a poem.

Wrap-Up

- Students share their poems with the class.

DAY 10 Guided Practice

Focused Instruction

Poets are always thinking about how readers will understand their ideas, so they have many decisions to make as they construct their poems. One is about the language they use (look back at the chart created yesterday) and the other is the way their words look on the page. They think about something we call "white space": the blank moments between words in a poem. This space is hugely important to poetry. Let's read "The Sidewalk Racer" by Lillian Morrison and "We Could Be Friends" by Myra Cohn Livingston. They are very different in terms of white space. Turn and talk with your partner about what you notice. How does each poet use white space to convey the ideas in the poem? What do you think their purpose was in organizing the poem like that?

- Read aloud "The Sidewalk Racer" by Lillian Morrison and "We Could Be Friends" by Myra Cohn Livingston.
- With a partner, students should identify where the poet used white space in the poem and discuss what the poet's purpose might have been.

Independent Practice

- Students take one poem they have written and write it two different ways to play with white space.
- Students talk with a partner about how each try influenced the way their poem feels and sounds.

Wrap-Up

- Students build a class chart with you (see Noticing White Space, Resource 5.7) that identifies how the poet uses white space to convey an idea.

DAY 11 Guided Practice

Focused Instruction

Poets write in different forms to convey their emotions and ideas. Many forms come from our history and culture. Today we will look at haiku. It comes from an ancient tradition in Japan in which a master poet travels around the countryside and admires the natural world. Haiku takes special consideration with white space, too. It is a beautiful and quiet form.

- Read several examples of haikus that model for students how haiku poets use white space to convey an idea.

Independent Practice

- Students use some of their observational writing to write haiku poems.

Wrap-Up

- Students share their haikus.

DAY 12 Guided Practice

Focused Instruction

We read a poem by Pablo Neruda called "Ode to My Socks." He has written a whole book full of odes. Odes are poems that admire and appreciate. They can be written in many ways but they are almost always about ordinary things seen in extraordinary ways. Let's try to write one today.

- Read aloud "Ode to My Socks." Identify how Pablo Neruda makes the ordinary extraordinary.
- Brainstorm ideas about which students could write odes.

Independent Practice

- Students write odes.

Wrap-Up

- Students share their odes.

DAY 13 Guided Practice

Focused Instruction

Let's create a Poetry Checklist (Resource 5.8) together of all of the things we have learned about in this unit that have helped us create great poems.

Independent Practice

- Students revise and edit their poems and prepare them for writing anthologies.

Wrap-Up

- Students share their revisions with partners.

DAY 14 Commitment

Focused Instruction

Use A Poet's Editing Checklist (Resource 5.9) to review your three favorite poems. It is a special editing checklist for poetry. Poetry may break many rules, but it still has structure.

Independent Practice

- Students edit their poems.

Wrap-Up

- Students share their editing checklist and one poem with a partner.

DAY 15 Commitment

Focused Instruction

An anthology is a collection of poems or stories. Today we are going to collect all of our poems that we have written during this unit and put them together into our very own poetry anthology.

- Model for students how to collect poems into an anthology using the read-aloud poems.

Independent Practice

- Students should collect the poems they wrote and compile a poetry anthology.

Wrap-Up

- Students should share their own poetry anthologies with the class.

Student poets can treasure what they love by capturing ideas in a poem.

DAY 16 Commitment

Focused Instruction

We have created anthologies of our poems, so we are going to celebrate the poem and our study of the poem. We are going to have a Poetry Café. We will each present our poetry anthology and read aloud one poem that we absolutely love!

- Begin a poetry celebration (see Poetry Celebrations, Resource 5.10).

Independent Practice

- For the Poetry Café, students set up a café atmosphere in the classroom, with tablecloths and festive flower arrangements and snacks. They invite students and teachers from other classes, as well as other special guests (school nurse, custodian, etc.) from the school community who would enjoy and appreciate a celebration.

Wrap-Up

- Final poetry share—each student reads one poem (see Resources 5.11 and 5.12).

Clubs Bring Voices to Life

In late spring, our students return to collaborations with renewed vigor. They had an earlier opportunity to learn how to collaborate in a group and to hear others' voices, adding their own ideas, and now they can return to that work with a foundational knowledge and take pleasure in reading new texts. Mix up the clubs! Give your students many opportunities to work with different configurations of peers.

Making Connections Across Books: Interest Clubs

STRATEGY

Why Teach This?

• To foster strong collaboration among readers.
• To reinforce types of connections readers make between books.
• To strengthen book-talk skills.

Framing Question

• How can we examine connections between books through reading clubs?

Unit Goals

• Students will participate in productive reading club conversation.
• Students will identify a reading interest and meet in a club based on similar interests.
• Students will make connections between books, plots, characters, and genres.

Anchor Texts

• *Chato's Kitchen* by Gary Soto
• *Thunder Cake* by Patricia Polacco
• *Too Many Tamales* by Gary Soto

Unit Assessment Making Connections Across Books: Interest Clubs			STRATEGY
Student name:	EMERGING	DEVELOPING	INDEPENDENT
Engages in productive, conversational book talk.			
Makes connections based on plot or story line.			
Makes connections across genres.			
Makes connections based on characters.			
Makes connections between authors.			

Stage of the Unit	Focused Instruction You will	Independent Practice Students will
IMMERSION 4 days	• read *Too Many Tamales*; address how readers often meet in groups to discuss books; revisit what a reading club looks like. • ask students what they need to do to have successful clubs (e.g., methods for taking turns talking, for choosing books, employ conversational talk). • generate a list of smart club behavior, building on the charts from the earlier unit. • model how readers choose good club books based on interests of all group members; jot down some interests that you may want to read about in your club (e.g., genre, specific authors, series books, nonfiction topics).	• identify one important characteristic of good reading club work. • jot down on a sticky note one way they will make their reading club successful (e.g., I will take turns in the group, I will ask great questions in my group). • jot down interests they may want to read about in their club.
IDENTIFICATION 2 days	• model how clubs choose books together, thinking aloud in the library to find a set of books (multiple copies of the same title) that fit their interest. • create a class list of conversational starters that increase talk in the club.	• meet with their interest club (assembled by you based on their interests) to choose a title they want to read, and create their first reading deadline to guide their work going forward. • meet with their club to talk about what they've read so far (they should have read some portion of the book at home or during independent reading between Days 5 and 6).
GUIDED PRACTICE 5 days	• read *Too Many Tamales* and model how readers make connections among books based on similar plot or story line; add a conversation starter to the list, "This plot reminds me of…" • model how book clubs choose new books based on similar or new interests. • model how readers make connections among different genres; add a conversation starter to the list: "This book reminds me of a similar book…"	• meet with their club to discuss connections among books based on similar plot or story line. • meet with their club to discuss the book (they may select a new book as a group, if needed). • meet with their club to discuss connections among different genres.

GUIDED PRACTICE *(continued)*	• model how readers make connections among books based on characters; add a conversation starter to the list: "This character reminds me of…" • read *Chato's Kitchen* and model how readers make connections among authors (e.g., comparing similar themes, characters, or story lines).	• meet with their club to discuss connections among books based on characters. • meet with their club to discuss connections among authors.

COMMITMENT 2 days	• talk about culminating book projects, showing examples or talking about each one. Projects include:
	  • creating a poster comparing two books or two characters in books
	  • writing an advertisement for a book that includes a comparison to a similar book
	  • writing business cards for the main characters in different books and compare the character descriptions
	• celebrate projects.
		• work with their group to select and produce a culminating project for one of their books, making sure to include information about the different connections their group discussed.
		• share the project with the other clubs.

TOTAL: 13 DAYS

Making Writing Connections: Interest Magazines

STRATEGY

Why Teach This?

- To allow students to share their writing in a new format.
- To give students the opportunity to reflect back on their writing.
- To invite students to rethink their writing in the context of a magazine.

Framing Question

- How do writers follow their interests to create magazines?

Unit Goals

- Students will create a magazine with content of their choice based on the writing that they have done all year.
- Students will organize their writing within a magazine structure.
- Students will create titles for their writing that reflects the feel of the piece.
- Students will select pieces that work together to reflect who they are as writers and the topic of their magazine.

Anchor Texts

- www.highlightskids.com (search for the following: "Bike Fright" by Linda Stephens, fiction; "Cactus Hotel" by Mona Hodgson, poetry; "Different Strokes: The Chinese Art of Writing" by Linda Petrucelli and Gary Hoff, nonfiction; "Junk Drawer" by Bridget Reistad, poetry; "A Night in the Desert" by Melissa Joy Scheidt, fiction)
- www.scholastic.com (search for the profile of author/illustrator Mark Teague)
- www.spaghettibookclub.org (search for the book review by Stephanie S. of *The Stories Julian Tells* by Ann Cameron)
- www.timeforkids.com (search for "Talking Trash" by Angelique LeDoux)
- Other children's magazines including *Ladybug, Spider, Ask, National Geographic Kids,* and *Sports Illustrated for Kids*

Unit Assessment Making Writing Connections: Interest Magazines			STRATEGY
Student name:	EMERGING	DEVELOPING	INDEPENDENT
Rewrites or revises entries for their magazines.			
Uses a magazine text to guide writing.			
Uses strong words in their writing.			
Researches their articles or stories, if necessary.			
Includes catchy titles for their stories and/or articles.			
Revises articles and/or stories (punctuation, grammar, spelling).			
Creates a magazine cover, including magazine title, catchy drawings or graphics, and the names of the articles and/or stories.			

Stage of the Unit	Focused Instruction You will	Independent Practice Students will
IMMERSION 1 day	• browse a variety of children's magazines (*Time for Kids*, *Sports Illustrated for Kids*, *National Geographic Kids*, *Ladybug*, *Spider*); ask students what they notice about the writing in magazines.	• read independently from a variety of children's magazines; meet with a partner to share their observations about magazine writing.
IDENTIFICATION 2 days	• create a list of things that make magazine stories/articles different from books (e.g., use of graphics/photos, length, variety of articles/stories in each issue, some magazines organized by topic or genre). • examine one narrative ("Bike Fright") and one nonfiction article ("Talking Trash"), and a poem ("Junk Drawer"); emphasize that magazine writers tend to write short pieces that get to the point quickly.	• reread writer's notebook to find short pieces that they would like to include in a magazine; think about what makes it feel like it would work in a magazine. • reread their selections to look for connections between writing; discuss how these pieces fit together.

GUIDED PRACTICE 8 days	• look at *Spider* to notice the theme of the magazine and how the writing in the magazine supports the theme; model thinking about a theme for a magazine. • select a magazine as a model; demonstrate how writers can use the model text to guide their writing (formatting, title, graphics/pictures, etc.). • look at *Spider* to notice how different genres are included in the magazine; model selecting a variety of types of writing from each of the genres students have written in throughout the year, including narrative, nonfiction, poetry, author blurbs (see the Scholastic author/illustrator blurb on Mike Teague). • model revising pieces of writing to use strong language, catchy leads, strong endings, and well-written sentences. • demonstrate how magazine writers come up with catchy titles for their stories or articles. • show students how magazine editors order how the stories or articles will appear in a magazine. • model how writers edit their work to make it easy to read, paying attention to punctuation, grammar, and spelling. • create a cover for your magazine, including the title, drawings and graphics, and the names of the articles in the magazine.	• decide on a theme for their magazines and jot down ideas on sticky notes. • reread notebooks to make sure that selections reflect a variety of types of writing from each of the genres they have written in throughout the year, including narrative, nonfiction, poetry, writing about reading, and any other writing they would like to include. • revise pieces to use strong language, catchy leads, strong endings, and well-written sentences. • add catchy titles to their stories or articles. • order their stories and writing. • edit writing, paying attention to punctuation, grammar, and spelling. • gather their writing and organize the pieces into the order they would like them to appear in the magazine. • create covers for their magazines, including a title, drawing or graphics, and the names of the articles in the magazine.
COMMITMENT 2 days	• share your finished magazine with a partner; model giving compliments on one another's magazines.	• share their finished magazines with a partner. • tell how this magazine reflects who they are as writers.
TOTAL: 13 DAYS		

Punctuation RULES!

Your students have been editing and thinking about conventions all year. A healthy dose of intensive instruction on one area of conventions will infuse their last month in school with the fun of conventions as well as their usefulness. The comma matters, after all.

Getting to Know Commas: Reading

CONVENTIONS

Why Teach This?

- To strengthen awareness of punctuation as the key to fluency by taking a closer look at commas.
- To continue to read with expression.
- To read with attention to sentence structure to assist in comprehension.

Framing Question

- How does punctuation challenge us to become better readers?

Unit Goals

- Students will use punctuation to help them read with fluency.
- Students will read with expression.
- Students will read with attention to punctuation by slowing down and taking a pause at each comma.
- Students will recognize commas as clues to reading complex sentences by looking for phrases and reading to the comma.

Anchor Texts

- *Because of Winn-Dixie* by Kate DiCamillo
- *Come On, Rain!* by Karen Hesse
- *Eats, Shoots and Leaves: Why Commas Really Do Make a Difference!* by Lynn Truss
- *Mr. George Baker* by Amy Hest
- *Yum! Ummmm! Que Rico!* by Pat Mora

Unit Assessment Getting to Know Commas: Reading			CONVENTIONS
Student name:	EMERGING	DEVELOPING	INDEPENDENT
Uses punctuation to read with fluency.			
Uses punctuation to read with expression.			
Uses commas to slow down and take a pause.			
Recognizes complex sentence structures by using the comma to read with phrasing.			

Stage of the Unit	Focused Instruction You will	Independent Practice Students will
IMMERSION 1 day	• read aloud *Mr. George Baker*, modeling reading with fluency and with expression.	• record what they notice about how the text was read aloud.
IDENTIFICATION 2 days	• read from an enlarged page from *Mr. George Baker* and name and define the punctuation marks students notice; emphasize how punctuation was used when reading aloud. • read from *Come On, Rain!* and discuss how commas slow down readers and cause them to pause before continuing; read an excerpt from *Because of Winn-Dixie*, identifying how commas give clues of how to read complex sentences.	• practice reading aloud their independent reading text to a partner. • continue to practice reading aloud their independent reading texts to a partner and write down sentences in which commas caused them to slow down and pause.
GUIDED PRACTICE 1 day	• place a passage from *Yum! Ummm! Que Rico!* on the overhead or chart paper that has no punctuation; put in the missing punctuation with the students, having them name and identify the punctuation marks that are missing.	• write out a short conversation they have with a partner using proper punctuation; read aloud the conversation and have other partnerships name and identify the punctuation being used.
COMMITMENT 1 day	• reflect on what you notice the students have come to understand about reading with fluency and expression.	• reflect on what they learned about punctuation that they can take with them to their next book.
TOTAL: 5 DAYS		

Getting to Know Commas: Writing

Why Teach This?

- To teach proper and effective use of commas in a series and in phrases.

Framing Questions

- How do writers use commas effectively?
- Why do writers use commas?

Unit Goals

- Students will demonstrate proper use of commas in a series.
- Students will demonstrate proper use of commas for dependent clauses (introducing the thought).
- Students will revise a piece of writing using their new knowledge of commas.
- Students will explain why writers use commas in their writing.

Anchor Texts

- *Big and Little* by Steve Jenkins
- *Eats, Shoots and Leaves: Why Commas Really Do Make a Difference!* by Lynn Truss
- *Fireflies* by Julie Brinckloe
- *Snow* by Uri Shulevitz
- *Yum! Ummmm! Que Rico!* by Pat Mora

Unit Assessment Getting to Know Commas: Writing			CONVENTIONS
Student name:	EMERGING	DEVELOPING	INDEPENDENT
Uses commas in a series.			
Uses commas for dependent clauses.			
Revises a piece of writing with new knowledge of commas.			
Explains why writers use commas in writing.			

Stage of the Unit	Focused Instruction You will	Independent Practice Students will
IMMERSION 1 day	• show students a variety of texts that have examples of comma usage; ask students to sift through the texts and find three examples of sentences using commas.	• write the three sentences on sticky notes and share with a partner how commas are being used in the sentences.
IDENTIFICATION 2 days	• read aloud *Yum! Ummmm! Que Rico!* or another text that models commas in a series; name and identify a variety of sentences that use the comma in a series; define the rules for this usage. • read *Big and Little* by Steve Jenkins or another text that models commas in phrases; name and identify a variety of sentences that use the comma for dependent clauses (introducing the thought); define the rules for this usage.	• revise a notebook entry by adding in the commas for a series of items, or generate a new entry. • revise a notebook entry by adding in commas for dependent clauses and/or phrases, or generate a new entry.
GUIDED PRACTICE 1 day	• model and think aloud how to revise a notebook entry by reflecting on when commas are to be used and why.	• pick a favorite entry where they tried to employ one of the comma uses for publishing; further edit it to publish.
COMMITMENT 1 day	• reflect on what you notice the students have come to understand about the effective use of commas in their writing.	• reflect on learning by thinking about how commas are used in their writing and how they can remember to continue to effectively use commas in their writing.
TOTAL: 5 DAYS		

Precious Days: Past and Future

We come to the end of the school year. The windows are open, attentions are scattered.

We are all eager for summer vacation. We need to measure our growth, like the height marks on the side of a door frame. It is time for our students to admire who they have become and where they are going next. They leave your room full of the gifts you have given them: the love of language and a confidence with text. Those gifts will be endless, always useful, and never forgotten. So, too, are their gifts to us.

Looking Back, Looking Forward: Making Summer Reading Plans

PROCESS

Why Teach This?

- To reflect on the reading students have done throughout the year.
- To make plans for summer reading.

Framing Questions

- How did you grow and change as a reader this school year?
- What are some reading goals you have for the summer?

Unit Goals

- Students will reflect on themselves as readers: favorite books read, book choices, reading activities, strategies learned across genres, reading successes and struggles.
- Students will create a reading plan to guide their reading life during the summer.

Anchor Texts

- "Books Fall Open," in *Good Books, Good Times!* selected by Lee Bennett Hopkins
- *The Hard-Times Jar* by Ethel Footman Smothers
- *The Library Dragon* by Carmen Agra Deedy
- *Mama, I'll Give You the World* by Roni Schotter and S. Saelig Gallagher
- "When I Was Nine" by James Stevenson
- "Yesterday," in *Hey World, Here I Am!* by Jean Little

Unit Assessment Looking Back, Looking Forward: Making Summer Reading Plans			PROCESS
Student name:	EMERGING	DEVELOPING	INDEPENDENT
Identifies qualities of self as a reader.			
Reflects on self as a reader: what has changed in his/her reading life since the beginning of third grade.			
Makes plans for summer reading.			

Looking Back...

Stage of the Unit	Focused Instruction You will	Independent Practice Students will
IMMERSION 1 day	• revisit the word *reflection* and explain how students will think back on their year as readers; read aloud "Yesterday" in *Hey World, Here I Am!* • reflect on reading goals they had for themselves as readers throughout the year.	• work with a partner and talk about one favorite book they read during the year. • work with a partner and reflect on the reading goals they accomplished this year.
IDENTIFICATION 1 day	• read "Books Fall Open" and name and identify ways they can reflect on themselves as readers: favorite books read, poems read, magazines read, book choices, reading activities, strategies learned across genres, reading successes and struggles, favorite genres.	• identify a time during the year when reading felt like a struggle and a time when they felt strong as readers.
GUIDED PRACTICE 2 days	• share books and other texts that represent you as a reader today: favorites, books that changed you as a reader. • read "When I Was Nine" and reflect on reading goals by modeling, "I grew as a reader because..."	• look over their reading logs and reflect on their personal book choices, noting what books they feel represent them as readers. • reflect on what types of comments they wrote and what this tells them about their thinking as readers; write, "This book changed me because..."; reflect on goals they set for themselves across the year by writing, "I grew as a reader because..."
COMMITMENT 2 days	• model drafting formal reading reflection ("How I Have Grown as a Reader"). • make a commitment to your reading plans this summer.	• gather all the information from the previous days and write a crafted reflection that celebrates who they are as readers. • make a commitment to their summer reading plans.
TOTAL: 6 DAYS		

Looking Forward...

Stage of the Unit	Focused Instruction You will	Independent Practice Students will
IMMERSION 1 day	• read *The Library Dragon* and discuss how readers can think about their reading lives over the summer and into the next grade and use the library to continue their reading.	• work with a partner and discuss what they are most proud of in reading this year and what they will continue to do as readers over the summer.
IDENTIFICATION 1 day	• discuss what your summer reading will look like, how you will find time to read, and what you will read.	• work with a partner to plan what their summer reading plans will be.
GUIDED PRACTICE 2 days	• read *Hard-Times Jar* and talk about the importance of libraries and access to books; make a list of books you would like to read (by author, genre, or series) and a list of topics you are interested in learning more about. • reflect how planning ahead as a reader means thinking about yourself as a reader and then setting realistic goals.	• explore the classroom library and interview their classmates to make lists of books they would like to read, organized by author, genre, series, or character, as well as things they are interested in learning more about. • work with a partner and list what goals they will set for themselves as readers, what they will continue to work on, and what new challenges they would like to take on.
COMMITMENT 3 days	• discuss how students will commit to their reading goals by writing about their reading goals for the summer. • make a group commitment to read regularly over the summer. • Read *Mama, I'll Give You the World* and plan who you will read with this summer and how the world is richer when you have friends and family to share in your special moments.	• write goals for their summer reading. • gather all the information from the previous days and create a contract committing to reading over the summer; place document in reading folder for the summer. • celebrate all the great reading work they have done this year.
TOTAL: 7 DAYS		

Looking Back, Looking Forward: Making Summer Writing Plans

Why Teach This?
- To reflect on the writing students have done throughout the year.
- To make plans for summer writing.

Framing Questions
- How did you grow and change as a writer this year?
- What are some writing goals you have for the summer?

Unit Goals
- Students will reflect on themselves as writers: favorite published piece, favorite genre, favorite writing activity and unit of study, favorite anchor texts, writing successes and struggles.
- Students will create a writing plan to guide their writing life during the summer.

Anchor Texts
- *The Gardener* by Sarah Stewart
- *Library Mouse* by Daniel Kirk
- *Live Writing: Breathing Life Into Your Words* by Ralph Fletcher
- *The Secret of Old Zeb* by Carmen Agra Deedy

Unit Assessment Looking Back, Looking Forward: Making Summer Writing Plans			PROCESS
Student name:	EMERGING	DEVELOPING	INDEPENDENT
Identifies qualities of self as a writer.			
Reflects on self as a writer: what has changed in writing since the beginning of third grade.			
Creates a summer writing plan to guide his or her writing life during the summer.			

Looking Back...

Stage of the Unit	Focused Instruction You will	Independent Practice Students will
IMMERSION 2 days	• revisit the word *reflection* and explain how they are going to think back on their year as writers. • read aloud *Library Mouse* and discuss goals students had for themselves as writers throughout the year.	• work with a partner and talk about one favorite published piece of writing. • work with a partner and reflect on the writing goals that they did and did not accomplish and why.
IDENTIFICATION 1 day	• name and identify ways students can reflect on themselves as writers: favorite published piece, favorite genre, favorite writing activity and unit of study, favorite anchor texts, writing successes and struggles.	• identify a time during the year when writing felt like a struggle and a time when they felt like strong writers.
GUIDED PRACTICE 4 days	• reflect on past writing by rereading various student pieces and discussing what they can do now as writers as compared to the beginning of the year. • share one of your own writing pieces and discuss why it means something to you. • discuss the anchor texts used during the year and how they helped students with their writing. • reflect on times when writing felt hard for students and times that they felt like strong writers.	• reread past writing and list what they can do now as writers. • share with a partner their favorite piece of writing, writing activity, and unit of study. • reflect on an anchor text that helped them learn more about themselves as writers. • reflect and list the strategies they can now use when they get stuck as a writer; share with a partner a time when they felt like strong writers and why.
COMMITMENT 2 days	• discuss how students will share how they have grown as writers by creating a written response. • make a commitment to write over the summer.	• gather all the information from the previous days and write a reflection that celebrates who they are as writers. • make a commitment to write over the summer.
TOTAL: 9 DAYS		

Looking Forward...

Stage of the Unit	Focused Instruction You will	Independent Practice Students will
IMMERSION 1 day	• read excerpts from *Live Writing* by Ralph Fletcher (pages 129–131) and discuss how students can plan their writing over the summer and into the next grade.	• work with a partner and discuss what they feel the most proud of in writing this year and what they will continue to work on.
IDENTIFICATION 1 day	• discuss what your summer writing will look like, how you will be finding a time and place to write, and in what genres you will try to write over the summer.	• work with a partner to plan what their summer writing will look like.
GUIDED PRACTICE 3 days	• model writing in a journal and how to use writing to remember special summer times. • read *The Gardener* and model how to write letters or e-mail to keep in touch with others. • show how planning ahead as a writer means thinking about themselves as writers and setting comfortable goals.	• decorate their small writing journals. • make a list of ways they will write over the summer, and share addresses with one another so that everyone has a summer writing buddy or two. • work with a partner and list what goals they will set for themselves as writers, what will they continue to work on, and what they would like to accomplish by the end of the summer.
COMMITMENT 3 days	• discuss how students will commit to their writing goals and how they will achieve them. • read aloud *The Secret of Old Zeb* and talk about the importance of reaching for the stars; make a commitment to write over the summer. • celebrate all the great writing work students have done this year by having a writing "museum" party.	• write about their goals and how they plan to achieve them. • gather all the information from the previous days and create a commitment to write over the summer; place the document in their writing folder for the summer. • lay out their writing and visit each other's work.
TOTAL: 8 DAYS		

Circular Seasons:
Endings and Beginnings

You will miss these children. And they will miss you. For the rest of their lives, they will remember your name. There should be more of a ritual for you to let go of these children and prepare to embrace the new ones.

In Japan every fall there is a traditional chrysanthemum festival to celebrate the last blooming before the winter comes. People journey to view the beautiful flowers and to celebrate the changing seasons. There are special horticulturalists who work for a full eleven months of the year to prepare for this festival, creating spectacular chrysanthemum arrangements, which they feature in *uwaya*, serene shelters for the beautiful plantings. In this way, people can contemplate and reflect upon the changing seasons.

I wish we had such a thing for the work we do. The seasons go around, and then come around again, and there is a beauty in that: we know they will always come again. But these, these precious, precious children, they will never come again quite like this. As we enter our summer and curl up on the couch with our mug of tea once again, let the last moments of this book be an *uwaya* for us— a serene shelter for reflection. The work you do with your students is, well, once in a lifetime. Remember this as the seasons of your teaching life begin once again.

Chapter 6

TRACKING STUDENT PROGRESS ACROSS THE YEAR

The C4 Assessment

Assessment is the beginning, the middle, and the end of our teaching. It is the heart of our instruction, the age-old dilemma, the most gratifying, frustrating, and rewarding aspect of our work, because it reveals in stark relief: How are we all doing? Done well, it is not offensive, harmful, hurtful, or unpleasant for children. Done well, it is engaging, reflective, fascinating, and insightful for teachers. Done poorly, it is demeaning, demoralizing, and useless to everyone. Done poorly, it is unhelpful, uninteresting, and slightly boring. We have created rubrics as formative assessments and a yearlong assessment tool we call the C4 Assessment that we believe will lead you to the "done well" column. Done well, assessment is meaningful, as J. Richard Gentry (2008) points out: "…you can loop together assessment and instruction and use both simultaneously to support your students in targeted and powerful ways."

Unit Rubrics as Formative Assessments

Within each unit we have written for this book, we have given you a model assessment rubric such as the following:

Unit Assessment Growing an Awareness of Theme and Time: Writing Fiction			GENRE
Student name:	EMERGING	DEVELOPING	INDEPENDENT
Writes an original narrative text in sequential order.			
Includes theme and evidence of theme.			
Uses descriptive words to give the reader a sense of time.			
Uses time to demonstrate theme.			

These rubrics can and should be used as formative assessments. By this we mean that you can construct rubrics such as these with your students during the Identification stage of any unit. As you name the expectations for process behaviors, or the elements of a genre, or the type of strategy or convention you would like to see your students use, you can add this list of performance indicators to your rubric. Then you can give the rubric to your students to use during their Guided Practice. If we give students our upfront expectations in writing, and they have helped to form and understand these expectations, we can be sure that they will know what we want them to do as readers and writers. They can use these rubrics as placeholders for our teaching—reminding them on a daily basis what we want them to practice, even when we are not sitting next to them.

By keeping the rubric alongside your conferring conversations with individual readers and writers, you will be able to focus your observations and record your comments on how each student is performing throughout the length of the unit. Using the rubric to supplement your conferring plans will also allow you to refer back on these conversations to plan for future instruction—either for the entire class when you see something that nearly everyone is having difficulty with, or for individual or small-group work.

Unit Rubrics as Summative Assessments

Of course these rubrics can also be summative. You may use them to measure your students' performance at the end of each unit, and you may gather these collective unit assessments to plan and draft your report cards. We believe these rubrics will be extremely helpful on several levels. They will help you focus your instruction towards the expectations listed on the rubric. They will help guide and focus your students practice within any unit of study, and they will allow for self-reflection— for our students and for ourselves. By the end of any unit, we should be able to see what students accomplished, and what we still need to work on.

The C4 Assessment

Rubrics are not the only form of assessment that we would like you to consider. As our entire year has been built around the premise of balanced instruction across process, genre, strategy, and conventions, we would like to suggest that you consider your students' growing skills and abilities within these four categories. To help you accomplish this task, we have created the C4 Assessment (C4A) forms seen at the end of this chapter. These forms merge many of the teaching points across the year into collective assessments of students' understanding of process, genre, strategy, and conventions. The C4A is clear and simple to use, and yet provides a great deal of information for teachers, so that we may differentiate our instruction for all students; for parents so we may share students' growth or challenges; and for schools.

Tracking Our Students Across the Grades

We have designed specific C4 assessments for each grade level. While their format and organization are the same, the content varies as we have given a great deal of thought to the articulation of instruction across the grades. We recommend that these assessment forms be filled out each year and passed on to the next year's teacher. This will give teachers a clearer sense of their students as readers and writers at the beginning of the year than traditional packaged reading or writing assessments.

Using These Forms

There are many different ways to incorporate these forms into your year. You may choose to:

- use them to conduct a more formal review of student performance at the beginning, middle, and end of the year.
- keep these forms with your other conferring materials and use them to note when students demonstrate progress within a particular unit.
- keep these forms with you as you read through your students' published writing, so you can use their written work as evidence of learning.

No matter which method you use, we ask you to consider how your children are developing as readers and writers inside the Complete 4 components. What have they learned to do as readers and writers? What have they come to understand about genre? What have they learned about reading and writing strategies? What do they now understand about the world of conventions? Our job is to create lifelong readers and writers in our classrooms. Instruction-linked assessment through the Complete 4 is the key to achieving this objective.

Complete 4 Component: Process Third Grade

KEY: **E**=emerging **D**=developing **I**=independent

Student: _____   School Year: _____

CAPACITIES:	BEGINNING OF THE YEAR	MIDDLE OF THE YEAR	END OF THE YEAR
Reads familiar text smoothly (fluency).			
Reads independently for 30 to 40 minutes (stamina).			
Reads at home independently for 15 minutes.			
Sustains book talk independently for 10 minutes (stamina).			
Selects books according to level and interest (independence).			
Explains personal criteria for choosing reading material (independence).			
Reads and understands written directions.			
Writes independently for 25 to 30 minutes (stamina).			
Writes at home independently for 10 minutes.			
Sustains a selected writing piece over three to five days (stamina).			
Rereads own writing to add on to it, revise, or fix grammar and spelling (independence).			

ROLES:	BEGINNING OF THE YEAR	MIDDLE OF THE YEAR	END OF THE YEAR
Is prepared for teacher conferences with reading and writing tools ready.			
Presents and discusses own writing in conferences with teacher.			
Presents and discuses own writing in a conference with a peer.			
Discusses peer's writing in a conference with a peer.			
Transitions from whole-class to independent practice without assistance.			

Complete 4 Component: Process Third Grade (continued)   KEY: **E**=emerging **D**=developing **I**=independent

Student: _____   School Year: _____

IDENTITIES:	BEGINNING OF THE YEAR	MIDDLE OF THE YEAR	END OF THE YEAR
Is able to express growth as a reader.			
Sets reasonable reading goals.			
Is able to express growth as a writer.			
Sets reasonable writing goals.			
Communicates with others using writing.			

COLLABORATION:	BEGINNING OF THE YEAR	MIDDLE OF THE YEAR	END OF THE YEAR
Hears advice from a partner respectfully.			
Shares advice with a partner respectfully.			
Articulates and shares reading experience with others.			
Participates in discussions about grade-level texts.			
Leads discussions about grade-level texts.			
Works collaboratively to comprehend text.			
Responds during conversation by adding on to ideas.			
Provides thoughtful feedback about a partner's writing with clear explanation.			
Articulates and shares writing experiences with others.			

Complete 4 Component: Genre Third Grade

KEY: **E**=emerging **D**=developing **I**=independent

Student: _____   School Year: _____

GENERAL:	BEGINNING OF THE YEAR	MIDDLE OF THE YEAR	END OF THE YEAR
Recognizes and articulates differences in genres of narrative, nonfiction, and poetry.			
Reads in a variety of genres.			
Writes in a variety of genres.			

NARRATIVE:	BEGINNING OF THE YEAR	MIDDLE OF THE YEAR	END OF THE YEAR
Identifies all story elements (character, problem, solution, setting, time).			
Relates the setting, plot, and characters in literature to own life.			
Relates the setting, plot, and characters in literature to other texts.			
Describes the mood or emotion of a story.			
Identifies themes in text.			
Identifies actual time period and passage of time in texts.			
Summarizes the main idea orally and in writing.			
Uses literary elements in writing.			
Writes clear beginning, middle, and ends with details.			
Writes texts that include characters, problem, solution, setting, and time.			
Uses dialogue in writing.			

Complete 4 Component: Genre Third Grade (continued)

KEY: **E**=emerging **D**=developing **I**=independent

Student: _____   School Year: _____

NONFICTION:	BEGINNING OF THE YEAR	MIDDLE OF THE YEAR	END OF THE YEAR
Relates data and facts from informational texts to prior information/experience.			
Identifies main ideas and supporting details in informational texts.			
Compares and contrasts information on one topic from two different sources.			
Identifies and interprets facts taken from visuals in a nonfiction text.			
Uses graphic organizers to record significant details from informational texts.			
Collects data, facts, and ideas from nonfiction texts.			
Uses multiple sources of information in writing a nonfiction text.			
Names and uses a variety of text features to make meaning from a text.			
Writes in response to the reading of informational texts.			
States a main idea and supports it with facts in written work.			

POETRY:	BEGINNING OF THE YEAR	MIDDLE OF THE YEAR	END OF THE YEAR
Recognizes different types of poems.			
Identifies common characteristics of poetry (rhyme, rhythm, repetition).			
Uses literary elements in written poems.			
Uses rhythm and rhyme to create short poems.			
Uses repetition in poems.			
Uses vivid language.			
Uses descriptive language.			
Uses white space to create a poem.			
Writes a poem based on the work of a mentor poet.			

Complete 4 Component: Strategy Third Grade

KEY: **E**=emerging **D**=developing **I**=independent

Student: School Year:

INPUT (the strategies readers use to comprehend text):	BEGINNING OF THE YEAR	MIDDLE OF THE YEAR	END OF THE YEAR
Makes logical predictions about events and characters.			
Draws conclusions about events and characters.			
Makes inferences about events and characters.			
Uses specific evidence from stories to describe characters and their actions and motivations.			
Uses knowledge of story structure and story elements to interpret stories.			
Identifies author's purpose.			
Distinguishes important and unimportant details.			
Identifies statements of fact and opinion.			
Infers underlying theme or message of written text (with support).			
Analyzes an author's use of setting, plot, and character.			
Connects at least two texts based on similarities in problem–solution or character.			
Compares and contrasts characters in literary works.			

Complete 4 Component: Strategy Third Grade (continued)   KEY: E=emerging D=developing I=independent

Student: School Year:

OUTPUT (the strategies writers use to create text):	BEGINNING OF THE YEAR	MIDDLE OF THE YEAR	END OF THE YEAR
Compares and contrasts characters, plot, and setting in literary works.			
Supports point of view with details from the text.			
Summarizes the main idea while writing about reading.			
Expresses opinions that demonstrate a personal point of view.			
Uses personal experiences and knowledge to analyze new ideas.			
Uses comprehension strategies to monitor own writing.			
Creates visual images in writing.			
Organizes writing with an awareness of paragraphing.			
Refines writing by incorporating craft elements into leads and endings.			
Takes notes to record data, facts, and ideas.			
Uses graphic organizers to record significant details about characters and events in stories.			
Demonstrates comprehension of grade-level text through written responses.			

Complete 4 Component: Conventions Third Grade

KEY: **E**=emerging **D**=developing **I**=independent

Student: _____   School Year: _____

SYNTAX:	BEGINNING OF THE YEAR	MIDDLE OF THE YEAR	END OF THE YEAR
Uses varied sentence structure in writing.			
Writes sentences in logical order.			
Uses paragraphs to organize topics.			
Effectively uses grade-level vocabulary in writing.			
Recognizes and writes sentences with adjectives and adverbs.			
Identifies the basic grammatical components of a sentence.			

PUNCTUATION/CAPITALIZATION:	BEGINNING OF THE YEAR	MIDDLE OF THE YEAR	END OF THE YEAR
Reviews work independently for spelling, capitalization, and punctuation.			
Uses a variety of punctuation in writing.			
Uses capitalization at appropriate points.			
Uses internal punctuation (ellipses, quotation marks, commas).			

SPELLING/DECODING:	BEGINNING OF THE YEAR	MIDDLE OF THE YEAR	END OF THE YEAR
Uses knowledge of letter–sound correspondence to blend sounds when reading unfamiliar grade-level words.			
Decodes by analogy using knowledge of syllable patterns.			
Decodes grade-level words using knowledge of word structure.			
Sight reads grade-level high-frequency words.			
Analyzes word structure to learn word meaning.			
Learns new vocabulary and concepts indirectly by reading books and other print sources.			
Uses a dictionary to learn the meanings of words.			
Uses a thesaurus to identify synonyms and antonyms.			

Chapter 7

Essential Reading for the Complete 4 Educator

The Complete 4 for Literacy
by Pam Allyn

Pam's book *The Complete 4 for Literacy* introduces us to the idea of the four major components for literacy instruction: Process, Genre, Strategy, and Conventions. She illuminates the components and how they interact throughout the year. In your school communities, we encourage you to form study groups around these components. Begin with Pam's book and study it together to orient yourself. Then, each year or each season, select one of the components to focus on. We can use each component to discuss not just whole-class instruction but also how best to confer with individual students, how to work with struggling readers and writers, and how to assess our students. We have prepared a special selection of professional texts to foster your investigation of each of the components.

Writing Above Standard
by Debbie Lera

Debbie Lera will help you to frame a year of teaching writing that really helps your students soar using your state standards as a guide. With the Complete 4 as the backbone of her thinking, Debbie takes us on a journey through state standards and how to make them work for us. In the spirit of the Complete 4 and the Complete Year which is all about building flexible frameworks, this book furthers your thinking by helping you to benefit from the structure provided by the standards while attending to the individual needs of your students.

Professional Books on Process

There are wonderful classics in the field of teaching reading and writing that help remind us why process work is so, so critical. Learning routines, talking about books, choosing topics: all the bedrock of a lifetime of success as readers and writers. Remind yourself that process is the key to a happy life: how you live your life is as important as what you did with it. The process work is the how.

Our favorites include:

- *Beyond Leveled Books: Supporting Transitional Readers in Grades 2–5* by Karen Szymusiak and Franki Sibberson

- *Classrooms That Work: They Can All Read and Write* by Patricia M. Cunningham and Richard L. Allington

- *In the Company of Children* by Joanne Hindley

- *Writing About Reading: From Book Talk to Literary Essays, Grades 3–8* by Janet Angelillo

Bonus!

- *Children's Books and Their Creators*, edited by Anita Silvey: A must-have for your shelf! It is a detailed collection of great authors' biographies and also excerpts from their most famous books. There is a lot of author information here that is excellent to incorporate into "where writers get ideas" lessons.

Professional Books on Genre

Genre units allow our third graders to try on many hats and be in the world of reading and writing. Genre is also power. If you know which genre matches your purpose, you can communicate most effectively.

Helpful books for your learning include:

- *For the Good of the Earth and Sun: Teaching Poetry* by Georgia Heard

- *Nonfiction in Focus: A Comprehensive Framework for Helping Students Become Independent Readers and Writers of Nonfiction* by Janice V. Kristo and Rosemary A. Bamford

- *The No-Nonsense Guide to Teaching Writing: Strategies, Structures, and Solutions* by Judy Davis and Sharon Hill

Professional Books on Strategy

In this book, you can see how strongly we believe in the strategic mind of the third grader! The third grader is deeply strategic in his planning and in the way he approaches problem solving when it comes to friendship and other social dynamics. So, too, can we help our students become strategic as readers and writers. The following books contain some helpful information on strategy work:

- *Guiding Readers and Writers: Teaching Comprehension, Genre, and Content Literacy* by Irene C. Fountas and Gay Su Pinnell

- *How Writers Work* by Ralph Fletcher

- *Learning Under the Influence of Language and Literature: Making the Most of Read-Alouds Across the Day* by Lester L. Laminack and Reba M. Wadsworth

- *The Resourceful Writing Teacher: A Handbook of Essential Skills and Strategies* by Jenny Mechem Bender

- *The Revision Toolbox: Teaching Techniques That Work* by Georgia Heard

- *Strategies That Work* by Stephanie Harvey and Anne Goudvis

- *What Really Matters for Struggling Readers: Designing Research-Based Programs* by Richard L. Allington

Professional Books on Conventions

We are lucky that these last few years have given us a new explosion in interesting perspectives on conventions: grammar, punctuation, and syntax. This is the hardest hurdle for us to overcome. Most of us grew up remembering either no grammar instruction or terrible grammar instruction. Spelling and grammar and punctuation can all be fun, truly! Conventions instruction is empowering and students want to learn how to spell and they want to be in on the secrets of language. The following can help:

- *The Fluent Reader: Oral Reading Strategies for Building Word Recognition, Fluency, and Comprehension* by Timothy V. Rasinski

- *A Fresh Approach to Teaching Punctuation* by Janet Angelillo

- *The Grammar Plan Book* by Constance Weaver

- *Grammar Study: Helping Students Get What Grammar Is and How It Works* by Janet Angelillo

- *Woe Is I Jr.* by Patricia T. O'Connor

Resource Sheets

Early Fall

- Resource 2.1   Parent Letter for Strengthening Sentences
- Resource 2.2   Sentences That Strike Me
- Resource 2.3   Admiring Sentences
- Resource 2.4   How Punctuation Affects the Sentence
- Resource 2.5   Noticing and Naming Sentences

Late Fall

- Resource 3.1   Parent Letter for Character Study
- Resource 3.2   Tracing a Character
- Resource 3.3   Pre-Draft Organizer
- Resource 3.4   Character Development Organizer
- Resource 3.5   End-of-Unit Reflection

Winter

- Resource 4.1   Parent Letter for Reading Clubs
- Resource 4.2   Noticing Conversations
- Resource 4.3   Preparing for Reading Talks
- Resource 4.4   Reading Club Reflection
- Resource 4.5   Parent Letter for Writing Clubs
- Resource 4.6   Finding Mentor Texts
- Resource 4.7   Noticing Text Features in Mentor Texts
- Resource 4.8   Writing Clubs Homework: Researching My Topics
- Resource 4.9   Editing Checklist for Writing Clubs

Spring

- Resource 5.1   Parent Letter for Exploring Poetry Connections Through Reading
- Resource 5.2   Sensory Images in Poetry
- Resource 5.3   Interpretation
- Resource 5.4   Parent Letter for Exploring Poetry Connections Through Writing
- Resource 5.5   Poetry Homework: Learning About Poets Through Their Words
- Resource 5.6   The Mood of Poetry
- Resource 5.7   Noticing White Space
- Resource 5.8   Poetry Checklist
- Resource 5.9   A Poet's Editing Checklist
- Resource 5.10   Poetry Celebrations
- Resource 5.11   Comments for the Poet
- Resource 5.12   Ways to Celebrate Our Writing

Parent Letter for Strengthening Sentences

Dear Parents,

We are beginning new units of study in both reading and writing. As readers we will explore how a well-crafted sentence helps us to create beautiful images of what we have read. As writers we will learn how to carefully choose and place words we use to best convey our message.

Throughout this unit, your children will collect sentences they love. When you find sentences that you think are really well-written in your newspapers, a letter or e-mail from a friend, or in a novel you are reading, please share them with your child.

I will be sharing with your children the elements of grammar, naming the parts of speech, including nouns, verbs, and adjectives.

Warmly,

Name _____ Date _____

Sentences That Strike Me

Sentences that strike me in _____.

(Title of Book)

Sentence	What We Notice
Example: It comes up round, ripe, and huge over autumn fields of corn and wheat.	These are three specific words to describe the moon that help the reader get a picture in her mind.

Name _____   Date _____

Admiring Sentences

Find three sentences in your reading that you admire and list those sentences in the space below. Then write why you admire it.

Book Title and Page Number	Sentences I admired	Why I admire this sentence
Example: *Come On, Rain!*	"It freckles our feet, glazes our toes."	"Freckles" and "glazes" are such surprising words to use to describe rain on skin!
Example: *Pleasing the Ghost*, Sharon Creech, page 1	"I'm Dennis, your basic, ordinary nine-year-old boy, and usually I live a basic, ordinary life."	The repetition of "basic, ordinary" to emphasize how normal his life is. It also makes me think that the story in the book is not going to be basic or ordinary because of how much he emphasizes his regular life.

Name _____

Date _____

How Punctuation Affects the Sentence

Text	Line From Text	Type of Punctuation	How the Punctuation Affects the Sentence

Noticing and Naming Sentences

Sentence	What we call it: • Painting a picture with words • Strong emotion • Right now moment • Drawing the reader into the story					
Example: "It comes up round, ripe, and huge over autumn fields of corn and wheat." —*Hello, Harvest Moon*, Ralph Fletcher	Painting a picture with words					

Parent Letter for Character Study

Dear Parents,

We are beginning a reading unit on studying character. For our whole-class study we will read the *Julian* books by Ann Cameron, and then students will have the opportunity to explore character on their own in different books of their choosing. Part of this work will be to collect information about a character from multiple books.

You can support our work at home by talking with your child about the characters in his or her book. Ask him to tell you about the character, what he knows about his or her personality and physical characteristics, and even if he would want to be friends with this person and why. Part of this work is finding examples from the text to explain your thinking. Remind your child to give you examples from the book to prove his or her thinking.

As always, if you have any questions, please don't hesitate to call.

Warmly,

Name _____ Date _____

Tracing a Character

Name of Character: _____

Physical Traits of Character:	Evidence From Text:
Personality Traits of Character:	Evidence From Text:

Dialogue Evidence From Story:	Reflections:
Interactions With Other Characters:	Reflections:
Problem-Solving Strategies of the Character:	Reflections:

Books Read:

1. _____

2. _____

3. _____

Name _____ Date _____

Pre-Draft Organizer

Who will my characters be?

Name: _____

Description: _____

_____

How/when will I introduce them? _____

_____

Where will my story take place?

Where? _____

When? _____

What are the events in my story?

Event 1: _____

Event 2: _____

Event 3: _____

Event 4: _____

If there is a problem, what is it? _____

_____

_____

_____

How will it be solved? _____

_____

_____

Name _____ Date _____

Character Development Organizer

Name of your character: _____

Character's physical traits:	Phrases to describe your character:
Character's personality traits:	**Phrases to describe your character:**
Character's problem-solving traits:	**Phrases to describe your character:**
Character's relationship with other people:	**Phrases to describe your character:**

Name _____ Date _____

End-of-Unit Reflection

1. Explain what you are the most proud of in this piece of writing. _____

_____

_____

_____

_____

2. List the ways you used Ann Cameron as a mentor to make your writing better.

- _____

_____

- _____

_____

- _____

_____

3. Explain which writing goals have now been met. _____

_____

_____

_____

_____

4. Name a goal you have for yourself as a writer. _____

_____

_____

_____

_____

Parent Letter for Reading Clubs

Dear Parents,

In reading, we are beginning a unit on Reading Clubs. Like adult book clubs, reading clubs provide an opportunity for students to come together with their peers to talk about what they read. This kind of experience builds students' speaking and listening skills and allows them to gain deeper understanding of and hear others' opinions on a shared text. As part of this unit we will be learning about how to have conversations with multiple people and to ground those conversations in a text.

You can support this work at home by having both text-based and non–text-based conversations with your children. Ask them for their opinions on different topics and model for them how to agree or disagree, change an opinion based on what someone else says, or add on to an idea in a respectful way. Your lively dinner conversations on all kinds of topics of interest will help us in class too, as conversations are all about building literacy!

Thank you for your continued support.

Warmly,

Name _____ Date _____

Noticing Conversations

What a Great Conversation Looks Like	What a Great Conversation Sounds Like

Name _____ Date _____

Preparing for Reading Talks

Book Title: _____

Select one sticky note that you would like to discuss with your group. Use the space below to write a response to your sticky note to think more about your topic. Remember to use examples from the text to support your thinking.

Place your sticky note here:

_____

_____

_____

_____

_____

_____

_____

_____

_____

_____

_____

RESOURCE 4.3

Name _____ Date _____

Reading Club Reflection

1. Please share your thoughts about how your club worked together.

_____

_____

_____

_____

2. Thinking: How did your club's conversation change your thinking about a text? Be specific.

_____

_____

_____

_____

3. Preparation: How did you prepare for your club's discussion? Do you feel that you were well prepared or that you will need to do something differently next time to be more prepared? Be specific and use examples.

_____

_____

_____

_____

4. Working Together: Were there moments that felt hard? If so, how did your club deal with them? What advice do you have for future clubs?

_____

_____

_____

_____

Parent Letter for Writing Clubs

Dear Parents,

We are beginning a unit in writing called Writing Clubs. The Writing Clubs unit is designed to allow students to choose their writing topic of interest and work with others who share that interest.

At home you can support our work by inviting your child to find texts in your home book collection, at the public library, or at the bookstore, that help him think more about his topic.

Thank you for your continued support in your child's learning.

Warmly,

Name _____ Date _____

Finding Mentor Texts

Search through your books at home or in the library or bookstore to find additional texts to add to your group's collection. Write the title of the books you found and why you selected them as mentor texts in the space below.

Name of Book	Why You Chose It

Name _____

Date _____

Noticing Text Features in Mentor Texts

Text Features	Leads (beginnings)	Endings	Language or Text Features That Strike Me	Special Text Features I Would Like to Try
Text Examples				
Text Examples				
Text Examples				

Name _____   Date _____

Writing Clubs Homework: Researching My Topics

Texts I found to help with my research:

Text Title	Where I Found It	Type of Text

New discoveries I made about my topic:

_____

_____

_____

_____

_____

Name _____ Date _____

Editing Checklist for Writing Clubs

	My Edits	Partner Edits
I use **capitals** for *I*, proper nouns, and first letters of sentences.		
I end my sentences with correct **punctuation** (. , ! ?).		
In narrative writing, I organize my writing into **paragraphs**.		
I circled and corrected all **misspelled words**.		

I checked all of my work carefully and thoughtfully.	Your Signature:	Partner's Signature:

Parent Letter for Exploring Poetry Connections Through Reading

Dear Parents,

We are beginning an exploration of poetry in reading and writing. Poetry is a joyous journey, and I want our classroom to become a little haven of words and the fun of them!

As part of this work, students will be reading and identifying poems they really like. They will collect these poems, illustrate and interpret them, and use them as inspirations for their own writing. Please try to tuck in a bit of time to read poetry with your child this month. Ask your child to read aloud to you from poetry he loves. Oral poetry reading is a great way to build fluency and language development, and it is also just a wonderful thing to do! Enjoy!

Warmly,

Sensory Images in Poetry

Title: _____

Poet: _____

1. Draw an image that you created in your mind as you read this poem.

2. What are the words in the poem that most illuminate the image for you?

_____

_____

_____

_____

_____

_____

_____

Name _____ Date _____

Interpretation

Title: _____

Author: _____

Put the poem into your own words. What do you think the poet is trying to convey?

_____

_____

_____

_____

_____

_____

_____

_____

_____

_____

_____

_____

_____

_____

_____

_____

Parent Letter for Exploring Poetry Connections Through Writing

Dear Parents:

Your children will bring home their poetry notebooks every day during this month. We are celebrating the idea that poetry is EVERYWHERE! So I will ask your children to find the extraordinary in the ordinary: look at all the things in their lives—people, objects, places—and see if they can "find a poem" in that thing. You can model for them how you see beauty everywhere by admiring the details of objects you love, or telling them stories about them, so your children can see you too find beauty and surprise in the world around you. That is really where poetry comes from.

Warmly,

Name _____ Date _____

Poetry Homework: Learning About Poets Through Their Words

Poem	Emotion/Feeling It Evokes in You	What This Might Tell Us About the Poet
Example: "In Daddy's Arms"	Proud, safe	This person loves and admires his daddy
Example: "dog"	Slow, lazy, comfortable, relaxed	The author notices small details of life

Name _____ Date _____

The Mood of Poetry

Poems We Like	Mood the Poet Conveys	How the Poet Conveys It
"Old Dog"	Loneliness	Few words, white space
"If I Were in Charge of the World"	Bold, different	Lots of words, repetition of key words
"The Dream Keeper"	Sadness, hope	Patterns of two or three words on a line, and then longer lines; repetition of key word *bring*

Date _____

Noticing White Space

Poem	Poet	White Space	What It Conveys	Who Will Try This?

Name _____

_____ Date _____

Poetry Checklist

Strong Idea (Matters to You)	Strong Image That Goes With the Idea	Word Choice and Repetition That Reflects Your Ideas	White Space That Conveys Some Mood About Your Idea

Name _____ Date _____

A Poet's Editing Checklist

Crafting Technique	Example of How I Used It
Artistic use of commas, question marks, periods	
Artistic use of verbs	
Artistic use of capitalization	
Artistic use of white space	
Form of poetry (ode, haiku, free verse)	
Spelling checked	
Title	
Poet's name	
Date	

Poetry Celebrations

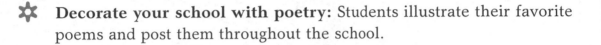

✿ **Poetry recitations:** Students who commit poems to memory can recite them in front of the class or visit another class to recite their poem and answer questions about it.

✿ **Decorate your school with poetry:** Students illustrate their favorite poems and post them throughout the school.

✿ **Participate in "Poem in Your Pocket Day":** Invite students to carry around multiple copies of their poem and hand them out to people throughout the day.

✿ **Interpret poetry:** This can be an anytime celebration. Invite students to share with the class their interpretation of a poem by saying what it means to them. They might talk about the picture it makes in their minds, retell the poem using their own words, or say how it makes them feel and why.

✿ **Have a Poetry Café:** Invite parents and students into your classroom to drink coffee, tea, or juice and listen to students read their poetry. Parents can share poetry they have written, too!

✿ **Create a class anthology of students' poetry:** You can select poetry around a common theme or particular craft.

Name _____ Date _____

Comments for the Poet

Share a compliment with:	

Ways to Celebrate Our Writing

✻ Author's Chair: Read your writing to the class

✻ Reading snippets and collecting comments: move around the room

✻ Looped Class Readings: bring in guest classes

✻ Frame our writing

✻ Author of the week

✻ Write a letter to someone (and get a response)

✻ Open mike at lunchtime

✻ Writing buddies

✻ Parent breakfast

Celebrate Your Writing at Home

✻ Read it to your whole family in the living room.

✻ Read it on the phone to someone far away.

✻ Share it with your family before dinner.

✻ Share your story over some cheese and crackers.

✻ Read your story to a friend on the bus.

✻ Read your story while you are taking a long car ride.

RESOURCE 5.12

Glossary of Terms for the Complete Year Series

We try to avoid jargon as much as possible, but it is inevitable that a community creates or uses specific terminology to identify important aspects of its work. We want you to feel comfortable with all the language inside this book. What follows are some of the key words we have used throughout this book and throughout the Complete Year series.

Anchor texts These are the books that moor us to the places of our learning. An anchor holds a ship in place, in water that may be moving fast. Texts are like that for us in our teaching. We are in moving water all the time, but great literature anchors us down to our teaching, to our learning, to our goals and outcomes. Anchor texts connect us to the teaching inside our units of study. They keep our teaching on course, steady, focused, anchoring our big ideas, our commitments and indeed, the essence of each unit. Anchor texts may also be used throughout the year in both the teaching of reading and the teaching of writing. For example, one text may be used in a reading unit for retelling, or sensory image, or prediction. The same text may also be used as a demonstration text for writing with detail, strong leads and endings, and the use of dialogue. There are some special texts that can travel with you throughout the year. They are great, lasting titles that transcend any one teaching point. These are considered anchor texts for the year.

Book clubs Working in book clubs allows students to build their collaboration skills and their ability to talk about texts. Book clubs may form from two sets of successful partnerships, or for a variety of teaching purposes. You may group a club according to skill sets or according to interests. Students in a club do not all have to be reading the same book. For example, in a nonfiction unit, the students may meet to discuss editorials or historical writing, using different texts at their own reading levels. You should give clear guidelines for the purposes of a club, its duration, expected outcomes, and how it will be assessed.

Commitment The fourth stage of a unit of study, the Commitment stage, is the bridge from the end of one unit to the beginning of the next one. Look for and make public examples of student work and behaviors that are becoming more integrated into the ongoing work of the individual and the community. This stage asks the question: How is what we have learned in this unit going to inform our learning as we begin the next one? It also requires a response to the question: What have you learned?

Conference/conferring This is a process for informally assessing your students' progress, and for differentiating your instruction for individual readers and writers. Ideally, you will meet with each student at least once a week in a brief, focused conference session. Stages of a conference are:

- **Preread/Research** (be very familiar with your student's work and processes in advance of the conference)
- **Ask** (pertinent questions relating to your lesson, the ongoing work, and the plans going forward)
- **Listen** (take notes, with attention to next steps)
- **Teach** (one target point)
- **Plan** (what the student will do when you leave the conference: today, tomorrow, throughout the unit and the year)

Conventions The fourth component of the Complete 4, Conventions refers to grammar, punctuation, and syntax. Understanding the conventions of the English language has a direct impact on reading comprehension and writing mechanics and fluency.

Downhill texts These are texts we can rest and relax into—to practice building our stamina or our fluency or to revisit favorite characters, authors, or series. They are books that do not require a great deal of decoding to be done by the reader, as the text is generally below the reader's independent reading level.

Focused Instruction The first part of every day's reading and writing time, Focused Instruction is the short, focused lesson at the beginning of each workshop session in the teaching of reading or writing. Each lesson should build on the ones before it. No lesson is taught in isolation.

Four Prompts In order to help our students learn how to find ideas for writing, we have developed a set of prompts to guide them. They are I wonder, I remember, I observe, and I imagine. You can use these to support your students' writing in any genre.

Genre The second component of the Complete 4, Genre typically refers to a type of text such as poetry, nonfiction, or narrative. Within each of these genres are subgenres, which may include a specific focus on persuasive nonfiction writing, or informational nonfiction writing in nonfiction studies. In a narrative study, the focus might be on the short story, the memoir, or story elements. We want students to focus on how they engage with a particular genre. How do we read a newspaper, for example, and how do we read a poem? How are they different, and how are they the same? We will talk about uses for a genre, the reasons we read inside one genre for a length of time, and how our thinking grows and changes as a result of that immersion.

Guided Practice In the third stage of any unit of study, Guided Practice, we use mentor texts, transcripts, teacher or student writing, think-alouds, role plays, and read-alouds to model exemplary attributes, behaviors, and qualities related to the unit. Over the course of this stage, students are given increasing responsibility for this work. It is generally the longest stage of a unit, as all students need time for practice.

Identification The second stage of any unit of study, Identification, is the time when we begin to develop the common language we will use throughout the study. We identify attributes of a genre, behaviors in a process, qualities of a craft element, rules for a convention or mark. Our thinking is recorded in public charts, student writing notebooks, and our notebook.

Immersion The first stage of any unit of study, Immersion, is the initial period of inquiry during which we surround our students with the sounds, textures, and qualities of a Genre, Process, Strategy, or Conventions focus. We marinate our students in the literature, the actions and reflections, and the attention to detail and conventions that are part of the study. During this stage, students construct a working understanding of the topic under discussion.

Independent Practice Following each day's Focused Instruction, Independent Practice provides time for students to read or write independently and authentically. Students independently read a variety of texts matched to their reading levels. Students also write a variety of texts independently, depending on the unit and their ability levels. They practice the skills and strategies taught in the whole-group sessions. We provide daily lessons to support their work, and confer regularly with the students to assess their individual needs.

Mentor text Somewhat interchangeable with an anchor text, we are more inclined to use mentor text to describe books that have particular appeal to individual students. Mentor texts inspire students' reading and writing, whereas anchor texts are specific texts chosen in advance by the teacher to prepare a unit. So in a poetry unit, one mentor text might be a Langston Hughes poem, "The Dream Keeper," because the student loves it and wants to write like that, whereas another student might choose a Valerie Worth poem because she likes the brevity of her language.

Partnerships At times you may choose to pair children for different reasons and different lengths of time. Partnerships can be very fluid, lasting for just one session, a week, or an entire unit. Partnerships may be based on reading levels, similar interests in particular books or subjects, or because you would like to work with the partners on a regular basis on small instructional reading or writing work.

Process The first of the Complete 4 components, Process asks readers and writers to become aware of their habits and behaviors, and to move forward in developing them. Process units can investigate roles, routines, capacity, or collaboration.

Read-aloud During read-aloud, you read from carefully chosen texts that reflect the reading and writing work the community is doing together. Listening to fluent and expressive read-alouds helps students identify the many aspects of text and develop their own deeper understandings of Process, Genre, Strategy, or Conventions. You may read from a book or short text that illustrates the topic of the Focused Instruction for the day, and encourage students to pursue that thinking in their independent reading and writing. During and at the end of the read-aloud, the whole class may have a conversation relating to the ideas in the story.

Reading notebook *See* Writing Notebook.

Shared reading/shared writing During this activity, you and your students read together from a shared text (on an overhead, chart, or a SMART Board, or using copies of the text). While teachers of younger children use shared reading and writing to help build decoding skills, teachers of older children may use shared reading to teach word analysis, new vocabulary, or punctuation skills. It's also a good way to work with older students on big-picture thinking such as developing an idea about a text, asking questions, or making inferences. Teachers of older students may use shared writing to guide their students toward new writing strategies in a public writing context, or model use of details and elaboration to improve their writing.

Small instructional groups This structure is used to differentiate and direct instruction to the specific needs of a small group of learners. You pull small groups of readers or writers with similar needs to explicitly teach targeted reading and writing skills. You select and introduce the texts for reading and make specific teaching points. You may prompt students in small writing groups to do a short, focused writing exercise based on their needs. These groups are flexible and will change as the year unfolds.

Stages of the lesson Each day, we should work with our students in a whole-small-whole routine. First we bring everyone together for the lesson (see Focused Instruction), then we send students off to practice something we have taught (see Independent Practice), and finally we call them back to join us for a recap and reiteration of our teaching (see Wrap-Up).

Stages of the unit Each unit of study follows a progression of instruction, from Immersion to Identification to Guided Practice to Commitment. These stages provide students with the necessary opportunities to notice, name, practice, and share their learning—all of which contribute to a deeper understanding and application of our teaching (see Immersion, Identification, Guided Practice, and Commitment).

Steady reader or writer This student is making steady progress and meeting appropriate grade-level expectations.

Strategy The third component in the Complete 4, Strategy consists of two types: reading and writing. In reading, Strategy refers to individual or grouped strategies for reading comprehension that impact reading development. These include visualizing, synthesizing, questioning, and inferring. A unit focused on strategy can be embedded in another study or illuminated on its own. Strategy units also include the study of theme, interpretation, building an argument, and story elements. In writing, Strategy refers to craft. This may include the external or internal structures of writing. Units in writing strategy may include structures of nonfiction or narrative texts, a focus on a particular author, or, internally, units focused on the use of repetition, varied sentence length, or the artful use of punctuation.

Strong reader or writer This student is performing above grade-level expectations.

Turn and talk This common technique helps students warm up for their reading or writing work. By asking students to "turn and talk" to someone in the meeting area to rehearse their thoughts, we give all students a chance to have their voices heard. It is an effective management technique for making sure students are prepared for the work ahead.

Unit of study A one- to six-week period of intensive study on one aspect of reading or writing. The Complete 4 curriculum planning system helps teachers and administrators plan an entire school year in the teaching of reading and writing.

Uphill texts This descriptor refers to a text that is above a student's independent reading level. Sometimes we want our readers to challenge themselves with a harder text. Sometimes readers have very good reasons for why they would like to keep an uphill book close by. Other times, though, we ask them to recognize that the book is too uphill for the task, and that they need to find a level text with which they can feel successful.

Vulnerable reader or writer This describes the reader or writer who struggles to keep up with the demands of the grade level. These are students who need extra support and scaffolding through appropriate texts or individualized or small-group instruction. Our vulnerable readers and writers need special care to feel successful and to flourish in our classrooms.

Wrap-Up The final step in each day's reading or writing time, the Wrap-Up is when we ask our students to return to a whole-group setting for reflection and reinforcement. For example, you may share one or two examples of student work or student behaviors ("Today I noticed . . . "), or one or two students might briefly share their thinking processes or the work itself.

Writing clubs These are recommended for all ages. Children may create clubs based on common interests, from the block area and writing in kindergarten to mystery writing in fourth grade. Give clear guidelines for the purposes of the clubs, the length of time they will last, the expectations, the outcomes, and how you will assess the progress of each club.

Writing notebook/reading notebook/ writing folder/reading folder These are containers for thinking and tools for collecting ideas, wonderings, observations, questions, research, lists, snippets of texts, and responses to literature. The form of the container is not the important thing; what is important is having containers for student work that make sense to your students and work well for you in terms of collecting and preserving a history of student reading and writing.

Grade 3 Anchor Texts

Early Fall

The ARCH: Setting Personal Reading Goals

- *The Boy Who Loved Words* by Roni Schotter
- *The Hundred Dresses* by Eleanor Estes
- *I Want to Be* by Thylias Moss
- *Whales* by Seymour Simon
- *What You Know First* by Patricia MacLachlan

The ARCH: Setting Personal Writing Goals

- *The Basket Moon* by Mary Lyn Ray
- *Emma's Rug* by Allen Say
- *A Family of Poems: My Favorite Poetry for Children*, edited by Caroline Kennedy
- *In Daddy's Arms I Am Tall* by Javaka Steptoe
- *Miss Rumphius* by Barbara Cooney
- *Nothing Ever Happens on 90th Street* by Roni Schotter
- *The Tarantula in My Purse and 172 Other Wild Pets* by Jean Craighead George
- *Wolves* by Seymour Simon
- *Wordsworth the Poet* by Frances H. Kakugawa

Making Choices in Reading: Strategies for Comprehension

- *The Firekeeper's Son* by Linda Sue Park
- *Hey, Al* by Arthur Yorinks
- *Sixteen Years and Sixteen Seconds: The Sammy Lee Story* by Paula Yoo
- *Super-Completely and Totally the Messiest* by Judith Viorst

Making Choices in Writing: The Four Prompts

- *All the Small Poems and Fourteen More* by Valerie Worth
- *Aunt Flossie's Hats (and Crab Cakes Later)* by Elizabeth Fitzgerald Howard
- *The Best Pet of All* by David LaRochelle
- *Calling the Doves/El Canto de las Palomas* by Juan Felipe Herrera

- *A Drop of Water* by Walter Wick
- *How I Spent My Summer Vacation* by Mark Teague
- *Snowmen at Night* by Caralyn Buehner and Mark Buehner

Growing Awareness of Theme and Time: Reading Fiction

- *The Art Lesson* by Tomie dePaola
- *Big Sister and Little Sister* by Charlotte Zolotow
- *The Chicken-Chasing Queen of Lamar County* by Janice N. Harrington
- *Crickwing* by Janell Cannon
- *Fly Away Home* by Eve Bunting
- *A Frog Thing* by Eric Drachman
- *Oliver Button Is a Sissy* by Tomie dePaola
- *The Other Side* by Jacqueline Woodson

Growing an Awareness of Theme and Time: Writing Fiction

- *The Art Lesson* by Tomie dePaola
- *Big Sister and Little Sister* by Charlotte Zolotow
- *Crickwing* by Janell Cannon
- *Fly Away Home* by Eve Bunting
- *Morning on the Lake* by Jan Bourdeau Waboose
- *Oliver Button Is a Sissy* by Tomie dePaola
- *Once Upon a Cool Motorcycle Dude* by Kevin O'Malley
- *The Other Side* by Jacqueline Woodson
- *Previously* by Allan Ahlberg

Understanding Sentences in Reading

- *Charlotte's Web* by E. B. White
- *Cloud Dance* by Thomas Locker
- *Come On, Rain!* by Karen Hesse
- *Fireflies* by Julie Brinckloe
- *Hello, Harvest Moon* by Ralph Fletcher
- *Mustang Canyon* by Jonathan London
- *Pssst!* by Adam Rex
- *Shortcut* by Donald Crews
- *Thunder Cake* by Patricia Polacco

- *When I Am Old With You* by Angela Johnson

Strengthening Sentences in Writing

- *Come On, Rain!* by Karen Hesse
- *Fireflies* by Julie Brinckloe
- *Hello, Harvest Moon* by Ralph Fletcher
- *Shortcut* by Donald Crews
- *Snapshots From the Wedding* by Gary Soto
- *Thunder Cake* by Patricia Polacco

Seeking Information: Strategies to Read Nonfiction

- *Bears: Polar Bears, Black Bears and Grizzly Bears* by Deborah Hodge
- *Big Blue Whale* by Nicola Davies
- *Can It Rain Cats and Dogs? Questions and Answers About Weather* by Melvin Berger and Gilda Berger
- *Duke Ellington: The Piano Prince and His Orchestra* by Andrea Davis Pinkney
- *Eleanor* by Barbara Cooney
- *National Geographic Explorer*
- *National Geographic Kids*

Naming Importance: Note-Taking Skills

- *Bears: Polar Bears, Black Bears and Grizzly Bears* by Deborah Hodge
- *Big Blue Whale* by Nicola Davies
- *Big Dig* by Meish Goldish
- *Can It Rain Cats and Dogs? Questions and Answers About Weather* by Melvin Berger and Gilda Berger
- *How to Talk to Your Dog* by Jean Craighead George

Late Fall

Building Multi-Genre Reading Skills: Test Prep

- *I Dream of Trains* by Angela Johnson
- *Seymour Simon's Book of Trains* by Seymour Simon
- "Song of the Train" by David McCord (from the collection *Far and Few*)
- *Train Song* by Diane Siebert

Building Response Skills: Writing About Reading

- *I Dream of Trains* by Angela Johnson
- *Next Stop Grand Central* by Maira Kalman
- *Seymour Simon's Book of Trains* by Seymour Simon
- "Song of the Train" by David McCord (from the collection *Far and Few*)
- *Train Song* by Diane Siebert

Making Wise Book Choices

- *Library Mouse* by Daniel Kirk

Mastering Dialogue

- *Cowboy & Octopus* by Jon Scieszka
- *I Will Never Not Ever Eat a Tomato* by Lauren Child
- *Little Night* by Yuyi Morales
- *My Dadima Wears a Sari* by Kashmira Sheth
- *The Stories Julian Tells* by Ann Cameron

Exploring Elements of Story: Reading About Characters

- Authors and Illustrators series, Scholastic
- Biographical information about Ann Cameron (childrensbestbooks.com)
- *Children's Books and Their Creators*, edited by Anita Silvey
- *Julian's Glorious Summer* by Ann Cameron
- *More Stories Julian Tells* by Ann Cameron
- *The Stories Julian Tells* by Ann Cameron

Exploring Elements of Craft: Writing About Characters

- *Julian's Glorious Summer* by Ann Cameron
- *More Stories Julian Tells* by Ann Cameron
- *The Stories Julian Tells* by Ann Cameron

Winter

Becoming Scientists and Historians: Reading Nonfiction

- *Duckling*, Watch me Grow Series, DK
- FOSSWeb Science Kit
- *Gandhi* by Demi
- Historic Communities series, and other books by Bobbie Kalman
- *...If You Lived with the Iroquois* by Ellen Levine, and other books in the series
- *Time for Kids, National Geographic Kids*
- True Book series by Stefanie Takacs
- *Vote* by Eileen Christelow
- *The Wright Brothers (In Their Own Words)* by George Sullivan, and other books in the series

Becoming Scientists and Historians: Writing Nonfiction

- *Can It Rain Cats and Dogs? Questions and Answers About Weather* by Melvin Berger and Gilda Berger
- *A Child's Day* and other books in the Historic Communities series by Bobbie Kalman
- FOSSWeb Science Kit reading materials and websites
- *...If You Lived with the Iroquois* by Ellen Levine, and other books in the series
- *Journey Around Boston from A to Z* and other books in the series by Martha Zschock and Heather Zschock
- *Martin's Big Words* by Doreen Rappaport
- True Book series by Stefanie Takacs
- *What Do Animals Do in Winter? How Animals Survive the Cold* by Melvin Berger and Gilda Berger

Paragraphing Power: Reading

- "The Lightwell" by Laurence Yep in *Home: A Collaboration of Thirty Distinguished Authors and Illustrators of Children's Books to Aid the Homeless*, edited by Michael J. Rosen
- *National Geographic Explorer*
- "Puffballs," in *Katya's Book of Mushrooms* by Katya Arnold

Paragraphing Power: Writing

- "The Lightwell," by Laurence Yep in *Home: A Collaboration of Thirty Distinguished Authors and Illustrators of Children's Books to Aid the Homeless*, edited by Michael J. Rosen
- "Puffballs," in *Katya's Book of Mushrooms* by Katya Arnold
- *Scholastic News*
- *Time for Kids*

Building Conversations: Reading Clubs

- *Ashley Bryan's African Tales, Uh-Huh* by Ashley Bryan
- *The Big Big Big Book of Tashi* by Anna Fienberg and Barbara Fienberg
- *Frog and Toad Together* by Arnold Lobel
- *Home: A Collaboration of Thirty Distinguished Authors and Illustrators of Children's Books to Aid the Homeless*, edited by Michael J. Rosen
- *National Geographic Kids*
- "The Rider" by Naomi Shihab Nye in *Fuel: Poems by Naomi Shihab Nye*
- *Scholastic News*
- *Time for Kids*

Nurturing Collaborations: Writing Clubs

- *The Best Pet of All* by David LaRochelle
- *Big Blue Whale* by Nicola Davies
- *Dumpling Soup* by Jama Kim Rattigan
- *Next Stop Grand Central* by Maira Kalman
- *Sports Illustrated for Kids*
- *Winter Poems* by Barbara Rogasky
- *Yoshi's Feast* by Kimiko Kajikawa

Spring

Exploring Poetry Connections Through Reading

- *Baseball, Snakes, and Summer Squash: Poems About Growing Up* by Donald Graves
- *The Dream Keeper and Other Poems* by Langston Hughes
- *The Flag of Childhood: Poems From the Middle East*, edited by Naomi Shihab Nye
- *From the Bellybutton of the Moon and Other Summer Poems* by Francisco Alarcón
- *Honey I Love* by Eloise Greenfield
- *Moon, Have You Met My Mother?* by Karla Kuskin
- "Ode to My Socks" by Pablo Neruda
- *The Place My Words are Looking For* ("Yellow Sonnet"), edited by Paul Janeczko
- *Poetry for Young People: Carl Sandburg*, edited by Frances Schoonmaker Bolin

- *Spring: A Haiku Collection* by George Shannon
- *Sweet Corn* (particularly "Old Dog") by James Stevenson

Exploring Poetry Connections Through Writing

- *Baseball, Snakes, and Summer Squash* by Donald Graves
- *Beach Stones* by Lilian Moore
- *Color Me A Rhyme* by Jane Yolen
- "dog" by Valerie Worth
- *The Dream Keeper and Others Poems* by Langston Hughes
- *From the Bellybutton of the Moon and Other Summer Poems* by Francisco Alarcón
- *Honey, I Love* by Eloise Greenfield
- *Horizons* by Jane Yolen
- *If I Were in Charge of the World* by Judith Viorst
- *Insectlopedia* by Douglas Florian
- "Old Dog" in *Sweet Corn* by James Stevenson
- "The Sidewalk Racer" by Lillian Morrison
- "Valentine for Ernest Mann," in *Red Suitcase* by Naomi Shihab Nye
- "We Could Be Friends" in *The Place My Words Are Looking For* by Myra Cohn Livingston
- *Winter Poems* by Barbara Rogasky
- "Write About a Radish" by Karla Kuskin

Making Connections Across Books: Interest Clubs

- *Chato's Kitchen* by Gary Soto
- *Thunder Cake* by Patricia Polacco
- *Too Many Tamales* by Gary Soto

Making Writing Connections: Interest Magazines

- www.highlights.com (search for the following: "Bike Fright" by Linda Stephens, fiction, "Cactus Hotel" by Mona Hodgson, poetry; "Different Strokes: The Chinese Art of Writing by Linda Petrucelli and Garry Hoff, nonfiction; "Junk Drawer by Bridget Reistad, poetry; "A Night in the Desert by Melissa Joy Scheidt, fiction)
- www.scholastic.com (search for profile of author/illustrator Mark Teague)
- www.spaghettibookclub.org (search for book review by Stephanie S. of *The Stories Julian Tells* by Ann Cameron)
- www.timeforkids.com (search for "Talking Trash" by Angelique LeDoux)
- Other children's magazines including *Ladybug, Spider, Ask, National Geographic for Kids,* and *Sports Illustrated for Kids*

Getting to Know Commas: Reading

- *Because of Winn-Dixie* by Kate DiCamillo
- *Come On, Rain!* by Karen Hesse
- *Eats, Shoots and Leaves: Why Commas Really Do Make a Difference!* by Lynn Truss
- *Mr. George Baker* by Amy Hest
- *Yum! Ummmm! Que Rico!* by Pat Mora

Getting to Know Commas: Writing

- *Big and Little* by Steve Jenkins
- *Eats, Shoots and Leaves: Why Commas Really Do Make a Difference!* by Lynn Truss
- *Fireflies* by Julie Brinckloe
- *Snow* by Uri Shulevitz
- *Yum! Ummmm! Que Rico!* by Pat Mora

Looking Back, Looking Forward: Making Summer Reading Plans

- "Books Fall Open," in *Good Books, Good Times!* selected by Lee Bennett Hopkins
- *The Hard-Times Jar* by Ethel Footman Smothers
- *The Library Dragon* by Carmen Agra Deedy
- *Mama, I'll Give You the World* by Roni Schotter and S. Saelig Gallagher
- "When I Was Nine" by James Stevenson
- "Yesterday," in *Hey World, Here I Am!* by Jean Little

Looking Back, Looking Forward: Making Summer Writing Plans

- *The Gardener* by Sarah Stewart
- *Library Mouse* by Daniel Kirk
- *Live Writing: Breathing Life Into Your Words* by Ralph Fletcher
- *The Secret of Old Zeb* by Carmen Agra Deedy

Professional References

Allington, R. L. (2005). *What really matters for struggling readers: Designing research-based programs.* Boston: Allyn & Bacon.

Allyn, P. (2007). *The complete 4 for literacy. How to teach reading and writing through daily lessons, monthly units, and yearlong calendars.* New York: Scholastic.

Alston, L. (2008). *Why we teach: Learning, laughter, love, and the power to transform lives.* New York: Scholastic.

Anderson, C. (2000). *How's it going? A practical guide to conferring with student writers.* Portsmouth, NH: Heinemann.

Angelillo, J. (2002). *A fresh approach to teaching punctuation.* New York: Scholastic.

Angelillo, J. (2008). *Grammar study: Helping students get what grammar is and how it works.* New York: Scholastic.

Angelillo, J. (2003). *Writing about reading: From book talk to literary essays, grades 3–8.* Portsmouth, NH: Heinemann.

Bender, J. M. (2007). *The resourceful writing teacher.* Portsmouth, NH: Heinemann.

Bomer, R. (1995). *Time for meaning: Crafting literate lives in middle and high school.* Portsmouth, NH: Heinemann.

Buckner, A. (2005). *Notebook know-how: Strategies for the writer's notebook.* Portland, ME: Stenhouse.

Calkins, L. (1994). *The art of teaching writing.* Portsmouth, NH: Heinemann.

Cole, A. (2002). *Better answers: Written performance that looks good and sounds smart.* Portland, ME: Stenhouse.

Daniels, H. (2002). *Literature circles: Voice and choice in book clubs and reading groups.* Portland, ME: Stenhouse.

Davis, J., & Hill, S. (2003). *The no-nonsense guide to teaching writing: Strategies, structures, and solutions.* Portsmouth, NH: Heinemann.

Fletcher, R. (2000). *How writers work.* New York: Harper Trophy.

Fountas, I. C., & Pinnell, G. S. (2001). *Guiding readers and writers: Teaching comprehension, genre, and content literacy.* Portsmouth, NH: Heinemann.

Gentry, J. R. (2008). *Step-by-step assessment guide to code breaking.* New York: Scholastic.

Goodlad, J. (2004). *A place called school.* New York: McGraw-Hill.

Graves, D. (1989). *Investigate nonfiction.* Portsmouth, NH: Heinemann.

Hahn, M. L. (2002). *Reconsidering the read-aloud.* Portland, ME: Stenhouse.

Harvey, S., & Goudvis, A. (2000). *Strategies that work.* Portland, ME: Stenhouse.

Heard, G. (2002). *The revision toolbox: Teaching techniques that work.* Portsmouth, NH: Heinemann.

Heard, G. (1999). *Awakening the heart: Exploring poetry in elementary and middle school.* Portsmouth, NH: Heinemann.

Hindley, J. (1996). *In the company of children.* Portland, ME: Stenhouse.

Hollingworth, L. (2007, December). Five ways to prepare for standardized testing without sacrificing best practice. *Reading Teacher.*

Hoyt, L. (2008). *Mastering the mechanics, grades 2–3: Ready-to-use lessons for modeled, guided, and independent editing.* New York: Scholastic.

Hoyt, L. (2004). *Spotlight on comprehension: Building a literacy of thoughtfulness.* Portsmouth, NH: Heinemann.

Janeczko, P. B. (1999). *How to write poetry.* New York: Scholastic.

Kaufman, D. (2000). *Conferences and conversations: Listening to the literate classroom.* Portsmouth, NH: Heinemann.

Keene, E., & Zimmerman, S. (2007). *Mosaic of thought: Teaching comprehension in a reader's workshop* (2nd ed.). Portsmouth, NH: Heinemann.

Krashen, S. (2004). *The power of reading: Insights from the research* (2nd ed.). Portsmouth, NH: Heinemann.

Laminack, L. (2007). Cracking open the author's craft: Teaching the art of writing. New York: Scholastic.

Laminack, L., & Wadsworth, R. M. (2006). *Learning under the influence of language and literature: Making the most of read-alouds across the day.* Portsmouth, NH: Heinemann.

Lera, D. (2009). *Writing above standard: Engaging lessons that take standards to new heights and help kids become skilled, inspired writers.* New York: Scholastic.

McAfee, D. (1991). *Effects of sentence combining on fifth grade reading and writing achievement.* Dallas, TX: University of Texas.

McLaughlin, M, & DeVoogd, G. L. (2004). *Critical literacy: Enhancing students' comprehension of text.* New York: Scholastic.

O'Connor P. T. (2004). *Woe is I Jr..* New York: Penguin Group.

Pearson, D., & Gallagher, M. (1983). The instruction of reading comprehension. *Contemporary Educational Psychology, 8*(3), 917–945.

Rasinski, T. (2003). *The fluent reader: Oral reading strategies for building word recognition, fluency and comprehension.* New York: Scholastic.

Ray, K. W. (2002). *What you know by heart: How to develop curriculum for your writing workshop.* Portsmouth, NH: Heinemann.

Ray, K. W. (1999). *Wondrous words: Writers and writing in the elementary classroom.* Urbana, IL: National Council of Teachers of English.

Ray, K. W., & Laminack, L. (2001). *The writing workshop: Working though the hard parts (and they're all hard parts).* Urbana, IL: National Council of Teachers of English.

Rich, M. (2007, November 19). Study links drop in test scores to a decline in time spent reading. *New York Times,* pp. E1, E7.

Routman, R. (2002). *Reading essentials: The specifics you need to teach reading well.* Portsmouth, NH: Heinemann.

Samway, K., Davies, & Taylor, D. (2007). *Teaching English language learners: Strategies that work, grades K–5.* New York: Scholastic.

Silvey, A. (1995). *Children's books and their creations.* New York: Houghton Mifflin.

Smith, M., & Wilhelm, J. (2007). *Getting it right: Fresh approaches to teaching grammar, usage, and correctness.* New York: Scholastic.

Stead, T. (2006). *Reality checks: Teaching reading comprehension with nonfiction K–5.* Portland, ME: Stenhouse.

Strunk, W., & White, E. B. (1999). *The elements of style* (4th ed.). New York: Longman.

Szymusiak, K., & Sibberson F. (2008). *Day-to-day assessment in the reading workshop.* New York: Scholastic.

Szymusiak, K., & Sibberson, F. (2001). *Beyond leveled books: Supporting transitional readers in grades 2–5.* Portland, ME: Stenhouse.

Welty, E. (1984). *One writer's beginnings.* Cambridge, MA: Harvard University Press.

HOW TO PAINT SHOREBIRDS

A Guide to Materials, Tools, and Technique

David Mohrhardt

North Kingstown Free Library
100 Boone Street
North Kingstown, RI 02852

Stackpole Books

Copyright © 1989 by
Stackpole Books

Published by
STACKPOLE BOOKS
Cameron and Kelker Streets
P.O. Box 1831
Harrisburg, PA 17105

Printed in the United States of America

10 9 8 7 6 5 4 3 2 1

Book and jacket design by Tracy Patterson

LIBRARY OF CONGRESS
Library of Congress Cataloging-in-Publication Data

Mohrhardt, David.
    How to paint shorebirds : a guide to materials, tools, and
technique / by David Mohrhardt.
        p.   cm.
    Bibliography: p.
    1. Shore birds in art.   2. Gouache painting—Technique.
3. Polymer painting—Technique.   4. Artists' materials.   5. Artists'
tools.   6. Artists' materials industry—United States—Directories.
7. Shore birds—Anatomy.   I. Title.   II. Title: How to paint shore
birds.
ND2280.M64   1989
751.42'2—dc19   88-21970
                                                                CIP